ALSO BY JEANNE VOLTZ

Barbecued Ribs, Smoked Butts, and Other Great Feeds
(Revised Edition)

Community Suppers and Other Glorious Repasts

Barbecued Ribs and Other Great Feeds

Gifts from a Country Kitchen
(edited)

How to Turn a Passion for Food into Profit
(with Elayne Kleeman)

The Flavor of the South

The Los Angeles Times Natural Foods Cookbook

The L.A. Gourmet
(with Burks Hamner)

The California Cookbook

THE
FLORIDA
COOKBOOK

▼

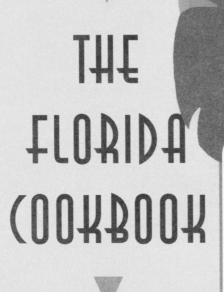

THE
FLORIDA
COOKBOOK

 FROM GULF COAST GUMBO
TO KEY LIME PIE

JEANNE VOLTZ AND CAROLINE STUART

ALFRED A. KNOPF NEW YORK 1996

THIS IS A BORZOI BOOK
PUBLISHED BY ALFRED A. KNOPF, INC.

Copyright © 1993 by Jeanne Voltz and Caroline Stuart
Illustrations copyright © 1993 by Linda Bourke
All rights reserved under International and Pan-American
Copyright Conventions. Published in the United States by
Alfred A. Knopf, Inc., New York, and simultaneously in Canada
by Random House of Canada Limited, Toronto.
Distributed by Random House, Inc.,
New York.

Library of Congress Cataloging-in-Publication Data
Voltz, Jeanne.
The Florida cookbook / by Jeanne Voltz and Caroline Stuart.
p.   cm.
Includes index.
ISBN 0-679-76575-1 (pbk.)
1. Cookery—Florida.   I. Stuart, Caroline.   II. Title.
TX715.V775   1993
641.59759—dc20   92-54284
CIP

Manufactured in the United States of America
Published February 16, 1993
First Paperback Edition, February 1996

For
young Luther and Jeanne Marie,
whose tastes were born and bred in Florida

—JEANNE VOLTZ

To
my husband, John,
and sons, Andy and Chris,
for their love and support,
and
in memory of my parents,
Alice and Kolb Stuart,
who encouraged a little girl to cook and
taught her to love Florida food

—CAROLINE STUART

CONTENTS

More than 450 years ago, Florida became the cradle of American cooking as we know it now, the place where European foods were first blended with the foodways of Native Americans. The great mix was set in motion in 1513, when Ponce de León staked a claim for Spain near Ponte Vedra. The exchange of multicultural food customs has never ceased, creating a cuisine of more ethnic diversity than any in America, and possibly in the world.

Ponce de León's party did not linger long enough to have much influence on the prevailing diets, but on his second trip in 1521, Ponce de León is believed to have brought farm animals and equipment, in hope of settling a colony on the west coast of the peninsula. Ponce de León was wounded by an Indian arrow, and he returned to Havana, where he died a few weeks later. The Hernando de Soto party, which arrived in 1539, brought more cattle and swine, and the progeny of these animals as they roamed the countryside launched a livestock culture in a land that had depended entirely on game and fish for meat. Two other early colonies, the Spanish at Pensacola in 1559 and the French Huguenots near the mouth of the St. Johns River in 1564, were short lived and left scant gastronomic lore.

It was the founding of St. Augustine in 1565 and, two years later, the Nombre de Dios mission that introduced European cooking to the new continent. Franciscans traveling the mission trail to Pensacola were making egg custards in the Spanish manner and using rice and spices unknown then in the Western world, and settlers in Florida were eating in the Spanish style long before Father Junípero Serra, the culinary trailblazer in the West, founded the first mission in California.

However, two powerful influences moderated the Spanish flavor of Florida. First, there were the people of African heritage. A small number of Moors and Africans came as free persons with the Conquistadors, then thousands were brought here as slaves, starting in the middle of the sixteenth century. The blacks carried with them sesame seeds, yams, eggplants, and okra for their own use. The second influential non-Spanish group was the Anglo-Americans, descendants of settlers in New England, Virginia, the Carolinas, and Georgia, who began to trickle into Florida before the American Revolution. They brought sweets, a taste for rice cooked differently from the Spanish, and quick hot breads. Not until the Spanish migrations to Key West and Tampa after the Civil War did European-type wheat breads come into general use, except in Pensacola where a unique hardtack was made for the salad called gaspachee.

The blacks and Anglos from Southern colonies introduced a style of cooking that is called Cracker cooking, country cooking, or soul food. Until this century Cracker cooking, with a touch of Spanish zest, prevailed. English blandness tempered the tang of Florida food, and never let it develop to the high spice of the chili and bean flavors of California-Mex cooking.

A group of Minorcans, brought as indentured laborers in 1768, added a new dimension to the Spanish Florida taste. The plantation where they had worked failed, and the six hundred survivors established a colony in St. Augustine. The datil peppers they favored gave their Minorcan pilaus and sauces a unique flavor, and their descendants still celebrate holidays with traditional coconut confections and cheese pastries.

Florida was shaped by adventurers and entrepreneurs, refugees and pirates. Key West was settled by Tories, many of them refugees from the American Revolution, but most of them from the Bahamas. Salvaging wrecked ships was a major occupation and some salvagers were suspected of leading navigators to treacherous waters for the riches the wrecks might yield. The Tories and others from the Bahamas contributed steamed puddings, conch salad, fiery with bird peppers, and peas and rice seasoned with the wild marjoram of the Bahamas, that now is translated to oregano. Living at the southern end of the sparsely settled peninsula, they created Key lime pie and "old sour" with the native lime, and used canned condensed and evaporated milk liberally in the absence of a safe supply of fresh milk, as is common in the tropics.

The Jewish population of Florida grew slowly. Some Jews were settled in Pensacola as early as the 1760s, and a Jewish fur trader was living in St. Augustine in 1785. Until the Civil War, small numbers of Jews came to Florida to earn their livelihoods as planters, farmers, and merchants. Jews historically adapt local foods to their dietary laws, and the early immigrants to Florida did just that. The real estate boom of the 1920s attracted Jewish as well as other investors, and Miami Beach was known as a center of Jewish culture; Jewish communities in other cities burgeoned, and restaurants catering to Jewish tastes sprang up. Many tourists consider a Miami Beach pickle and pastrami sandwich or slice of cheesecake a high point of a winter holiday.

New Smyrna was the first Greek community in Florida, but the best-known one is Tarpon Springs. Once a sponge fishing port, today it is a tourist center and a great place to try Greek food. Greek salad is popular at home and in restaurants everywhere, and a simple olive oil and lemon sauce on grilled snapper is Greek inspired.

In the late 1880s Northern tycoons began to build the railroads that opened land routes to south and central Florida and the hotels that set a style for grand living. But it was the workers, who stayed on in Florida, and the farmers and businessmen, whom the railroads brought in, that had a longer-lasting effect on the real food. In South Dade county, after the final spur of the railroad to Key West was completed, men quit their work crews and homesteaded near the town that was aptly named Homestead. The wives they imported from Northern states to help build the family stakes in the fruitful land would remember forever eating their first mangoes and making them into pie, as they had made apple pies back home. These women and railroad wives everywhere in Florida developed countless ways to use guavas, carambolas, fresh ginger, and local seafood. They left their mark on the cookery of Florida when their inventions were circulated through home demonstration clubs, community cookbooks, and by word of mouth.

The real estate bust after the hurricane of 1926 put a damper on change until the 1950s, when men and women came home from World War II, eager to restart their lives. Servicemen who had been stationed in Florida returned with families, bought tract houses with GI loans, and equipped them with refrigerators, blenders, and the latest kitchen gadgets. Newcomers learned to love papayas, guavas, and avocados. The average child in south Florida knew mangoes before apples, and snacked on such fruits as loquats and carambolas.

Then, in December 1959, began the largest migration of all time, the refugees from Cuba. Southwest Eighth Street in Miami became Calle Ocho, with a Cuban-style restaurant every two or three doors, and black beans and arroz con pollo were soon daily fare everywhere in Florida. Even in small towns, there were Cuban sandwich take-out shops.

The blending of peoples and their foods continues, with Haitians, Nicaraguans, and Dominicans adding their bits. Mexicans, Indonesians, Cambodians, and Vietnamese are farming in south Florida, in the enormous vegetable and melon fields near Lake Okeechobee, in the central citrus belt—actually in almost every part of the state. The Chinese community in Miami that numbered a few families in the 1950s has grown so large that several Oriental markets have opened to cater to them.

Today innovative flavors are being introduced by bright young chefs, inspired by the bounty of fresh foods. Allen Susser and Mark Militello in Miami, Doug Shook and Phil Heimer in Key West, and Lionel Nicaise, Marty Blitz, and Tony Granahan in Tampa are combining garden-fresh fruits and vegetables, locally caught seafood, and other first-rate ingredients in surprising ways. Gilbert LeCoze, the young Frenchman who made a great splash in New York City with a seafood restaurant in the 1980s, has opened a place in Coconut Grove to highlight Florida seafood. Geoffrey Tomb, who writes about food for the Miami *Herald* and, at times, has been a stern critic of dullness of the local diet, anticipates a Florida cuisine as adventurous as that of California, if the public can be lured into accepting the new tastes. "The raw materials are here," he says. "There's no reason that our chefs cannot do as well or better than those in California."

Time will tell if New Wave cooking will add to the rich blend of Hispanic, southern United States, and dozens of other cuisines that Floridians enjoy daily. Will mango and pineapple salsas outdo grits and greens? It's a toss-up, and a delicious one.

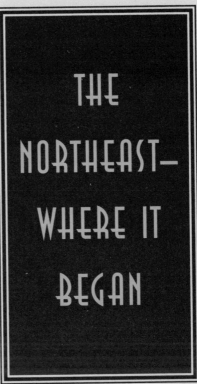

THE NORTHEAST— WHERE IT BEGAN

APPETIZERS

Fromajardis

Marinated Green Beans with Dill

Okra Appetizer

Those Toasts

Tallahassee Chicken Salad

Veggie Riders

Jacksonville Tabbouleh

ENTRÉES

Fernandina Shrimp Gravy

Green Sauce for Seafood

Minorcan Chicken Pilau

Shrimp Broth

Oyster Pie

Broiled or Grilled Rock Shrimp

St. Augustine Beef Chuck Barbecue

Sfeeha (Syrian Meat Pies)

VEGETABLES

Eggplant in Italian-Style Sauce

Florida Smoked Beans

Country Baked Beans

Indian Corn

Grits à la Summerfield

BREADS

Jane Burbank's Hushpuppies

Refrigerator-Freezer Yeast Biscuits

DESSERTS

Minorcan Christmas Candy

Stirring Fruitcake

Peanut Butter Pie

Open-Face Blueberry Pie

Pecan Pie

The gateway to Florida for many tourists and newcomers is I-95, crossing into the state over the St. Marys River. For a first taste of real food, take the second ramp off the Interstate to Fernandina Beach. In the fall or winter, often you'll find notices of oyster roasts posted in the historic district. Buy a ticket for a feast that goes back to the days when Spanish explorers came upon natives roasting their oysters, a handy way of opening the sharp shells without cutting their hands. Later, in the seventeenth century, English and African Americans from the Low Country of Georgia and the Carolinas came across the border into Florida and brought with them their versions of an oyster roast, a convivial spread shared at communal tables; the people of Fernandina Beach still carry on the tradition for community benefits and backyard supper entertainments.

When Ponce de León landed a few miles south of the St. Marys River in 1513, natives were farming corn, beans, and other vegetables, foods that helped the explorers survive in the unknown land. Cornbread and vegetables still figure prominently in the Florida diet. The Indians ate swamp cabbage (hearts of palm) and a huge variety of fish; they, too, remain on the Florida menu. Natives smoked mullet, mackerel, and shrimp; smoked seafood is still highly prized on both coasts of Florida.

Fifty-two years after Ponce de León, St. Augustine was founded as a mission town. As nuns and priests took religion across the territory, their larder was limited, but they knew what to do with corn and vegetables that were grown, the wild boar descended from pigs that were left to run free by Spanish landing parties, the wild fruits, and vegetables, game, and seafood.

Two hundred years after the founding of St. Augustine, Minorcans settled there, to reinforce the Spanish culture. Greek, Portuguese, Ital-

3

ian, and other seagoing folk sailed into ports to trade, and some stayed, tossing other Mediterranean tastes into the cooking pot.

Since pre-Colonial times, Anglos and African-Americans have trickled in from Alabama and Georgia, the Carolinas, and Tennessee to work in the turpentine and lumbering forests. They brought "Cracker cookin'" and a Southern taste for fried chicken, biscuits, gravy, and desserts.

This is seafood country. No wedding reception is complete without pickled shrimp, and in restaurants in St. Augustine, fried shrimp invariably draws long waiting lines. Today, frying is giving way to grilling, broiling, and poaching fish and seafood, but northeast Florida still produces what may be the best fried seafood you'll ever have, as chefs here take special pains with it.

Drive west to Tallahassee, the territorial capital and now the seat of state government, and hear the soft Southern accents. Grits and cornbread are daily food; markets carry a special chowchow for the Presbyterian church chicken salad; the coffee frappe that has been ladled out at receptions for more than a century is as delicious as ever. Near town are hunting lodges that house wealthy sportsmen, who dine on country-cured hams, as well as quail, and other game. Ocala to the south is cattle country and winter home to horsey folk, who indulge in grand buffets to rival those of Kentucky or Saratoga.

Tomatoes and summer squashes come from Lake Butler to fresh markets in Jacksonville, Tallahassee, and other cities. Hastings near St. Augustine provides "the finest potatoes in the world," says Mark Rodriguez, owner of a restaurant in Maitland. Pecan trees shade yards and provide Florida's favorite nut in the autumn. Food traditions of the region reflect the diversity of the people. Pilau is a two-faced dish, burning with the fire of datil peppers, if it is made the Minorcan way, well seasoned but not so spicy if the rice dish is done Southern American–fashion.

Two of Florida's best-known food writers, Marjorie Kinnan Rawlings, whose *Cross Creek Cookery* was a classic in the 1950s, and Ernest Matthew Mickler, whose book *White Trash Cooking* became a runaway best-seller for a few months in 1986, honed their tastes in northern Florida; Rawlings as a young writer in Cross Creek, near Gainesville, and Mickler from birth at a crossroads town, Palm City, near St. Augustine.

The stew is rich—a grand mixture of Florida-produced foods set to the tune of hundreds of personal culinary traditions.

FROMAJARDIS

MAKES 24 3-INCH OR 8 TO 10 6-INCH PASTRIES.

After visiting St. Augustine in 1843, William Cullen Bryant included the Fromajardis hymn in Mahonese dialect in his "Letters of a Traveller." Fromajardis are the traditional cheese pastries that Minorcan women would bake in the weeks before Easter. On the eve of the feast day, serenaders would walk through the streets, singing the salute to Mary, mother of Jesus, and rap on the wooden shutters of Minorcan homes. A good host would swing open the shutters and distribute the pastries to the serenaders, then the song, translated into English, would end:

> The owner of this house
> Is a polite gentleman.

If the host failed to offer Fromajardis, the hymn ended loudly for the neighbors to hear:

> The owner of this house
> Is an impolite gentleman.

The Fromajardis custom is still observed at 8 p.m. each Easter Eve at the Oldest House in St. Augustine. And the crisp cheese turnovers are served at parties as an accompaniment to wine and other drinks.

3 cups all-purpose flour
¼ teaspoon nutmeg
1 teaspoon salt
1 cup vegetable shortening
8 to 10 tablespoons cold
    water
4 large eggs

½ pound sharp Cheddar
    cheese, shredded
½ teaspoon minced datil
    pepper or other small hot
    chile pepper or ⅛ teaspoon
    ground red pepper
    (cayenne)

In a medium-size bowl, mix the flour, nutmeg, and salt until blended. Add the shortening in spoonfuls and cut it in with a pastry blender or two table knives until the mixture resembles coarse meal. Add 2 table-spoons of the water and blend it in thoroughly with a fork, then add the remaining cold water by the tablespoon, using only enough to make the dough cling together. Gather into a ball, wrap in waxed paper, and refrigerate while preparing the filling, or refrigerate up to 24 hours.

Preheat the oven to 425 degrees. For the filling, beat the eggs, then stir in the cheese and chile. Roll out the dough, half at a time, to sheets ⅛ inch thick. Cut in rounds with a 3- to 6-inch cutter. Place the rounds on baking sheets, drop 1 teaspoonful filling for small size up to 2 teaspoons for large pastries near the center of each round. Fold over to half-moon shapes and press edges together with the tines of a fork. Cut across the top of each pastry with short snips of scissors or a sharp knife. Place on ungreased baking sheets. Bake 10 minutes, until crisp and pale brown. Move to the top rack of the oven and bake 2 to 3 minutes longer, to brown; the filling will ooze through the cuts in the top.

If there is leftover pastry dough, women in St. Augustine would use it to make "crispies"; they roll out the dough thin, sprinkle it with cinnamon sugar, cut the pastry into small wafers, and bake the "crispies" along with the cheese pastries. If there is leftover filling, it can be spread on bread, cut in fingers or triangles, and baked with the cheese turnovers.

Serve Fromajardis warm or hot. If baked beforehand, put them on a cookie sheet and reheat them in a preheated 375-degree oven for 5 to 10 minutes.

THE NATIVES

Three native peoples, the Seminoles, Miccosukees, and Creeks, live in Florida today, and none traces its roots to the people that Ponce de León came across in 1513. In 1492, 750,000 natives, mistakenly called Indians, lived in Florida, writes Gary R. Mormino, historian at the University of South Florida. The Ais, Tequestas, Calusas, and other groups living south of Cape Canaveral and Charlotte Harbor were nomadic, and they were so warlike that explorers chose to land to the north, where the Apalachees and Timucuas were more friendly. They lived in houses in permanent villages and raised corn and other food crops. In the hundred years after St. Augustine was settled, thousands of natives succumbed to European diseases, such as smallpox, and were killed in battles. When Spain ceded Florida to the English in 1763 in exchange for Havana, the few surviving natives fled to Cuba and Mexico, never to return.

The Seminoles, the best-known Native Americans of today, are a conglomerate—their name means "runaways." Most of them were fugitives from the whites, including the Yamasees driven from the Carolinas in 1717, Oconees from the Apalachicola River Valley, and Creeks from Georgia. Runaway slaves joined the natives in such numbers that the United States launched campaigns led by Andrew Jackson in 1814 and 1818 to return the slaves to their owners. The white warriors were unsuccessful at capturing the slaves, but fighting to take lands for white settlers continued until the Seminoles' chief Osceola was captured by trickery in 1837, to die in prison later. The Seminoles then fled to the Everglades, where they still live, farming, herding cattle, hunting, fishing, and working as fishing and hunting guides to the mysterious watery land.

The Miccosukees, a smaller tribe, operate a tourist village and restaurant on U.S. 41 about thirty-five miles west of Miami. There they show off their handicrafts, including the bright skirts and shirts painstakingly stitched of many hues of cotton fabric. The Miccosukees still preserve their native religion, whereas many Seminoles have been converted to Christianity. Both tribes observe traditional Green Corn and Hunting Dances that few whites have witnessed.

These south Florida natives lived in chickees, small open-sided pavilions with palm-thatch roofs, and cooked over open fires. They farmed corn, coconuts, fruits, and other foods, and proved to be good cattlemen, many of them running small herds. For more than one hundred years their diets consisted of the foods they raised, game and fish of the Everglades, wild fruits and berries, and sugar and other items obtained in bartering. But young people attending public schools and working at jobs outside the Seminole settlements easily adopted the burger-and-Coke diets of white teenagers, and elders worry that the young are eating too much fried food. Today cars and television sets are as much a part of their lives as they are of whites'. Some Indians live in houses in nearby towns, but go home to the 'Glades for special occasions.

Creeks whose forebears came from Alabama and other Southeastern states are the largest tribe in Florida, but the least visible, as the people farm quietly in rural communities of northwest Florida. Creek schools in Blountstown, Panama City, Bruce, and Pensacola are operated to perpetuate the Creek language and history, and traditional Green Corn, Little Green Corn, and Harvest festivals are celebrated each year in Blountstown.

MARINATED GREEN BEANS WITH DILL

MAKES 4 TO 6 SERVINGS.

Farm stands and home gardens once were the only sources of fine produce in Florida. As in other regions, specialty produce markets and many supermarkets featuring a delicious variety of vegetables and fruits grown nearby are springing up. Helen Brown of Jacksonville, who also is into the fitness movement that has struck the nation, regularly patronizes a neighborhood produce market, well lighted, with a knowledgeable staff, and filled with an enormous array of fresh things. She does this fresh pickle with snap beans or broccoli, whichever is in season. Broccoli is better, as the vinegar turns the beans a dull brown.

1½ pounds green beans or broccoli

1 small clove garlic, minced

¼ cup tightly packed minced fresh dill

3 tablespoons olive oil

2 tablespoons cider vinegar or lemon juice

¼ teaspoon salt, or to taste

Wash, trim, and cut the beans if they are large. The broccoli stalks should be peeled and diced, with the flowerets broken apart. Cook the beans or broccoli in boiling water until just crisp-tender. Remove from the hot water and cool in a bowl.

Combine the garlic and dill in a small bowl. Whisk in the oil, then the vinegar and salt. Pour over the vegetables and toss lightly. Cover and refrigerate. Serve at room temperature.

OKRA APPETIZER

MAKES 4 SERVINGS.

If you detest flabby okra, these tender-firm spears with lemony hollandaise sauce will be a refreshing surprise. We have converted this recipe for okra from *Cross Creek Cookery* by Marjorie Kinnan Rawlings to a lighter sauce that looks and tastes like hollandaise, and is perfectly safe. Using sour half-and-half in place of butter enables you to cook the sauce like a custard to a temperature high enough to make the egg yolks completely safe. (See Note.)

40 to 48 small tender spears of okra	**2 tablespoons lemon juice**
2 egg yolks	**Dash ground red pepper (cayenne)**
1 cup sour half-and-half	

Choose okra of uniform size for even cooking, and small tender spears are best. Bring a large saucepanful of lightly salted water to a boil. Wash the okra and leave it whole; do not cut off the stems. Drop it into the boiling water. Do not crowd it; cook it in two batches, if necessary. Boil 2 to 3 minutes, just until the okra is crisp-tender. Test with a fork. Drain the okra immediately and dry on paper towels, then put on a plate. Cover with foil to keep warm.

In the top of a double boiler or small heatproof glass mixing bowl set over boiling water, stir together the egg yolks and sour half-and-half. Heat and stir about 5 minutes. When the sauce begins to thicken add the lemon juice and red pepper. Continue to stir and cook until the sauce mounds slightly on a spoon.

Place a small custard cup, tiny bowl, or hollowed-out lemon half in the center of each salad plate. Spoon some of the sauce into each cup. Arrange the okra spoke-fashion around the sauce cups, 10 to 12 spears per serving. Okra spears are picked up by the stem ends and dipped in the sauce to eat.

NOTE: Partially cooked eggs as in hollandaise sauce may be unsafe. But the virulent strain of salmonella that contaminates a few fresh eggs is destroyed if heated to 160 degrees. When the sour-cream, egg-yolk mixture thickens, the temperature will be 160 degrees or higher. Test with an instant-reading thermometer, if you wish.

THOSE TOASTS

MAKES 5 TO 6 DOZEN TOASTS.

A caterer in Jacksonville kept the secret of these non-crumbly canapé bases until she retired in the 1960s. A friend got the recipe and spread it around. Her "secret" has been adopted throughout Florida. Families serve it as a snack, as croutons to sprinkle over gazpacho and other soups, and occasionally as the base for spreads. Those Toasts, as they are invariably called, keep well, so they are a godsend for holiday snacking and entertaining. When making these, don't be stingy with the butter, and note that cottony bread makes flabby toasts with weak flavor.

1 large loaf (1½ pounds)
   firm-type sandwich bread
½ cup (1 stick) butter,
   melted
¼ cup freshly grated
   Parmesan cheese

Optional toppings: minced
   garlic or green onion tops,
   parsley flakes, dried dill
   weed, sesame, caraway, or
   poppy seed

Preheat the oven to 250 degrees. Line a large cookie sheet or jelly-roll pan with foil. Cut the crusts off the bread, working with 4 slices stacked, then cut in quarters—squares, rectangles, or fingers. Fit closely together in the pan. Brush generously with the melted butter, then sprinkle with Parmesan cheese. For variety, add one or more of the optional toppings, though the simpler toast is more adaptable to soups, salads, and so on. Bake near the middle of the oven until dry and golden brown, 1½ to 2 hours. Cool and pack in airtight containers. Keep up to 1 week at room temperature, several weeks in the freezer.

BULLBAT TIME

*S*ocializing is easy and usually informal for all except ceremonial events in Florida. The invitation is casual, a friend or neighbor saying, "Come over for supper (a drink, tea, or other friendly gathering)." A newcomer is apt to ask, "What time!" "About bullbat time," the host or hostess will answer.

Bullbat time is the hour for almost any evening socializing, especially a cocktail party, and people at home often say, "Let's have a drink, it's 'bout bullbat time."

Bullbats are not bats at all, but a type of nighthawk that swoops down from country courthouse cupolas and church steeples, and some say they roost in and soar from the state capitol dome. The graceful flight of a dozen or two of the birds against the evening sky fading to gold or mauve is one of the natural beauties of north Florida.

TALLAHASSEE CHICKEN SALAD

MAKES 4 SERVINGS.

The original recipe for this treasured dish called for "five fat hens, 1 quart chow-chow pickle, and 1 dozen eggs (for making the mayonnaise)." For many years it was called Presbyterian Chicken Salad, and was the main dish at the old church's annual bazaar. Cross & Blackwell's Chow-chow pickle, which still is stocked by markets in Tallahassee and some other Florida towns, makes this salad authentic. To a Tallahassean nothing else will do, though taste as you add the chowchow, as some people like a milder mustard flavor. Home folk still make the salad this way for parties, large and small. This recipe uses poached chicken breasts and thighs in about equal parts.

2 cups chopped poached chicken thighs and breasts (see Note)	Dash hot pepper sauce
1 cup diced celery	1/3 cup mayonnaise, or as needed to moisten
Half a 9 3/8-ounce jar chowchow	Garden or Boston lettuce

In a medium-size mixing bowl, combine the chicken, celery, chowchow, and pepper sauce. Mix lightly; add the mayonnaise and mix again. Add more mayonnaise if needed to moisten well. Chill 1 to 2 hours before serving. Line a bowl or platter with greens and spoon the salad onto the greens.

NOTE: To poach chicken: Combine 1 pound each of skinned chicken thighs and breast pieces in a large skillet with a carrot, peeled and sliced; a rib of celery, cut in chunks; a small onion, cut in halves but not peeled; and water to barely cover the mixture. Add 1/2 teaspoon salt, 1/4 teaspoon pepper, a sprig or two of parsley, and a lemon half. Cover, and simmer 30 to 45 minutes, until juices run clear or golden when the chicken is pierced with a fork. Cool the chicken in the broth. Cut meat off the bone and chop it coarsely. Refrigerate until ready to make the salad. If desired, the broth should be saved for soups or other uses.

British travel writer F. Trench Townshend wrote of a camping trip through sparsely settled areas of Florida and Cuba in 1884. He seemed surprised to find that Jacksonville, the party's starting place, provided most of the foods and cooking equipment for the journey. He wrote:

> The stores we laid in were strictly necessaries and consisted of the following articles: A demi-john of whiskey, tea, coffee, sugar, flour, baking powder, bacon, ship's biscuits, hominy, lard, preserved milk, a few cans of potted meats and sardines, salt, and tobacco; also a saucepan, coffee pot, tin plates, knives, forks, spoons, tin cups, matches, and last, but not least, an axe, perhaps the most important article for equipping for travel in the backwoods.

> from *Wild Life in Florida with a Visit to Cuba*
> by F. Trench Townshend, captain, Second Life Guards;
> Hurst and Blackett, London, 1875

VEGGIE RIDERS

MAKES 4 TO 6 SERVINGS.

Doctors, nurses, patients, and folk from nearby offices and shops lunch on Veggie Riders at a modest cafe near St. Vincent's Hospital in Jacksonville. The "Riders" are pita-bread pockets that are filled with the bulgur wheat and vegetable salad called tabbouleh, and a slice of cheese, and then grilled. Other quick-lunch spots serve them as well. This kind of sandwich is a contribution of Syrians, whose parents and grandparents settled in Jacksonville almost a century ago. Many a mother of Syrian ancestry serves these sandwiches as family lunch or party food, as they are easy to do at home. A Rider is grilled in a well-oiled skillet, or on a griddle, or it is wrapped in plastic and heated in a microwave.

4 to 6 large pita pockets
1⅓ to 2 cups Jacksonville
   Tabbouleh (recipe follows)
4 to 6 ounces Swiss, Cheddar,
   feta, or other cheese

Oil or vegetable cooking spray
   for grilling (optional)

Slit the pita pockets at one edge and open up for filling. Spoon about ⅓ cup Tabbouleh into each and insert a slice or finger of cheese. Wrap each sandwich in plastic film and microwave two sandwiches at a time for 2 minutes on high, until cheese is melted and salad warmed. Or heat the sandwiches on a hot grill or skillet greased with oil or cooking spray, for about 3 minutes, turning once. Serve warm.

AN OYSTER ROAST

In a typical back garden in Fernandina Beach stands a massive stone table surrounded by benches. This is an oyster-roast table, with a deep trough behind the table top. A piece of sheet metal is laid over a fire built in the trough or a nearby grill, and oysters are cooked there. The fresh oysters are first scrubbed well, then placed on the hot metal and cooked until the shells open, 15 minutes or longer. During cooking, the oysters are raked with a short-handled tool to turn them, and when done they are lifted to serving dishes.

Each guest is given a bowl of melted butter seasoned with lime or lemon juice and Worcestershire sauce. The host or helpers pry the shells loose; some guests even bring their own personal oyster knives to extract the oysters. There are many Fernandina natives who value their old-fashioned knives that were made by flattening railroad nails.

The oysters of old were dug off Amelia Island, on which Fernandina stands, but with the ups and downs that occur in oyster beds, the shellfish sometimes has to be shipped in for roasts.

Old-time oyster roasts were only the first course of a dinner that might consist of a pilau, rice, and peas, hot biscuits, and a dessert. Today, oyster roasts are likely to be the main course, with garlic bread and a salad on the-side.

Oyster roasts provided wintertime entertainment to the earliest white and African settlers of Savannah and south Georgia, where many Floridians trace their roots. A popular excursion now is to sail from Fernandina in the morning to Cumberland Island, which lies in full view off the harbor, enjoy an oyster roast, and sail home before nightfall.

JACKSONVILLE TABBOULEH

MAKES 6 TO 8 SERVINGS.

Greens and fresh herbs are abundant in Florida, so standard recipes often get an extra measure of them. This classic Middle Eastern salad is lightened with more than the usual amount of parsley and is faintly scented with fresh mint. The recipe is large enough to serve as a side dish for dinner, *and* provide the filling for Rider sandwiches at the next day's lunch.

1½ cups fine bulgur (cracked wheat)

2 cups very hot water

2 cups minced parsley, preferably flat leaf

2 tablespoons minced mint leaves or 1 teaspoon mint flakes

¾ cup diced sweet onion

1 ripe tomato, diced

¼ cup olive oil

¼ cup lemon juice

½ teaspoon salt, or to taste

¼ teaspoon freshly ground pepper

Romaine or Belgian endive leaves

Place the bulgur in a medium-size mixing bowl, add the hot water, and let the mixture stand 1 to 2 hours, until the wheat is softened and most of the water absorbed. Remove as much of the water as possible, squeezing the damp grain between your hands. Return the bulgur to the bowl and mix in the parsley, mint, onion, and tomato. Drizzle the oil and lemon juice over the salad, add the salt and pepper, and toss lightly to mix it thoroughly. Pile the salad into a bowl or onto a platter and surround it with greens.

DONAX BROTH

The donax, also called coquina or periwinkle, is a tiny mollusk in a varicolored round shell about the size of your fingertip. Dozens of them wash in on a wave and scurry to burrow into the sand, so you have to be nimble to capture them. Once they've been scooped up, they are put in a colander and lowered into the sea to flush out the sand. Six quarts of donax will flavor a quart of broth.

The making of donax broth used to be the high point of great summer outings along any coast of Florida. With the advent of air conditioning, such sun-kissed play is less seductive, but stalwarts still gather donax and hurry home with them to make broth in air-conditioned comfort.

Joan Adams Wickham dedicates this recipe to Pedro Menéndez de Avilés, founder of St. Augustine, in *Food Favorites of St. Augustine:*

> Place the donax in a large kettle filled with enough preheated water to barely cover the shellfish. Slowly bring the mixture to a rolling boil and simmer two or three minutes. Do not add salt, as fresh sea water seasons donax broth. Strain the delicate liquid through cheesecloth or a fine sieve, pour into small soup cups, and season it lightly with freshly ground pepper, dots of butter, and a bit of cream and chopped parsley. Serve the broth very hot or well chilled.

For heartier flavor, make donax broth double-rich fashion. Simmer the broth as directed by Joan Wickham, then use this stock for cooking a fresh batch of the shellfish. The donax are discarded, as chipping off the circular cover of the shell is difficult; the meat has a rubbery texture and depends on a vinegary sauce or butter for flavor. However, the tiny fish may be extracted with a small pick, dipped in butter or a mignonette (oil and vinegar) sauce, and consumed after cooking.

FERNANDINA SHRIMP GRAVY

MAKES 4 TO 6 SERVINGS.

Shrimp nets that are used around the world are woven in Fernandina. It was the local fishermen who pioneered modern deepwater shrimping early in this century. The most famous dish made here of the wiggling crustacean is known as Shrimp Gravy—shrimp in a savory brown sauce that is served over rice. Old-timers make the coloring for the sauce by caramelizing sugar, but commercial gravy coloring is substituted by cooks in a hurry. But don't tamper with the recipe, or people here protest. When a writer from west Florida once came to Fernandina in search of recipes, one of her finds was Shrimp Gravy; Helen Litrico, who gave her the recipe, was horrified at the writer's adaptation. "She called for only a half pound of shrimp, and celery instead of bell pepper!" exclaimed Helen. "And I suspect she thought a pound and a half of shrimp too expensive." In Fernandina, if cost is a concern, a cook is likely to serve it less often, but Shrimp Gravy is full of what it is—mostly shrimp.

1 tablespoon sugar

1 tablespoon plus 1 cup water

2 ounces salt pork, diced

½ cup minced onion

½ cup diced green bell pepper

½ cup diced red bell pepper

½ cup diced celery

1½ pounds shrimp, shelled, cleaned, and, if large, cut in pieces

1 teaspoon salt

¼ teaspoon freshly ground black pepper

⅛ teaspoon crushed dried red pepper

2 cups hot cooked rice

In a heavy medium-size skillet, stir the sugar over moderate heat until it begins to melt. Continue to cook until the syrup turns golden. Add the tablespoon of water, protecting your hands with a pot holder as the hot sugar may spatter. Stir until the sugar is dissolved. Set this caramel aside.

In a large skillet or sauté pan, cook the salt pork until browned, stirring now and then. Remove the pork bits with a slotted spoon, and set aside. Pour off all but 1 tablespoon of pork drippings. Add the onion, green and red peppers, and celery. Sauté until the vegetables are tender. Add the shrimp and cook until they turn bright pink and are opaque, 2 to 3 minutes. Remove the shrimp and vegetables with a slotted spoon and keep them warm on a plate. Add the remaining 1 cup water and 1 teaspoon of the caramel to the pan drippings. Bring to a boil, stir, and simmer 1 to 2 minutes. Season with salt, black pepper, and crushed red pepper.

Return the shrimp and vegetables and the salt pork bits to the gravy and heat a minute or two. Serve hot over rice.

GREEN SAUCE FOR SEAFOOD

MAKES 1½ CUPS, DIP FOR 10 TO 12 PERSONS OR SAUCE FOR 4 TO 6 SERVINGS.

St. Augustine is the shrimp-eating capital of Florida, say local folk, and this sauce on steamed or fried shrimp is a tasty alternative to ketchup-based mixtures. The bread base of this sauce is reminiscent of the famed *skordalia* of Greece. Many persons of Greek ancestry live here, and festivals at the Greek Orthodox church offer fabulous foods. The Green Sauce is so widely used that nobody is quite sure that it is Greek.

1 slice white bread with crust
   removed
5 tablespoons distilled white
   vinegar
4 tablespoons olive oil, or
   as needed
¾ cup minced parsley,
   preferably flat leaf

2 cloves garlic, minced
3 anchovy fillets, minced
   fine
1 teaspoon sugar
1½ teaspoons capers,
   drained

Tear the bread into pieces and place in a small bowl. Add 3 tablespoons of vinegar and soak until the bread is saturated, about 30 minutes. Using a hand-mixer (or you may do the puréeing in a blender or mini-chopper), add the olive oil, parsley, garlic, anchovies, and sugar to the bread and vinegar. Beat (or process) until well mixed. Add the capers and the remaining 2 tablespoons vinegar. Spoon into a small serving bowl and let stand 15 to 20 minutes to blend the flavors or chill up to 3 hours. Serve as a dip with steamed or poached seafood or as a sauce with broiled, poached, or grilled fish.

THE HOSPITAL—BEST FOOD IN TOWN

The best food in town is at the hospital, said Anne Heymen, food editor of the St. Augustine *Record,* and several other writers in the busy city room between editions chimed in, "Ummh, that catfish!" A society writer told of three guests at a tea leaving early to get front places in line at the Flagler Hospital's cafeteria. Asked how the hospital cafeteria earned such high praise for catfish, Jo Coleman, director of food services, said, "I buy the best catfish available!" She admitted that the board of Flagler Hospital allows enough slack in her budget so that she can shop for quality as well as price. She buys a top brand of farm-raised catfish, cut in 8-ounce fillets. The fillets are sprinkled with seafood seasoning mix and dipped in a prepared coating (both available in most supermarkets), and fried a few fillets at a time in 365-degree deep oil. The fish is then whisked to the serving counter. The cafeteria line moves fast, and the trays are replenished constantly, so the fish never loses its flavor and crispness by languishing on a steam table. Catfish is served every two weeks, on "payday Fridays," explains Coleman. The hospital cafeteria was established for the convenience of hospital staff and families of patients, and later opened to elderly persons as a place for economical meals and socializing. Now St. Augustine people of all ages and economic status eat there, indulging in the cafeteria's prizewinning version of Minorcan clam chowder, a choice of hot and cold foods, as well as the catfish and hushpuppies.

PILAU AND ARROZ CON POLLO—
THE RICE SUPERSTARS

Pilau and arroz con pollo illustrate the cultural mix that makes Florida cookery unique. The rice mixture has two distinct forms, Minorcan and southern United States. The Minorcan pilau is Spanish in character, showing the influence of the Moors who occupied southern Spain for centuries. The southern United States pilau is milder, with an African-American zest in some versions. Both combine chicken or seafood with the rice and seasonings.

The Minorcan-style pilau is spiced, sometimes fiercely, with the tiny datil pepper unique to Minorcan cookery, and is russet colored with tomato and aromatic with onion, garlic, and bell peppers.

Rice plantations flourished in the Low Country of Georgia and South Carolina in the seventeenth and eighteenth centuries, and to this day some Low Country folk eat more rice than wheat or corn products. The pilau they made and brought to Florida can be quite simple, with little or no tomato, no garlic, or high seasoning. Or Southern pilau may be spicy hot with black pepper or tiny bird peppers, tastes that were dear to African Americans working on the rice plantations. The Southern-style pilau has chopped hard-boiled egg mixed into it or sliced over the top.

The best-known of all Florida-Cuban dishes, arroz con pollo, came with cigar workers in the nineteenth century. The rice is colored golden by saffron, bijol (a less expensive, less flavorful derivative of the annatto tree), or annatto seeds. Lots of garlic and onion season the combination; roasted sweet red peppers and green peas or asparagus garnish the steamed yellow rice and chicken flamboyantly.

In the 1940s and 1950s the foremost gathering place of Hispanics in Miami was Club Latino at the corner of Northwest Fifth Street and Miami Avenue. Lean and handsome jai alai players would cluster at one end of the bar, talking in a Basque dialect, old men pored over checkerboards in the patio, and young men drank Hatouey beer from Havana at tables while their pretty dark-eyed dates sipped Cokes. Many Cuban-style foods were listed on the menu, but arroz con pollo was the one that attracted Anglos, out on the town for "exotic food." Arroz con pollo is no longer exotic. Today you find it in thousands of eating spots and in homes from Pensacola to Key West. It is almost as popular at church suppers and potlucks as pilau, and most Floridians who cook make an arroz con pollo of some sort.

MINORCAN CHICKEN PILAU

MAKES 4 SERVINGS.

Pilau is a one-pot meal of rice and seasonings with chicken, seafood, or meat. Those who cook pilau regularly may simmer the cut-up chicken and pour rice and seasonings into the broth around it. We cook the chicken separately, take the meat off the bones, then measure the cooking liquid and adjust the right amount of rice to liquid. The chicken is then returned to the pot to reheat. The traditional garnishes are hard-cooked egg and lots of minced parsley.

3 tablespoons olive or vegetable oil	½ teaspoon salt, or to taste
1 3-pound chicken, cut up	¼ teaspoon freshly ground pepper, or to taste
2 onions, chopped	
2 cups chicken broth	1 can (16 ounces) whole tomatoes, chopped, or 2 cups fresh ripe tomatoes peeled and chopped
2 ounces salt pork or country-smoked ham, diced	
½ green bell pepper, coarsely chopped	
1 large clove garlic, minced	1 datil pepper, 1 inch long, or other hot chile pepper
1 rib celery, diced	1 hard-cooked egg, sliced
2 cups long-grain rice	2 tablespoons minced parsley

Heat 2 tablespoons of the oil in a Dutch oven, add the chicken, and brown lightly. Push the chicken to the side, add half of the onions to the drippings, and sauté a minute or two. Rearrange the chicken evenly, add

1 cup of the broth, cover, and simmer 30 minutes or until the chicken is tender. Remove chicken and pour the pan juices into a 2-cup measure. When cool, skin the bird, remove the meat from the bone in large pieces, and set aside.

In a large deep skillet or Dutch oven, heat the remaining 1 table-spoon of oil and the salt pork or ham. Sauté until the pork bits are lightly browned. Add the remaining onion, green pepper, garlic, and celery. Sauté until the onion is tender. Add the rice and sauté, stirring, until it looks opaque. Add the ½ teaspoon salt and ¼ teaspoon pepper. Pour enough chicken broth into the measure with the pan juices to make 1½ cups and add along with the tomatoes to the vegetables. Cover and sim-mer 25 minutes, until the rice is tender and liquid absorbed. Mix the datil pepper or chile pepper and chicken lightly into the rice; heat 2 to 3 min-utes. Taste and add salt and pepper, if needed. Turn onto a platter, arrange sliced egg around the edge, and sprinkle with parsley.

LOW COUNTRY CHICKEN PILAU
CHICKEN PERLOO

Follow the recipe for Minorcan Pilau, omitting the datil pepper and gar-lic, and using only 1 cup tomato and 2 cups broth. Use the tiny bird pep-per found in Southern gardens in place of the datil pepper, if a spicy pilau is wanted. Low Country Pilau may have chopped hard-cooked egg stirred through it, as well as egg slices as garnish.

MINORCAN OR SOUTHERN SHRIMP PILAU

Begin the pilau by sautéing the onions, salt pork, and other vegetables in the oil. Use Shrimp Broth (recipe follows) in place of the chicken broth. Add 1½ to 2 pounds shelled shrimp to the pilau when the rice is almost tender, cover, and steam the shrimp with the rice for 5 to 6 minutes.

SHRIMP BROTH

MAKES 6 TO 8 CUPS.

If a fish dealer shells the shrimp for you, ask for the shells to make the broth. Some dealers have shells that they give to good customers or sell for a few cents a pound.

Shells from 1½ to 2 pounds shrimp

2 quarts water

1 cup dry white wine (optional)

2 teaspoons salt, or to taste

¼ teaspoon freshly ground pepper

2 teaspoons seafood seasoning, liquid or dry*

½ lime or lemon, squeezed and dropped into the pot

1 medium unpeeled onion, cut in wedges

1 carrot, peeled and cut in chunks

2 ribs celery, cut in chunks

1 to 2 small chile peppers, minced

*Seafood seasoning is available in fish markets and the spice sections of most food markets.

Combine all ingredients except chiles in a large pot. Cover, bring to a boil, and simmer 45 minutes. Add chiles and simmer 5 minutes longer. Cool, strain, and refrigerate in a covered bowl until needed. Extra broth can be frozen in sealed containers up to 6 months.

FIRST CAME DINNER, THEN MARRIAGE

Pedro Menéndez de Avilés, the founder of St. Augustine in 1565, may have been the first host at a state dinner in the Continental United States. After driving off many of the French at Fort Caroline and slaughtering most of the others at Matanzas Inlet, Menéndez set about making friends with the neighbors. He invited Calusa Chief Carlos to a dinner of Spanish food, served with fine silver and other appointments of a high-class European table, wrote the historian Arva Moore Parks in a contribution to *Biscayne Bights and Breezes*. Carlos was so impressed that he offered his sister in marriage to Menéndez. Parks reports that Menéndez couldn't resist the advantage that such a marriage would give him with the natives, so accepted the offer, despite the fact that he already had a wife.

OYSTER PIE

MAKES 4 SERVINGS.

On the northeast Florida coast, a main-dish pie may be a macaroni and cheese or seafood casserole with crumbs, following the custom of ancestors from the Carolina and Georgia Low Country. But some of the finest have crispy crusts over bubbly aromatic fillings, like this one. Oyster pie makes a great luncheon or supper dish and miniature versions are often served as a stylish starter for dinner. The oysters are covered with a sauce of the reduced oyster liquor, cream, and gentle seasonings. Simmer the oysters in their juices only until plumped to avoid toughening them. The pie is best baked in individual dishes to brown the pastry quickly.

1 quart shucked oysters with their liquor	10 whole allspice
	1 tablespoon minced parsley

¼ teaspoon dried or 2 teaspoons minced fresh thyme	½ cup heavy cream

¼ teaspoon dried or 2 teaspoons
minced fresh thyme

½ teaspoon dried or 1 tablespoon
minced fresh marjoram

¼ teaspoon salt

⅛ teaspoon ground
white pepper

½ cup heavy cream

2 tablespoons cream sherry

1 sheet frozen puff pastry,
thawed but cool, or flaky
pastry for a 2-crust 9-inch
pie

Combine the oysters in their liquor with allspice in a large skillet or sauté pan. Simmer over moderate heat until the oysters are plumped, 2 to 3 minutes. Lift out the oysters with a slotted spoon onto a plate. Add the parsley, thyme, marjoram, salt, and pepper to the liquor. Simmer briskly until the liquid is reduced to about ½ cup. Add the cream and sherry, and stir over moderate heat until slightly thickened. Skim out the allspice and return the oysters to the sauce. Spoon the oysters and the sauce into 4 individual shallow baking dishes or a 9-inch pie plate. Roll out the pastry very thin and cut it into shapes to fit the pies. Place the pastry over the pies and crimp the edges to the rims of the dishes. Cut several slits in the top of each pie. You may refrigerate the pies at this point up to 2 or 3 hours. To bake, preheat the oven to 425 degrees. Bake until the pastry is golden brown and the oyster filling bubbly, 12 minutes for individual pies, 15 to 18 minutes for a large pie. Serve at once.

ROCK SHRIMP—A "NEW" SEAFOOD

When rock shrimp first came to market in the 1980s, zealous salesmen and restaurateurs hailed it as a new species. It's not at all new. Florida fishermen had eaten it for generations, but assumed its tough shell made it unsaleable.

Its flavor is between lobster and shrimp, and the texture is as firm as lobster. A favorite way to prepare large rock shrimp is to split them, and grill or broil them with butter and lemon juice. In spite of the considerable obstacle of the hard rigid shell, rock shrimp is sold heavily around most ports in Florida, usually at bargain prices, and often is found in New York and other northern markets.

Retailers will split rock shrimp for you to ready it for grilling, and getting the shrimp out of its shell is not as hard as it seems, once you know a trick or two. Shelling hot steamed rock shrimp is a bit easier than tackling the uncooked ones.

Wear rubber gloves to prevent cuts from the shell. With the tail section in one hand and "legs" in the palm, pop the third joint from the end with sharp kitchen shears. Snip and crack off the rest of the shell, and peel it off. The very distinct sand vein is grasped with the points of the scissors or your finger tips and pulled out. Shelling rock shrimp goes faster and is more fun with a helper or two.

To split the shrimp, lay them back side down and "legs" up on a chopping board. With a sharp knife, cut between the "legs" from the softer undershell through to the hard shell. Open the shrimp up like a book and wash well in cold water to remove the sand vein. Flatten and broil it, cut side up; or the meat can be pulled out of the split shells and cooked—only about half a minute in seasoned boiling water. Do not overcook rock shrimp, as they become tough and flavorless.

Rock shrimp is more perishable than ordinary shrimp, so it always is frozen when caught. Shell and thaw it just before cooking to protect the fresh-frozen quality.

BROILED OR GRILLED ROCK SHRIMP

MAKES 4 SERVINGS.

In Fernandina or St. Augustine, rock shrimp is fun for a patio supper. The split shrimp is brushed with seasoned butter and cooked on a patio grill or at a tabletop broiler with guests gathered around. It can be the main dish, served with a big bowl of salad and garlic bread, or it may be the appetizer before the main course.

4 tablespoons (½ stick) butter	½ teaspoon dried or
2 tablespoons vegetable oil	1 tablespoon minced fresh
2 tablespoons lime or lemon	oregano leaves
juice	2 pounds rock shrimp, split

Combine the butter and oil in a small saucepan and place over low heat until the butter has melted. Beat in the lime juice and oregano. Remove from the heat and let the sauce stand. Open the shrimp in their shells out flat and brush with the butter mixture. Place the meaty sides down over hot coals and grill 2 to 3 minutes, until the flesh is opaque throughout. Be careful not to overcook rock shrimp. Brush with the butter sauce again. Reheat the remaining sauce and serve a small cupful of it with each portion of shrimp.

To broil, place the shrimp shell side down on a greased broiler pan. Brush lightly with the sauce and broil 4 inches from the heat 2 to 3 minutes, until the flesh is opaque. Serve hot with the remaining sauce.

DATIL—THE PEPPER THAT CAME HOME AGAIN

Minorcans who came to St. Augustine in 1777 changed the cooking of Florida forever. One of their contributions is the datil pepper, a slender, yellow-green capsicum, a couple of inches long. The flavor is very hot, "atomic," some chile lovers say. Columbus and his men thought they had found the black pepper that he had promised to bring Queen Isabella if she raised the money for his voyage. The capsicums that the party took to Europe included bell peppers, pimientos, and many hot chiles. Spanish and Italian cooks took to them enthusiastically.

Minorcan women so loved a rare capsicum, the datil pepper, that they brought the seeds here. For more than two hundred years, their descendants have kept the unique pepper alive, sowing, harvesting, and saving the seeds, then replanting them. Today the peppers still are home grown, as the seeds have not been commercially produced, and St. Augustine gardeners believe that datils thrive only there. But gardeners grow them around Jacksonville.

The mystery of how the peppers were nurtured for almost three hundred years on the island of Minorca, then brought back to an ideal environment in the New World, probably never will be solved. But Minorcan-style cooking isn't the same without datil peppers. They make the difference between Minorcan and standard Southern pilau and are a major ingredient of a table sauce called Bottled Hell that is everywhere in St. Augustine.

Bottled Hell is made by puréeing in a blender two cupfuls of datil peppers, seeds included, with a half cup of cider vinegar, then simmering the mixture with the contents of two bottles of ketchup, plus two and a half cups more of the vinegar. The sauce is bottled and stored in a cool place. A commercial version of the sauce is called Dat'l Do It. It can be ordered from Dat'l Do It, Inc., P. O. Box 4019, St. Augustine, FL 32085.

For those who wish to try growing the peppers, seeds occasionally are listed for sale in the Florida Market Bulletin, Fifield Hall, Gainesville, FL 32611. Peppers require a frost-free climate; one grower winters over the plants by bringing them indoors when temperatures drop.

ST. AUGUSTINE BEEF CHUCK BARBECUE

MAKES 6 TO 8 SERVINGS.

Floridians years ago discovered the juicy goodflavor of "a hunk of meat" barbecued on a grill. Before air-conditioning and microwaving, cooking a chuck or rump roast on the grill made more sense than heating up a kitchen. One steamy August morning a meat man in an Albertson's Market in St. Augustine was piling the cases high with chuck roasts. Asked what shoppers did with this cut of meat in hot and humid weather, he replied without a pause, "Chucks go out of here like wildfire. They barbecue them!"

His customers marinate them first with spicy seasonings and cook them very slowly on a covered grill, Cajun style, he called it, but the method is similar to Texas brisket barbecue. The meat is then sliced thin (a sharp knife wielded by a skilled carver is the greatest tenderizer of all).

This recipe employs commercial tenderizer, derived from papaya or pineapple, but old-time Floridians used to tear leaves off a papaya plant to wrap around the meat to soften it. Tenderizing is optional; if you use marbled meat, keep the fire very low, and baste the meat often, tenderizer is not needed.

2½ to 3 pounds boned beef chuck, rump, or top round	¼ cup red wine
2 teaspoons chili powder	¼ cup olive or vegetable oil, or as needed
½ teaspoon dried oregano	¼ teaspoon freshly ground pepper
2 cloves garlic, minced	Meat tenderizer, as directed on label (optional)
2 tablespoons red wine vinegar	

Pierce the meat at intervals with a fork. Rub chili powder, oregano, and garlic over it. Place in a plastic bag. Mix together the vinegar, wine, ¼ cup oil, and pepper. Pierce the meat again with a fork, then pour the marinade over it. Close the bag, turn to coat the meat, and marinate it in the refrigerator 3 to 8 hours. Remove the meat from the bag, reserving the marinade. If used, apply the tenderizer as directed.

Place a drip pan in the grill and position the meat over it to cook over indirect heat. Brush the meat with the reserved marinade. With a poker, push the coals to the side of or around the drip pan. Keep the fire low. Cover the grill and cook slowly, turning the meat from time to time to cook evenly. Allow about 2 hours of cooking time.

Brush with additional oil occasionally if the meat appears dry. Meat is rare when a thermometer inserted in a thick part of the roast registers 120 degrees, medium at 140 degrees. This cut of meat should not be cooked well done, or it will be tough.

Remove the meat from the grill. Cover with foil to keep warm and let rest 20 minutes before carving. Slice thin and serve with salsa. Leftovers are wonderful in sandwiches or salad the next day.

"A hunk of meat" can be oven-roasted—at 300 to 325 degrees for 1½ to 2 hours.

SFEEHA
SYRIAN MEAT PIES

MAKES 8 TO 10 PIES, 4 TO 5 SERVINGS.

This open-face pie resembles pizza, but has less tomato and no cheese. Julia Rady, one of a large Syrian colony in Jacksonville, serves these meat pies with other traditional foods to her grown children, nephews, or nieces when they yearn for Mom's and Grandmom's cooking.

1 onion, chopped fine	6 tablespoons (½ 6-ounce
1 tablespoon butter	can) tomato paste
1 pound coarsely ground lean	2 tablespoons water
lamb	⅓ cup pine nuts
½ teaspoon salt	Juice of ½ lemon
¼ teaspoon freshly ground	Dough for Meat Pies (recipe
pepper	follows)
½ hot chile pepper, minced	
(optional)	

In a large skillet, sauté the onion in the butter until tender but not browned. Add the lamb, salt, pepper, and chile. Cook, breaking up the meat with a fork so that it does not clump together. When the lamb is crumbly and loses its red color, pour off the fat in the pan. Add the tomato paste, water, and pine nuts. Mix well and keep warm for filling the pies.

Preheat the oven to 450 degrees. Roll the dough out thin and cut in 5- to 6-inch rounds. Place a spoonful of filling on each round and squeeze the lemon juice over the fillings. Crimp the edges to raise narrow rims, or pinch the pies into flat triangles or fat crescents with shallow rims. Place the pies on a pizza tile or baking sheet that has been lightly buttered. Bake 20 to 22 minutes, until the dough is lightly browned and the filling is hot. Serve hot, warm, or at room temperature.

DOUGH FOR MEAT PIES

Makes enough dough for 8 to 10 pies.

1¼ cups warm water
1 package active dry yeast
½ teaspoon sugar
2½ to 3 cups bread or all-
    purpose flour

½ teaspoon salt
2 tablespoons butter, melted
    and cooled

Place ¼ cup of very warm water in a large bowl. Sprinkle the yeast and sugar over it. When the yeast is dissolved, stir in ½ cup of the flour, the salt, then the remaining warm water. Stir in 1 cup more of the flour, then the melted butter. Work in enough more flour to make a dough that leaves the sides of the bowl. Turn out onto a floured surface and knead 8 to 10 minutes, using as much flour as needed to prevent sticking. Shape the dough into a ball and place it in a warm bowl that has been buttered. Turn to grease the top of the dough, cover with buttered wax paper, then a towel, and let the dough rise in a warm place until doubled, about 1 hour.

Punch the dough down, turn out onto the work surface, and invert the bowl over it. Let the dough rest 10 to 15 minutes. Working in two portions, roll out the dough very thin and cut into 8 to 10 5- to 6-inch rounds, tracing around a saucer with a knife if you lack a 5- or 6-inch cutter. Proceed with the recipe for Syrian Meat Pies to fill and bake the pies.

TO FLORIDA FOR HEALTH

Since Ponce de León's mythical search for the Fountain of Youth (serious historians say he was looking for gold and jewels, not a fountain) Florida has been a mecca for health seekers. Numerous spas in the state today cater to health and beauty fans of the 1990s.

The earliest Indians migrated from the Northwest eight to ten thousand years ago in search of a life free from famine and the other rigors of a cold climate, some authorities surmise. Ralph Waldo Emerson was one of the first New Englanders to write of retreating to Florida for his health. In the 1830s, he found a land "that can beguile the months of banishment to the pale travelers whom disease has sent hither for genial air from Northern homes." Emerson survived his consumption, because of or in spite of his stay in Florida, and lived another half century. From the time Florida became a United States territory in 1821, the state was a haven to people suffering "weak lungs," one of the many euphemisms for tuberculosis or consumption.

Soon health- and diet-peddlers came in droves to the sunny clime trying to sell their fitness programs. In the 1920s John Harvey Kellogg, the cereal mogul, opened a sanitarium near Miami.

The Kellogg nuts, grains, and berries diet and exercise program outlived the boom, and dozens of cured patients stayed on in Miami Springs, the village where the sanitarium was located, to become permanent residents. As late as the 1950s, the center was a haven of stage and sports celebrities seeking rest and seclusion.

In the 1930s, Bernar Macfadden, the publisher of *Physical Culture* magazine, *True Story*, and *True Confessions*, established a health and tanning institute in a Miami Beach hotel. It became the model for any number of gymnastic and tanning centers in hotels that sprang up before the dangers of excessive sun were recognized. Men and women slathered with coconut oil would be tanned and turned, then worked out in the roof garden of the hotel, while Macfadden drove around town in a convertible with the top down, his tan a striking contrast to his mane of white hair billowing in the wind.

And these days millions of individuals retire to Florida, seeking a "cure" to the discomforts of aging in icy climes.

EGGPLANT IN ITALIAN-STYLE SAUCE

MAKES 4 SERVINGS.

More eggplant is grown in Florida than in any other state, and any good Florida cook has several fine recipes for it. Dishes such as this are served hot as a dinner side dish, and the leftovers are saved and served cold as a salad or spread for pita bread the next day.

1 eggplant, about 1 pound
¼ cup olive or vegetable oil
1 medium onion, chopped
1 clove garlic, minced
2 cups peeled, seeded, and chopped
    tomatoes or drained canned
    tomatoes, chopped

1 tablespoon capers with
    juice
1 tablespoon anchovy
    paste
⅓ cup chopped pitted black
    olives, preferably Mediter-
    ranean style

Wash the eggplant, slice off the stem and bud ends, and cut the unpeeled vegetable in ½-inch slices. Heat the oil in a large skillet, add the eggplant slices, and sauté until lightly browned, but not soft. Transfer to a plate and keep warm. Sauté the onion and garlic in the pan drippings until the onion is tender but not browned. Add the tomatoes and cook, stirring often until thickened. Place the sautéed eggplant in the sauce, cover, and simmer 10 minutes, or until the eggplant is tender. Lift the eggplant from the sauce and place on a platter. Stir the capers, anchovy paste, and olives into the sauce until blended, and spoon over the eggplant. Serve hot. Refrigerate leftovers and serve cold as a salad or spread for pita bread.

FLORIDA SMOKED BEANS

MAKES 8 TO 12 SERVINGS.

We sampled smoked beans both at Carl Allen's Historical Cafe in Auburndale, where back-woods food is offered, and in a short-order spot in Tallahassee, where casual barbecue has been sanitized to Formica-top tables, and FSU coeds in snappy red uniforms were servers. Allen's beans were served with deep-fried alligator tail, rattlesnake, turtle, armadillo, and other foods to brag about eating in order to horrify friends. The canned beans were doctored up with added seasonings (more sugar and such) and smoked for several hours in the same smokehouse where fish is smoked.

The fast-food version was served with barbecued pork ribs, chicken, or beef, and garnished as neatly as a burger plate in any number of fast-food eateries. But the beans apparently were cooked from scratch, seasoned well, and wafted a pleasant smoke aroma when they were put on the table.

This recipe is our adaptation for home use, the best of the smoked beans we tasted. The beans are baked in a kitchen oven, then finished in a smoke oven or at very low heat in a barbecue grill with a hood. Halve the recipe, if you like, but beans freeze and reheat successfully, and we think having beans in the freezer is a plus, whenever you want a quick supper with grilled chicken or pork.

1 pound dried great northern or navy beans	**¹⁄₂ cup water**
3 teaspoons salt	**¹⁄₄ cup molasses**
3 ounces thinly sliced country ham or salt pork, diced	**¹⁄₄ teaspoon freshly ground pepper**
1 medium onion, diced	**1 teaspoon dry mustard**
1 small green bell pepper, seeded and diced	

Place the beans in a large bowl, add enough water to cover by 2 inches, cover the bowl, and let soak overnight. Drain off the soaking water. Place the beans in a large pot and add water to cover by 2 inches. Cover, bring to a boil, and turn the heat to low. Simmer 1¼ hours, or until the beans are almost tender when tested with a fork. Add 2 teaspoons of the salt and simmer 25 to 30 minutes longer, until the beans are soft, but not mushy. Drain the beans, reserving the liquid to moisten beans while baking.

Preheat the oven to 275 degrees. Spritz a 2½-quart bean pot or deep casserole with nonstick cooking spray or butter it well. Spoon a layer of beans into the pot. Sprinkle with a third each of the ham, onion, and bell pepper. Layer the remaining beans, ham, and vegetables in this order, ending with the beans.

In a small saucepan, combine the water, molasses, pepper, mustard, the remaining 1 teaspoon salt, and ½ cup of the reserved bean liquid. Bring to a boil and pour over the beans. Heat the remaining bean liquid and add to the pot until the liquid level shows just below the top of the beans. Bake uncovered 5 hours, stirring occasionally. Add a small amount of bean liquid or water, heated to boiling, as the liquid is absorbed by the beans while cooking. Smoke beans immediately or reheat them before smoking.

To smoke, set the uncovered pot of hot beans on a rack in a smoker that has been preheated to medium. Or place the pot of beans on a rack in a kettle-type grill with the fire built at the other end to provide low, indirect heat. Spread dampened wood chips (mesquite, hickory, oak, or fruit wood) on the fire, and cover the smoker or grill. Smoke 1 to 1½ hours, stirring beans now and then to allow penetration of the smoke flavor. Serve beans immediately, or refrigerate and reheat them for serving.

COUNTRY BAKED BEANS

MAKES 8 TO 10 SERVINGS.

This is a good shortcut recipe for baked beans, for those times when starting from scratch with dry beans is too much trouble. Preparation is a snap, but the long cooking gives them homemade taste. Or try them smoked for even more flavor.

2 1-pound cans pork and beans
1 medium onion, chopped
1 cup chopped green bell pepper
⅔ cup packed brown sugar
2 tablespoons dry mustard

1 tablespoon Worcestershire sauce
1 cup ketchup or chili sauce
2 strips of uncooked bacon in 1-inch pieces (optional)

Preheat the oven to 325 degrees. Combine the pork and beans with the remaining ingredients and mix well. Pour into a buttered 1½-quart casserole. Cover and bake 1 to 1½ hours, uncovering for the last 20 minutes.

INDIAN CORN

MAKES 8 SERVINGS.

This spread for corn roasted over charcoal is popular in Fernandina Beach. And if fresh sweet corn is not available, menfolk in the town make a run to the farmer's market in Jacksonville, twenty-five miles away, for the main ingredient. The spicy sauce is not for timid palates, say locals, but dozens of ears of corn are eaten with it each summer.

16 ears corn	Dash ground marjoram
1 tablespoon ground cumin	Dash turmeric
1 tablespoon ground coriander	Dash ground red pepper
2 teaspoons salt	(cayenne)
1 teaspoon chili powder	½ cup (1 stick) butter, melted
1 teaspoon curry powder	2 limes, cut in wedges

Shuck the corn, remove silks, and place in a large bowl or glass dish and cover with ice water. Refrigerate at least 1 hour before grilling.

Mix together thoroughly the dry spices and seasonings. Stir one-third of the spicy mixture together with the butter in a bowl. Put the remaining seasoning blend in another bowl and arrange the lime wedges cut side down in the spices.

Remove the corn from the water and grill, 4 or 5 ears of the wet corn at a time, turning often until lightly browned. To eat: Dip a pastry brush in the butter-spice mixture and brush up and down each ear of corn. For spicier flavor, dip a lime wedge into the dry mixture and rub and squeeze the spiced lime up and down the ear.

NATHAN MAYO'S CRACKER BREAKFASTS

athan Mayo, Florida's commissioner of agriculture from 1923 to 1960, proudly called himself a Cracker. He made a big Cracker breakfast famous by inviting VIP groups to partake of it and showing off Florida foods in the breakfast.

Mrs. Mayo's grits, a highlight of the breakfasts, immortalizes Summerfield, the village near Ocala, where the Mayos lived and brought up their family.

Lefthand hams were served, holding to the legend that the meat from the left side is more tender than that of the right. Crackers believe that a pig scratching his right leg does a vigorous jig, developing the muscle. The left side scratches in a gentle shimmy, so is tender, say country folk.

For several days before a breakfast, producers in the state collected double-yolk eggs that they found by candling. Fried over light in Florida butter, they were a novelty since double-yolk eggs rarely are sold fresh.

This is a partial menu:

Orange Juice
Broiled Grapefruit Halves
Fried Double-Yolk Grade AA Eggs
Hickory Smoked Ham (Grilled Slice)
Historic Suwannee River (Red-Eye) Gravy
Grits à la Summerfield
Hot Biscuits, Fresh Florida Butter
Guava Syrup

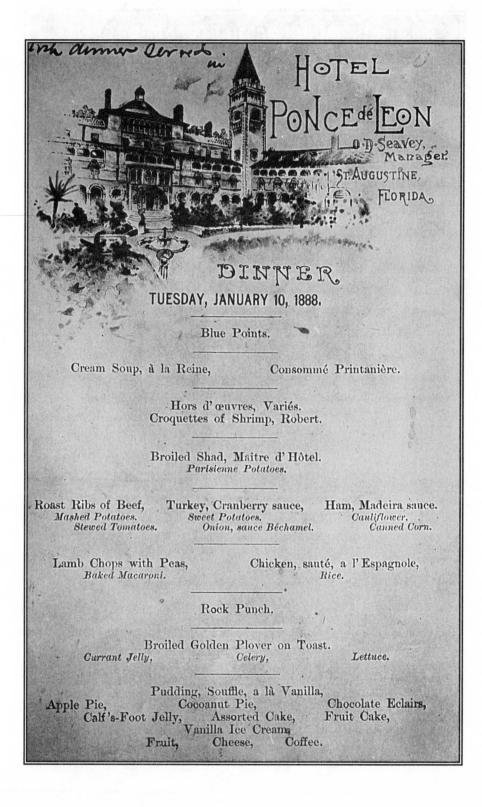

HOTEL PONCE de LEON

L.o D. Seavey, Manager.

St. Augustine, Florida.

DINNER

TUESDAY, JANUARY 10, 1888.

Blue Points.

Cream Soup, à la Reine,   Consommé Printanière.

Hors d' œuvres, Variés.
Croquettes of Shrimp, Robert.

Broiled Shad, Maître d' Hôtel.
Parisienne Potatoes.

Roast Ribs of Beef,   Turkey, Cranberry sauce,   Ham, Madeira sauce.
Mashed Potatoes.   *Sweet Potatoes.*   *Cauliflower.*
Stewed Tomatoes.   *Onion, sauce Béchamel.*   *Canned Corn.*

Lamb Chops with Peas,   Chicken, sauté, a l' Espagnole,
Baked Macaroni.   *Rice.*

Rock Punch.

Broiled Golden Plover on Toast.
Currant Jelly,   *Celery,*   *Lettuce.*

Pudding, Souffle, a là Vanilla,
Apple Pie,   Cocoanut Pie,   Chocolate Eclairs,
Calf's-Foot Jelly,   Assorted Cake,   Fruit Cake,
Vanilla Ice Cream,
Fruit,   Cheese,   Coffee.

FRIED GRITS

Leftover breakfast grits are the foundation for this favorite supper dish, side dish to quail, or next-day breakfast food.

With the back of a spoon, press the cooked grits into a shallow pan or dish that has been buttered or spritzed with nonstick cooking spray. Chill until firm. Cut the firm grits in squares, wedges, or finger shapes. Flour the pieces lightly and sauté in a mixture of half vegetable oil and half butter until golden brown and heated through. Serve hot with molasses or as an accompaniment to game, pork, poultry, or beef.

GRITS À LA SUMMERFIELD

MAKES 4 SERVINGS.

Floridians of Southern ancestry and those indoctrinated in the pleasures of this country staple revere grits and give them the care they deserve—long, slow cooking with milk in a double boiler. This method is from Mrs. Nathan Mayo, whose recipe became well known at her husband's famous Cracker breakfasts.

¾ cup regular white grits (not quick or instant)

¼ cup water

½ teaspoon salt

2¼ cups milk (can use low-fat or skim)

Butter

Place the grits in a sieve and run hot water through the grains, then drain them. Put the damp grits and the ¼ cup water in the top of a double boiler. Cook and stir over low heat until moistened throughout, a minute or two. Place over boiling water and stir in the salt and milk. Cover and cook 1 to 1½ hours, stirring now and then. Stir in more milk if the grits become too firm. They should be creamy but not runny. Serve hot with lots of butter or red-eye gravy.

HUSHPUPPIES—BREAD OF LEGEND

Legend says that hushpuppies were discovered, not really invented, at a fish fry at a turpentine camp in northwest Florida. Cooks there fried cornbread cakes, and tossed them to the barking dogs, shouting, "Hush, puppy!" Then a man took a bite, and hushpuppies were born. The story probably is apocryphal, but in the 1950s when *The Saturday Evening Post* called Tallahassee the birthplace of hushpuppies, the

Chamber of Commerce graciously accepted the honor, but knew not where or when the first cornbread fritters were made.

Hushpuppies became known nationwide. From the Chesapeake to the southernmost tip of Key West, to Texas and California, hushpuppies invariably go with fried fish. They accompany barbecue in the Carolinas, and, in the 1980s, you could buy a bagful of freshly fried hushpuppies at the Barking Fish, a take-out shop and restaurant a few steps from Times Square in New York City.

The mother of hushpuppies are corn dodgers, fried corn cakes, that probably were made by Native Americans before the Europeans arrived. Corn dodgers served as plain food in the South for generations.

No homemade hushpuppy looks or tastes like the leaden balls called hushpuppies in fast-food America. Artists at hushpuppy-making keep the batter light enough to drop from a spoon, not a ball scoop. Traditionally hushpuppies are cooked in the drippings after fish is fried or at the cooler edges of a skillet full of fish. The pups rising in the hot fat take free-form shapes a bit thicker than pancakes.

There are literally hundreds of recipes, most unwritten and without measured ingredients. "Shorty" Hodges, a fisherman out of Cedar Key, uses ketchup in place of water or milk in the batter. Others use beer. Fishing boats ration fresh water, so seawater or any liquid in the galley moistens hushpuppies.

Onion is a must in Southern hushpuppies, usually lots of it. Many hushpuppy experts pepper the batter heavily; or hot sauce or minced chiles may spice hushpuppies.

Hushpuppy batter is made of corn meal, but flour is added for smoothness. Some women and men insist on self-rising flour, claiming it makes lighter hushpuppies. Others use pancake mix in place of plain flour.

JANE BURBANK'S HUSHPUPPIES

MAKES ABOUT 28 TINY HUSHPUPPIES, ENOUGH FOR
4 TO 5 SERVINGS.

Mrs. Burbank, mother of a family of netweavers, makes "the lightest hushpuppies ever," say folks in Fernandina Beach. One time she fried two thousand hushpuppies for a town supper. Light and crispy-brown, they have a wonderful flavor. Hushpuppies are fried in hot drippings left after frying fish, picking up some of the fresh fish flavor.

1 cup self-rising corn meal	¼ teaspoon freshly ground
(preferably white stone-ground)	pepper
½ cup self-rising flour	1 egg
¼ cup pancake mix (see Note)	1 medium onion, diced
Pinch salt	½ cup milk, or as needed
½ teaspoon sugar	Oil or fish drippings for frying

Combine the corn meal, flour, pancake mix, salt, sugar, and pepper in a bowl. Beat the egg lightly in a measuring cup, and add the onion and enough milk to fill to the 1-cup mark. Mix the liquids into the dry mixture well. If not moist throughout, add a tablespoonful or two more of milk, blending well.

Put any fish drippings you may have in a heavy frying pan and add enough oil to a depth of ¼ inch. Heat and drop a small amount of batter into the fat. If it sizzles, the fat is hot enough. Make a test hushpuppy: Drop a teaspoonful of batter in; if it spreads like a pancake, the batter is too thin, so stir a tablespoonful or two of corn meal into the uncooked batter. If, after the test hushpuppy has cooked, it is dense and dry, stir 2 or 3 teaspoons of milk into the batter. When the batter consistency is right, drop the batter from the tip of a teaspoon into the pan; cook 6, 8, or 10 at a time, being careful not to let the hushpuppies overlap while frying. Cook until lightly browned, 3 to 4 minutes, turn, and brown the other side, about 3 minutes. Drain on paper towels and keep hot while frying the remaining hushpuppies. Add more oil to the pan as needed, a little at a time, to prevent cooling. Fat should be kept medium-hot, to brown hushpuppies. Check often so that hushpuppies do not scorch.

NOTE: In Florida many like to use self-rising flour and corn meal as well as pancake mix in hushpuppies and other breads. If you wish, substitute all-purpose flour for self-rising and the pancake mix; use plain corn meal in place of the self-rising type. Then to the dry ingredients add 1 tablespoon baking powder and 1 teaspoon salt. Add the liquid ingredients, then proceed with the recipe as directed.

FLOUR CHOICES

Many cake and biscuit bakers in Florida use self-rising flour to save time and to get a tender, light texture. Southern flour companies, Martha White or White Lily, for example, add baking powder and salt to soft-wheat flour to make it self-rising flour. To mix biscuit dough, a home baker need only to work in the fat and milk.

A newcomer is dismayed by the choice of flours in Florida. Standard all-purpose, unbleached, and whole-wheat flours are on the supermarket shelves, along with self-rising and soft-wheat flours. Whole grains are in thin supply. They turn rancid or mold quickly in the humid warmth, so markets stock them sparsely or seasonally. Cake flour (with no leavening) is everywhere, attesting to a strong interest in cakes. This is a fine soft-wheat flour that gives cakes a velvety light texture, and it should be used only in recipes adjusted for it.

Don't despair if you grab a bag of self-rising flour when you wanted all-purpose. Markets exchange unopened bags, but if you open it before you look, self-rising is adaptable to most uses except yeast breads. For baked goods omit the leavening and salt called for in a recipe. To use all-purpose flour in a recipe that calls for self-rising, add 1½ teaspoons baking powder and ¼ teaspoon salt for each cupful of flour.

REFRIGERATOR-FREEZER YEAST BISCUITS

MAKES 5 TO 6 DOZEN BISCUITS.

Country ham sliced paper thin in hot biscuits is as popular for parties in Florida as in Georgia, the Carolinas, and Virginia. This recipe, also called Angel Biscuits or Risen Biscuits, makes it possible to serve the little breads with a minimum of last-minute fuss. The biscuits are mixed and shaped up to six weeks ahead of time, frozen, thawed, and baked at the last minute.

1 package active dry yeast	½ cup (1 stick) butter, melted
½ cup warm (105 to 115 degrees) water	and cooled
	¼ cup corn or vegetable oil
6 to 6½ cups self-rising flour (see Note)	2 cups buttermilk or sour cream
2 tablespoons sugar	

NOTE: If using all-purpose flour, stir in 3 tablespoons plus 1 teaspoon baking powder and 1¾ teaspoons salt with the sugar in the recipe.

Dissolve the yeast in the warm water in a cup; let stand in a warm place 5 minutes, until the yeast is softened. In a large bowl, stir together 4 cups of the flour and the sugar. With a fork, mix in the yeast mixture, butter, and oil until crumbly, then stir in 1½ cups flour and the buttermilk. With a few strokes, knead the dough until smooth. Turn out onto a floured board and gently knead in more flour to make a soft dough. Pat out to a 1-inch-thick round, and cut with a floured 1½-inch round cutter. Place the biscuits on ungreased baking sheets and freeze until firm. Transfer to freezer bags, working quickly so that the biscuits do not thaw. Seal and freeze up to 6 weeks. Or refrigerate the dough overnight or up to 3 days, then pat out, cut, and bake.

To bake frozen biscuits, place ½ inch apart on baking sheets. Brush with melted butter, if desired, cover with waxed paper, and let stand until thawed, about 1½ hours. Preheat the oven to 400 degrees and bake 18 minutes or until golden brown.

To bake refrigerated biscuits, let rise about 45 minutes and bake at 400 degrees, 15 to 18 minutes.

MINORCAN CHRISTMAS CANDY

MAKES 1¼ POUNDS, 60 TO 70 PIECES.

This candy requires skill and patience, and per-haps a few drops of Minorcan blood coursing through your veins to make the trouble worthwhile. Let your mind wan-der a second, and the syrup turns tawny, ruining the gleaming white that makes it pure memory food of Old St. Augustine. The chore of shelling and grating coconut puts off some cooks. It still makes Christmas for most people of St. Augustine. Frozen shredded coconut can be substi-tuted for fresh, but packaged coconut is not suitable, as it scorches easily.

3 to 3½ cups (1 large) shredded fresh coconut (see page 159)	3 tablespoons white corn syrup
2 cups sugar	1 teaspoon vanilla extract (optional)
½ cup coconut water or fresh milk	

Combine the coconut, sugar, and coconut water in a large bright heavy sauté pan or Dutch oven. (Do not use a dark pan, which makes it diffi-cult to see the boiling candy color.) Stir over moderate heat until the sugar is dissolved, then stir in the corn syrup. Bring to a boil over medium-low heat, stirring often to prevent burning. Turn the heat low, cover, and cook 2 minutes to dissolve crystals on side of pan. Uncover and stir constantly until the candy is thick, 20 to 30 minutes. You can cease stirring for a half minute, maybe, but do not answer the phone or look away for more than a second in the final stages, when the syrup thickens. If it begins to turn the least bit ivory colored, stir in 1 table-spoon cold water and continue cooking very slowly. If the candy becomes golden, it is good confection, but not the traditional holiday treat. The candy is ready when a teaspoonful dropped onto a waxed paper–lined tray stands with no syrup running from edges. Stir in the vanilla, if wanted, but many prefer the pure flavor of coconut. Drop by teaspoonfuls onto waxed paper–lined trays. If the candy should become too hard to drop, stir in a tablespoon cold water and stir over medium heat until liquid enough for dropping. Cool the candy. Store in cake tins in layers separated by waxed paper. This candy improves with age up to 2 or 3 weeks, and remains in excellent condition for several weeks.

STIRRING FRUITCAKE

MAKES ABOUT 4 POUNDS OF CAKE, 50 OR MORE
SERVINGS, IF OFFERED IN THIN, SMALL SLICES.

This version of pineapple and cherry fruitcake came down from Georgia, and remains a holiday tradition for north Floridians, after years of successes. Stirring the batter at intervals while baking may seem a waste of time, but the total baking time is only three hours, and many a working man or woman bakes this cake after office hours. Since the batter is rearranged with each stirring, the oven temperature can be higher than usual without the risk of burning; it also allows the cake to be evenly light-brown throughout, and there is no problem of heavy fruits and nuts settling to the bottom.

This light fruitcake is adapted from the recipe of Mrs. Glen Terrell, now deceased, of Tallahassee. Her cake was flavored with vanilla and almond extracts, but we think brandy or bourbon gives it pizazz.

4 cups (1 pound) shelled pecans	4 large eggs
1 pound each candied red cherries and candied pineapple	1 cup self-rising flour (see Note)
1 cup (2 sticks) butter, softened	2 tablespoons brandy or bourbon
1 cup sugar	

Chop the pecans coarsely and put in a bowl. Cut the fruit into ½-inch pieces, using scissors dipped in water from time to time. Combine with the pecans. Cover loosely and let stand until ready to mix.

Butter a Dutch oven or large baking pan and set aside. Preheat the oven to 375 degrees. In a large bowl, cream the butter well, then add the sugar gradually and beat until fluffy. Beat in the eggs, one at a time, mixing well after each. Stir in the flour in four additions. Add the spirits, then the pecans and fruits, working them in with a sturdy spoon or floured hands.

Pour the batter into the buttered pan, bake 15 minutes, remove from the oven, and stir well from the bottom and sides of the pan. Repeat the baking and stirring every 15 minutes, for a total of 3 times.

While the batter is baking, butter a 10-inch tube pan or two 8½- by 4½-inch loaf pans, line the bottoms of the tube or loaf pans with brown paper or cooking parchment, and butter the paper. Pour the hot batter into the prepared pan and pack carefully around the tube and into edges of the pan. Return to the oven and bake 15 minutes.

Let the cake cool in the pan on a rack for 20 minutes, then turn out and cool completely. Wrap in foil or plastic film and store in a cool pantry or cupboard for several days, in the refrigerator for several weeks, or in the freezer for several months. Chill before serving, and slice thin.

NOTE: If self-rising flour is not available, sift together 1 cup all-purpose flour, 1½ teaspoons baking powder, and ¼ teaspoon salt.

PEANUT BUTTER PIE

MAKES 6 TO 8 SERVINGS.

Peanut butter pie is as popular in north Florida as Key lime pie is in the Keys. Our version is less sweet than those offered in roadside cafes and tearooms. It is inspired by the one at a restaurant called The Sisters, in Orange Park. The early bird gets the pie, in this case, so local folk, tourists, and men from the Jacksonville Naval Air Station nearby vie for early seating and a chance at the famous pie. It sells out fast, sometimes before lunch hour is half over.

Peanut Butter Pie (continued)

¾ cup confectioners' sugar

⅓ cup chunky peanut butter

½ cup granulated sugar

¼ cup cornstarch

1 tablespoon flour

½ teaspoon salt

3 cups milk (can use low-fat or skim)

3 egg yolks, beaten until blended

1½ teaspoons vanilla extract

1 tablespoon butter

1 9-inch pie shell, baked and cooled

Three-Egg-White Meringue (recipe follows)

Combine the confectioners' sugar and peanut butter in a shallow bowl. Work together with a fork until crumbly and blended, finishing with fingers, if necessary. Set the crumbs aside.

In a heavy saucepan, mix the granulated sugar with the cornstarch, flour, and salt. Stir in the milk until smooth, then stir over moderate heat until thickened, about 4 minutes. Stir 2 or 3 spoonfuls of the hot mixture into the egg yolks; then stir the mixture back into the hot filling. Cook, stirring, over low heat 2 to 3 minutes, until thickened. Remove from the heat and stir in the vanilla extract and butter until incorporated.

Preheat the oven to 350 degrees. Sprinkle the peanut butter crumbs in the pie shell, reserving 2 tablespoons. Pour the filling over the crumbs. Prepare the meringue and spread over the warm filling, sealing to the crust at the edges. Sprinkle the remaining peanut butter crumbs over the meringue. Bake 15 minutes, or until golden. Cool 1 hour before slicing; this pie is best if served the day it is made.

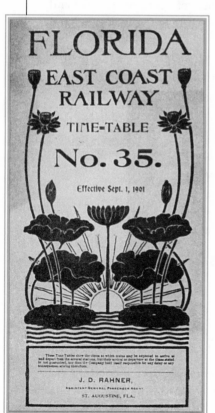

FLORIDA

EAST COAST RAILWAY

TIME-TABLE

No. 35.

Effective Sept. 1, 1901

J. D. RAHNER,
Assistant General Passenger Agent
ST. AUGUSTINE, FLA.

THREE-EGG-WHITE MERINGUE

Makes enough to top a 9-inch pie.

3 egg whites, at room
temperature

¼ teaspoon cream of tartar
6 tablespoons sugar

Beat the egg whites at high speed until foamy throughout. Add the cream of tartar and continue beating until soft peaks form. Add the sugar, a tablespoonful at a time, and beat until stiff peaks form.

OPEN-FACE BLUEBERRY PIE

MAKES 6 TO 8 SERVINGS.

Blueberries, once considered a northern fruit, today are grown commercially near Gainesville and in other parts of Florida. This pie, which some might call a tart, is an alluring way to serve the fresh fruit. Uncooked berries added when the pie comes from the oven provide an incredibly fresh flavor and texture.

Butter Pastry, chilled (recipe
follows)
5 cups (2 baskets) blueberries
½ cup plus 3 tablespoons sugar
¼ cup flour

Pinch salt
1 tablespoon lemon juice
4 tablespoons (½ stick) butter,
cut in small pieces
Pinch cinnamon

Roll the chilled pastry out on a floured pastry cloth to a round about 2 inches larger in diameter than a 9-inch pie plate with 2-inch sides. Gently fit the pastry into the pie plate, trim it, and crimp the edge to the rim of the pie plate.

Preheat the oven to 400 degrees. Wash and pick over the blueberries carefully, removing debris and any stems remaining. Set aside 1 cup of the berries.

In a medium-size bowl, combine the remaining 4 cups berries, the

½ cup sugar, flour, salt, lemon juice, butter, and cinnamon. Mix lightly. Spoon the berry filling into the pie shell. Redistribute the butter among berries if it is clumped together. Place the pie plate on a rack set in the lower third of the oven and bake 50 minutes to 1 hour, until the rim of the crust is lightly browned and the filling bubbly. Remove from the oven and sprinkle the reserved 1 cup of berries over the filling. Sprinkle with the remaining 3 tablespoons sugar. Cool slightly on a wire rack. Serve warm or at room temperature with ice cream or whipped cream.

BUTTER PASTRY

Makes enough for a 9-inch single-crust pie.

1½ cups all-purpose or
  pastry flour
¼ teaspoon salt
3 tablespoons vegetable
  shortening

3 tablespoons cold
  butter
3 tablespoons (about)
  iced water

In a shallow bowl, mix the flour and salt thoroughly. Add 2 tablespoons of the shortening and the butter. Cut in with a pastry blender or 2 table knives until the mixture resembles crumbs. Add the remaining 1 tablespoon shortening and cut in until particles are the size of small peas. Add the water, a teaspoon at a time, then by drops, working it in with a fork. Use only enough water to make the dry ingredients cling together. Gather up the pastry in a ball, wrap in waxed paper or plastic film, and refrigerate at least 1 hour before rolling.

PECAN PIE

MAKES 6 SERVINGS.

This pie is appealing to many because it is not as sweet as most versions, and extra eggs make it very light.

5 eggs

1 cup sugar

¾ cup dark corn syrup

2 tablespoons butter, melted

½ teaspoon salt

1 teaspoon vanilla extract

1 cup pecan halves

1 unbaked 9-inch pie crust

Preheat the oven to 375 degrees. Break the eggs into a mixing bowl and beat well. Add the sugar, corn syrup, butter, salt, vanilla extract, and pecans, blending well after each addition. Carefully pour into the pie shell and bake for 45 minutes or until the filling is firm and the pastry has browned. Serve warm or at room temperature.

THE
PANHANDLE

APPETIZERS

Boiled Peanuts

Parched Peanuts

Sweet Potato Chips

Florida Coleslaw

Gazpachee Salad

West Indies Salad

Smoked Honeyed Chicken Wings

SOUPS

Southern Turnip Green Soup

Gulf Coast Gumbo

ENTRÉES

Broiled Scamp with Hollandaise

Stifado (Greek-Style Fish Stew)

Linda's Barbecued Shrimp

Shrimp Stuffed Eggplant

Bourbon Marinated Chicken Breasts

Campbell Family Chicken

Smothered Quail

Farm-Supper Pork Chops

VEGETABLES AND STARCHES

Green Beans with Potatoes

Country Butter Beans

Grilled Whole Onions

Nassau Grits

Baked Cheese Grits

Pecan Brown Rice

BREADS

Baked Corn Cakes

Florida Spoon Bread

DESSERTS

Blackberry Dumplings

Peach Ice Cream

Old-Fashioned Pound Cake

Peanut Butter Snack Cakes

Lemon Butter Cookies

Robert's Peanut Brittle

The Florida Panhandle stretches its narrow way roughly two hundred miles from Tallahassee to Pensacola, just east of where Alabama clings to a tiny scrap of Gulf-front. It is a laid-back part of old Florida, with comparatively cold winters, and a down-home sensibility. Along the way are cypress swamps, giant oaks draped with Spanish moss, and miles of white sand beaches that rank as some of the most beautiful in the country.

Traveling from the east across the Panhandle, one finds vast peanut and tobacco fields, acres of soybeans, watermelons, canteloupes, and farm stands filled with locally produced fruits and vegetables. Literally and figuratively entering another time, you pass into the Central Time Zone at the Apalachicola River, and into a more unspoiled region of fishing villages and small towns that owe their allegiance to the Old South. A heritage of Spanish, English, and French occupations combine with a natural reliance on the Gulf waters to inspire a style of cooking and eating that is too casually inherent to be called "cuisine." Such a highfalutin word does not belong to this slice of Florida.

What does belong here are the fishing boats that fill Apalachicola Bay, one of the major oyster beds of Florida; as do the shrimp boats farther out in the Gulf. A wealth of seafood is readily available wherever you go, and shrimp, crabs, and oysters can be bought fresh off the boats. Snapper, scamp, mullet, and mackerel are also at home in the warm coastal waters and appear on tables throughout the area. Cornbread, slaw, and hushpuppies are frequent accompaniments, in addition to local specialties like gazpachee salad and Nassau grits.

Chowders, gumbos, and creoles make good use of native ingredients and often draw on the spicy influences of Spanish, French, and African-American roots. The Apalachicola National Forest lures hunters, and game such as venison and quail show up on Panhandle plates beside turnip greens and hand-shelled lima beans. Pecans, peaches, and persimmons thrive in backyards, to be picked for pies, puddings, and cobblers.

The casual lifestyle of the Panhandle lends itself to lots of outdoor entertaining and barbecues, crab and shrimp boils, fish fries, and all manner of cookouts are prevalent.

Of course, not all of the Panhandle is rural. Along the Gulf Coast, communities have sprung up featuring condos, resorts, and attractions for visitors, most of whom come from neighboring Southern states. In addition to tourists, the city of Pensacola has long been a hub of Panhandle activity. It is the second-oldest permanent settlement in the United States, after St. Augustine, and it is called the "city of five flags," symbolizing as many governments in four centuries.

The Native Americans who preceded the first white settlers are not counted in this succession of occupants, and not represented by flags, but were nonetheless a part of the varied food heritage of the Panhandle.

It is an exciting recipe for good eating: Equal parts rich resources and creative cooks, a dash of Cracker ingenuity, a pinch of sophistication, mixed with good ol' boy modesty, and served with low-key hospitality.

BOILED PEANUTS

MAKES 6 TO 8 SERVINGS.

A young man from north Florida we know yearned so hard for boiled peanuts that his dad would pack freshly dug green peanuts in ice and Federal Express them to the hungry freshman in Boston. A specialty produce dealer might be persuaded to order a few freshly dug green peanuts, but the genuine article is hard to find, even in peanut regions. You may find them at farm stands and a few markets in certain sections of the state.

2 quarts green peanuts, pulled   ¼ cup salt
  off the vines and washed
2 quarts water, or enough
  to cover

Place the peanuts in a large saucepan. Add water to cover and stir in the salt until dissolved. (Some use much more salt, but we think this gives a salty, but not briny flavor.) Bring to a boil, turn the heat low, cover, and simmer until the peanut shells are tender and the kernels swollen to fill the shells. Add boiling water, if needed, to keep the peanuts covered while cooking. This will take 30 to 45 minutes. Taste a sample, cooled in cold water, for doneness; it should taste mealy and salty throughout. Cool the peanuts in the cooking brine, drain, and serve.

Boiled peanuts are shelled and eaten, though some folk eat the tender but fibrous soft shells with the kernels. Provide plenty of napkins, any way you choose to eat the peanuts, as they are damp. Leftovers can be refrigerated in a bag or covered jar and served within 2 or 3 days. Or boiled peanuts can be dried on clean kitchen towels or paper towels, put in freezer containers, frozen, and kept for 2 or 3 months. In season, some peanut growers who fancy this nibble prepare them by the gallon and freeze lots for holiday parties.

BOILED PEANUTS

This snack is little known outside peanut-growing regions of south Alabama, Georgia, and north Florida. Nobody knows why peanut growers of Virginia and the Carolinas overlooked Boiled Peanuts, the most addictive of all snacks to munch with beer, bourbon and branch water, or even Coke.

The essential ingredient is immature peanuts, harvested a few weeks before they ripen sufficiently to dry and parch or send off to peanut butter and oil factories. The green peanuts feel more like peas in a pod than dry raw peanuts that are allowed to grow a few weeks longer. The green peanuts are shucked off the vines and washed to remove any dirt. The old-time way of boiling them was to put the peanuts in a large iron wash pot with water and lots of salt; then they were simmered over pine-knot fires in farmyards.

The time? That depends. A senator with his roots in peanut country prescribed several hours, to allow time to tell jokes, lie, and engage in other activities connected with politics. Home cooks, who boil them in large pots on a kitchen range, say about half an hour is enough for the nuts to become mealy and the shells tender, just right to eat.

PARCHED PEANUTS

MAKES 6 TO 8 SNACK SERVINGS.

You may call these roasted peanuts, but farm folk in the peanut-growing regions of Florida, Georgia, and Alabama hang on to the old-timey name, "parched peanuts." The aroma of peanuts parching in the oven of an old black-iron stove is a delicious memory of anybody who grew up on a Southern farm. The stove warmed the kitchen as families sat at kitchen tables and popped the nuts into their mouths. When electricity came to the country, parching peanuts became easier. Today farm women roast the legumes in their microwaves. Pat Basford, whose husband, Steve, is a peanut grower in Jackson county, swears by the microwave method. When the skins of the peanuts are dry enough to blow off your hand, they are ready to eat. Roasting the goobers in the microwave is quick, easy, and foolproof, says Mrs. Basford.

2 cups shelled red-skin peanuts   **Seasonings (see Note)**

Spread the peanuts one layer deep in a 9-inch round shallow baking dish or pie plate. (Choose a dish that fits your microwave with space to turn freely, and adjust the amount of peanuts to fit in one layer.) Microwave at full power 2 minutes. Stir, then microwave at medium-high for $1\frac{1}{2}$ minutes. Repeat the step of stirring and microwaving at medium-high for $1\frac{1}{2}$ minutes, until the peanuts are parched to taste. This should take 3 to 5 cooking periods. Cool one or two peanuts, place them on your hand, crackle the skins, and if they waft away when you blow at them, the peanuts are parched. Or taste a cooled peanut to test for doneness. If desired, rub the skins off all the peanuts.

Season the peanuts to taste and serve warm or store in a tightly covered jar or food storage bag.

NOTE: Garlic powder, chili powder, curry powder, or mixed herbs with salt are popular seasonings; some people like cinnamon sugar or confectioners' sugar with grated orange or lime zest. Melted butter or peanut oil may be added to the legumes, but we think peanuts are rich enough without the added fat.

OVEN-PARCHED PEANUTS

Place the peanuts in an oiled shallow baking pan. Roast in a preheated 325-degree oven 35 to 40 minutes, stirring every 10 minutes. After 20 minutes, taste a peanut to check if it is done and parch a little longer. Cool, rub the skins off the peanuts, if desired, and season to taste.

SWEET POTATO CHIPS

MAKES 4 SERVINGS.

Fried sweet potatoes and fried fish are an old Florida food partnership worth reviving. Sweet potato chips are even better, full of flavor, and as crackly-crisp as an autumn leaf underfoot. The chips make fabulous snacks or you can serve them with fish, poultry, beef, or pork. A mandoline for cutting them is a big help, but the thin slices can be successfully cut with a sharp knife.

1 quart water

2 tablespoons lemon juice

2 large or 3 medium sweet
    potatoes, preferably
    red-meated

Oil for deep frying

Salt

Chili powder, brown sugar,
    or garlic powder

Pour the water into a deep bowl and add the lemon juice. Prepare the sweet potatoes one at a time, to minimize darkening by exposure to air. Peel them with a swivel-blade peeler, and cut in 1/8-inch slices on a mandoline or with a very sharp knife. Place the potatoes in the water with lemon juice immediately after cutting.

Pour 3 to 4 inches of oil into a deep fryer, and heat to 375 degrees. Dry a few potatoes at a time on kitchen towels or paper towels and place in a frying basket. Lower into the oil, and fry until lightly browned, about 2 minutes. Remove from the hot oil, drain a moment or two on the edge of the fryer, and spread on a waxed paper–lined tray. Sprinkle with salt, then the seasoning of your choice. Serve hot or cooled.

FLORIDA COLESLAW

MAKES 4 TO 6 SERVINGS.

Coleslaw is a year-round food in Florida; it is almost obligatory at a fish fry, just the right fresh crisp dish to pack for a picnic or potluck, and a good side dish to sandwiches at home or eating out. This all-purpose slaw can be varied by adding red or green bell pepper, celery, or carrot. For a different approach, see the Pineapple Coleslaw (page 258).

½ head (¾ to 1 pound) cabbage
3 green onions or scallions with
    tops, sliced very thin
1½ teaspoons dried dillweed or
    2 tablespoons minced fresh dill
½ teaspoon salt

¼ teaspoon freshly ground
    pepper
3 tablespoons red wine vinegar
2 tablespoons vegetable or
    olive oil
⅓ cup mayonnaise

Shred the cabbage fine with a sharp knife or in a food processor. Cut out the core; this is the cook's bonus if it is sweet, discard it if it is bitter. In a medium-size bowl, combine the cabbage with the green onions, dill, salt, pepper, and vinegar. Toss lightly, add the oil and mayonnaise, and toss again. Cover and chill 1 hour before serving.

GAZPACHEE SALAD

MAKES 4 TO 6 SERVINGS AS A FIRST COURSE
OR SIDE SALAD.

Which came first, gazpachee or gazpacho? Those in the Panhandle say gazpachee, which originated among descendants of Spanish settlers. The bready salad was Pensacola's most famous food for perhaps a century before gazpacho became the rage in big cities and trendy food spots in the 1950s.

Authentic gazpachee contains hardtack, a rock-hard seabiscuit valued for its keeping qualities when voyages from Europe took several weeks. While it is something of a rarity, two bakers in Pensacola still provide hardtack for gazpachee makers, and it can be mail-ordered from the Premier Baking Company, 1124 W. Garden Street, Pensacola, FL 32501. It's the real thing and worth the effort.

At home, this hand-me-down salad can be served upscale as a first course for sit-down dinners, or it can be offered casually, as a salad to accompany fish or chicken, corn on the cob, and grits, at a cookout supper.

2 hardtack, 2½ ounces each
Water
2 large ripe tomatoes, chopped
1½ to 2 cucumbers, peeled, seeded, and chopped
1 medium onion, chopped
1 green bell pepper, chopped
¾ teaspoon salt
¼ teaspoon freshly ground pepper

½ teaspoon dried leaf oregano or 2 tablespoons minced fresh
1 teaspoon dried basil leaves or 3 tablespoons minced fresh
2 cloves garlic, pressed
2 to 3 tablespoons mayonnaise
Salad greens

Soak the hardtack in water to cover for several hours or overnight. Squeeze out the water with your hands, then roll in a cloth to squeeze as dry as possible. Crumble the damp bread into a salad bowl and add the tomatoes, cucumbers, onions, and the bell pepper. Season with the salt, pepper, oregano, basil, and garlic. Stir in enough mayonnaise to moisten, but not too much or the salad will be runny. Serve on greens. Gazpachee is best served the day it is made.

NOTE: Pensacolans away from home without access to hardtack use Uneeda biscuits as a substitute or use dried French and Italian bread.

FLORIDA "CAVIAR"

Each autumn's first cold front from Canada brings a frantic fishing day to west Florida bays and estuaries, where mullet come down from brackish water to spawn. On a blustery November morning in 1990, we chugged out on a motor trawler into St. Joseph Bay, to see dozens of small boats bobbing precariously on white caps. Occupants of the small craft were buffeted by the brisk winds, as they stood to cast out nets. In minutes, the nets would be pulled in, laden with flopping fish. The roe is sold to the Japanese, paying two or three times the price that fishermen get for mullet sold for its meat. To connoisseurs, mullet roe is a luxury to be sought, "better than caviar," says one Floridian. In this country, it rarely is sold as roe, but in the fall, mullet with roe is found in first-class fish markets. Ask your fish dealer, and he may be persuaded to save it for you. If you are so lucky, cut out the roe (red of the female, white of the male), flour it lightly, and sauté it two or three minutes in butter. A squeeze of lemon juice or a bit more melted butter over it is all it needs. The white roe is more delicate flavored, but both are excellent. They remind you of the better known shad and salmon roe, but the mullet "caviar" has a sea-fresh flavor of its own. The texture is similar to shad roe.

WEST INDIES SALAD

The beauty of this elegantly simple salad is that the fresh blue crab-meat flavor is not overwhelmed by competing tastes. It was originally concocted at Bayley's Steak House on Mobile Bay in Alabama, but the top-quality crab-meat dish is just as abundant in neighboring states, where it has been a specialty for years.

This is a recipe that truly makes the most of fine fresh crab. Only a bit of onion, mild-flavored oil, vinegar, and salt and pepper season it, though some cooks add a touch of garlic. Many home-cooks and restaurant chefs in the area offer superb West Indies Salad, but beware of stale crab, and even imitation crab meat used in some budget cafes.

1 pound lump crab meat	½ cup vegetable oil
½ teaspoon salt	6 to 8 tablespoons distilled
¼ teaspoon freshly ground pepper	white or cider vinegar
1 onion, chopped fine	½ cup ice water

Pick over the crab meat to remove any cartilage and bits of shell, fluff up the crab meat, but do not cut it up. Season it with the salt and pepper. Place half of the chopped onion in a serving bowl. Top with the seasoned crab meat, then add the remaining onion. Pour the oil, vinegar, and ice water, in that order, over all. Cover and refrigerate several hours or overnight. The liquid in the dish can be spooned off and discarded although you should leave enough to make the salad moist. To serve as a salad, toss gently and serve on crisp greens. As appetizers, spoon into a bowl and serve with water biscuits, melba toast, or crackers.

FRIED SEAFOOD SANDWICHES

Fried shrimp, soft-shell crab, or oyster sandwiches are to the Panhandle's Gulf Coast what lobster rolls are to New England seaside resorts. The hot, fried seafood is heaped into hamburger buns or hoagies for you to doctor up with tartar sauce or make-your-own red cocktail sauce. Many casual restaurants do them, and The Oyster Bar Restaurant in Pensacola is especially fun because you can go by boat and dock right outside.

SMOKED HONEYED CHICKEN WINGS

MAKES 6 TO 8 ENTRÉE OR 12 TO 20 APPETIZER SERVINGS.

Two-bite-size chicken drumlets, mini-drumsticks shaped from wing joints, make handy party food on a buffet table, are convenient for tailgate parties, and children love them as a main dish.

**3 pounds chicken drumlets (see
    Note)
Juice and shell of 1 orange
    (¼ to ⅓ cup juice)
Juice and shell of 1 lime or lemon
    (3 tablespoons juice)
1 tablespoon Dijon-style mustard**

**1 clove garlic, minced
3 tablespoons honey
Salt
Hot pepper sauce
Handful hickory or oak chips,
    soaked**

Place the drumlets in a plastic bag. Mix the citrus juices, mustard, garlic, honey, salt, and pepper sauce in a measuring cup. Pour the marinade over the chicken, close the bag, and turn it to coat the chicken well. Place the bag in the refrigerator for 2 hours or longer.

Build the fire 45 minutes before cooking to allow time for it to burn down to hot coals and until the heat indicator shows the smoker is at the correct temperature. Place the orange and lime shells in the water pan of the smoker, drain the marinade from the chicken into the pan, and almost fill it with water. Put the pan in place and heat it a few minutes to allow smoke to build up. Place the chicken drumlets slightly apart on the smoker racks to allow smoke circulation. Cover the smoker and smoke the chicken for 1½ to 2 hours. Add the dampened chips to the fire. Cover and smoke 1 hour longer, or until juices of the chicken run clear when thick parts of the drumlets are tested with a fork. Serve the drumlets warm or cold as an appetizer or entrée. Refrigerate leftovers and serve cold or reheat them before serving.

NOTE: Drumlets are the meatiest wing joint of a broiler fryer with the meat pushed toward the larger end to form miniature drumsticks. Some processors pack drumlets. If you cannot find them, buy 4½ pounds wings and snip off the tips and second joints and reserve them for other uses. Loosen the skin on the meatier joints and push the meat to the rounded ends.

TUPELO HONEY—THE WORLD'S FINEST

Tupelo honey, esteemed in Europe, Asia, and in this country, is produced exclusively in a small area of northwest Florida. The swampy terrain of the basins of the Apalachicola, Ochlockonee, and Choctawhatchee rivers is the only place in the world where the tupelo gum tree blooms when nothing else is in flower to compromise the purity of the tupelo nectar. In April, beehives are trucked from south Georgia to the river basins. The bloom is over by early May, and the hives are taken to other nectar-hunting grounds.

Tupelo honey's most admirable quality is that it does not crystalize. It is extremely clear, pale amber colored, and has an elegantly light flavor. Before the Shah of Iran was deposed, his household had a standing order for barrelsful of the precious sweet each year, and discerning Americans invariably purchase it after the harvest.

Because the bloom season is short, and the swampy land makes nectar collecting and handling of the beehives difficult, tupelo honey may be a bit more expensive than other varieties, but it still is an affordable luxury.

Pure tupelo honey is identified on the label. Wildflower honey with tupelo may have some of the qualities, but is not the same. The precious sweet can be purchased at markets in the Panhandle or mail-ordered from Donald E. Lanier, P.O. Box 382, Wewahitchka, FL 34625.

SOUTHERN TURNIP GREEN SOUP

MAKES 6 TO 8 SERVINGS.

Many people may not consider Florida as part of the "Deep South," but in fact it shares many of the same characteristics of neighboring Alabama, Georgia, and Mississippi. This soup is one example of the "soul food" that exemplifies the African-American heritage of the area.

Turnip green soup is chicken stock–based, streaked with turnip greens, and flavored with onions and lemon juice. A bit of cooked grits is added for contrasting texture. It makes a good soup when fresh turnip greens are in season. If the turnips are not sold attached to the greens, purchase them separately. This recipe comes from Dee Davis.

1 bunch (1 pound) young turnip greens with turnips	5½ cups chicken stock
6 tablespoons butter	2 tablespoons lemon juice
1 cup chopped onions	2 cups half-and-half
1½ teaspoons salt	4 tablespoons cooked grits
1¼ teaspoons sugar	Salt and freshly ground pepper to taste

Cut the turnip roots off the greens. Clean and wash the greens, discarding any blemished or yellowed edges. Tear the large leaves into smaller pieces. Trim the ends and peel the turnips. Cube into bite-size pieces, enough to make 4 cups.

Melt 3 tablespoons of the butter in a large skillet over moderate heat. Add the turnips and sauté until crisp-tender, about 10 minutes. Add the onions, and sauté 5 minutes or until tender, but not browned. Add ½ teaspoon salt, ¼ teaspoon sugar, and 1½ cups of the chicken stock. Blend well, stir in the lemon juice, and set aside.

In another skillet, melt the remaining 3 tablespoons of butter. Add the greens and sauté over medium heat for 10 minutes, until crisp-tender. Add the remaining 1 teaspoon of salt, 1 teaspoon of sugar, and remaining 4 cups chicken stock. Blend well and remove from the heat and cool for

15 minutes. Purée the greens in a food processor or in batches in a blender. Add the puréed greens to the turnip mixture. Mix together and reheat. Add the half-and-half and the cooked grits, and adjust the salt and pepper to taste. Serve hot.

FUN-LOVING PENSACOLA

Cock fighting was a regular Saturday afternoon diversion in Pensacola before the Civil War, and the owner of the deceased bird was allowed to bring it home to enrich the family's chicken-oyster gumbo. Women of the household made the *roux* and started the gumbo while the men played away the afternoon at the cock pit.

In the early 1800s, Mardi Gras was celebrated in Pensacola with as much merriment as in the neighboring Gulf cities, New Orleans and Mobile. The festival included a parade, gaudily costumed and masked people, and a feast, candies and sweets to end the days of revelry.

Community picnics in the city's parks were important social events, with the Fourth of July the grandfather of all picnics, drawing hundreds of people to the parks, lugging their picnic baskets laden with fried chicken, pilaus, cold meats, and other delectables.

from *Old Customs of Pensacola and Favorite Recipes of the Times*
by Catherine L. Stewart and Maude Hallowell,
Pensacola Historic Preservation Society, 1974

Cleaning crabs before cooking ensures grit-free stocks and stews. In Florida and other coastal areas, your dealer may supply precleaned crabs. Otherwise, look for live crabs or cleaned cooked ones in the shell, usually, broken in halves. If the crab is cooked, you won't have the benefit of the flavor that the live crab and shell give the stew, but you won't have to clean the shellfish yourself.

To clean a live crab, protect your hands with work gloves or rubber gloves, and use a towel to handle the creature. Tongs or pliers may help you grasp the shellfish without getting nipped.

1. With the tongs or pliers or your protected left hand (if you are a right-hander), grasp the crab body from behind the claws and feelers that curve toward the front. Twist off the two large claws, and rinse them. Break off the feelers, rinse, and add to the stew.

2. Turn the crab over, shell side down. The apron or skirt is easily identified. In a male, it is a long thin part of the soft shell; in the female, a rounded segmentation of shell with a point toward the center. Lift the point of either sex apron and twist to remove it.

3. Working from the underside of the pointed end of the shell, lift the flap to reveal the body meat, any roe in the female, and other parts that are discarded.

4. Remove any roe and juices, and add them to the stew. Remove and discard the spongy lung tissue, called the "dead man's fingers" by old-timers. It is not deadly, but is inedible.

5. Crack the body in half with your hands or a cleaver. Crack the claws with a mallet or meat pounder. Drop the body pieces and claws into the pot. When the crab stew or soup is served, the body pieces and claws are distributed to diners along with nut- or lobster-crackers, and picks.

GULF COAST GUMBO

MAKES 6 TO 8 LARGE SERVINGS.

"First you make a roux . . ." so the saying goes. The mixture of fat and flour, slow-cooked to an even, dark color, often is the base for an ideal gumbo—a spicy stew made with an assortment of vegetables and meat and/or seafood. It is thickened with okra or filé powder (ground sassafras leaves), and served with rice.

Closely associated with Louisiana, the rich heritage of gumbo is a combination of Spanish, French, Native American, and African influences. It was African slaves who gave the dish its name, from the word "gombo," or "ngombo," meaning "okra." A salad and a crusty loaf of bread are the only accompaniments needed.

This gumbo, made with okra, reflects the Cajun influence in the Panhandle, and makes good use of fresh local seafood. Longtime Pensacola residents Joe Crona and his wife, Diane, serve this year-round whether entertaining corporate executives or friends.

¾ cup bacon drippings or
    vegetable oil

¾ cup all-purpose flour

1 medium onion, chopped

¾ green bell pepper, chopped

1 pound okra, sliced ½ inch thick

2 large ribs celery, chopped

4 cloves garlic, minced

¼ cup chopped parsley

6 bay leaves

½ teaspoon dried thyme

½ teaspoon dried oregano

1 teaspoon salt

1 teaspoon freshly ground
    black pepper

1 teaspoon ground red
    pepper (cayenne)

Hot pepper sauce to taste

2 quarts Shrimp Broth (page
    25) or chicken stock,
    heated

1 15-ounce can tomato sauce

4 pounds shrimp, shelled and
    cleaned

1 pound crab meat, preferably
    claw meat

6 to 8 crab bodies, cleaned but
    not cooked (page 74)

3 cups hot cooked rice

Heat the drippings or oil in a large heavy pot, and gradually stir in the flour. Cook over medium-high heat, continuing to stir constantly until the mixture is a dark nut-brown. This can take up to 30 minutes. Remove from the heat for a few seconds if it darkens too quickly, then reduce the heat slightly. If the flour burns and black specks appear, discard and begin the roux again. Stir in the onion, green pepper, okra, celery, garlic, and parsley, and cook until the onion, pepper, and celery are tender, and the okra stops "roping" (the white threads produced by the okra disappear). Add the bay leaves, thyme, oregano, salt, pepper, cayenne, and hot pepper sauce, if using, and mix well. Slowly pour in the warm broth and the tomato sauce. Partially cover and simmer 30 to 40 minutes. Add the shrimp, crab meat, and crab bodies and cook 5 minutes more, until the shrimp turn pink. Adjust the seasoning with additional salt and pepper, if wanted. To serve, remove the bay leaves, and ladle the gumbo into deep plates or bowls over a mound of rice (and a crab body if so desired). Provide nutcrackers for cracking the claws.

SCAMP—THE PRIZE OF THE GULF

The scamp is a small grouper with very white flesh and delicate texture and flavor. Many people of the Panhandle, where it is caught, consider it to be the best of all saltwater fish. Seafood markets in this area carry it and south Alabamians and Georgians who holiday there ask for it, so their markets back home offer it.

In north Florida scamp may be fried, sautéed, or broiled. It is not often grilled, as the fillets are thin, with fragile flesh, and are difficult to turn without breaking. Lemon or lime juices complement the flavor of scamp; relishes and sauces should be understated, so they aren't overpowering.

Some scamp is shipped to fish wholesalers in the Northeast, but often it is sold as ordinary grouper, since the public and restaurant chefs are unfamiliar with its qualities.

BROILED SCAMP WITH HOLLANDAISE

MAKES 4 TO 5 SERVINGS.

The delicate flesh of this fish demands tender handling. Heavy or spicy sauces mask the fine flavor and texture of this Gulf Coast favorite.

½ cup (1 stick) plus 2 table-spoons butter	Dash hot pepper sauce
2 egg yolks	2 tablespoons lemon juice
¼ teaspoon salt	2½ pounds scamp fillets
	Lemon wedges for garnish

Cut the stick of butter into 3 pieces. Stir the egg yolks until smooth in the top of a double boiler. Add 1 hunk of the butter, place the pan over

Broiled Scamp with Hollandaise (continued)

boiling water, and stir the sauce vigorously until the butter is almost melted. Add another hunk of butter, stir until almost melted, then add the third hunk of butter and stir until thickened and smooth. Add the salt and pepper sauce, then the lemon juice. Remove from the heat and stir a minute or two to stop the sauce from cooking.

Preheat the broiler. Butter the rack in the broiler pan and place the fish fillets on it. Spread the remaining 2 tablespoons of butter over them. Broil 6 to 7 minutes. Spread generously with the sauce and broil 2 to 3 minutes longer, until the sauce is bubbly. Watch carefully to see that the fish is not scorching. Serve hot and garnish with the lemon wedges.

STIFADO
GREEK-STYLE FISH STEW

MAKES 4 SERVINGS.

There is a large Greek community in Pensacola, where the Silivos family owns and operates Skopelos On The Bay, a first-rate Greek restaurant. Gus Silivos left the family long enough to sharpen his skills at the Culinary Institute of America and is now executive chef at the restaurant. One of his warmest childhood memories is the *stifado* that his mother still makes.

6 cups water

5 tablespoons tomato paste

1 teaspoon minced garlic

A 2½-inch length of cinnamon stick

7 whole cloves

1 small bay leaf

16 pearl onions, peeled

1 teaspoon salt, or to taste

¼ teaspoon freshly ground pepper

4 tuna, swordfish, or mackerel steaks, ¾ inch thick (2 pounds in all)

5 tablespoons cornstarch, blended smooth with a small amount of water

Bring the water to a boil in a large saucepan or deep skillet. Add the tomato paste, garlic, cinnamon stick, whole cloves, and bay leaf. Mix well, cover, and simmer 20 to 25 minutes to blend flavors. Add the onions, salt, and pepper. Simmer, covered, 10 to 12 minutes longer, until the tip of a sharp knife slips easily into the center of an onion. Place the fish in the sauce, baste with the liquid, then cook slowly 10 to 12 minutes, or until the fish is firm when tested with a fork. Remove the fish with a slotted spatula to a plate and keep warm. Taste the sauce, and add more salt and pepper, if wanted. Remove the cinnamon stick and bay leaf, and bring the sauce to a boil. Add the cornstarch mixture and cook, stirring until smooth, thickened, and boiling. If a thicker sauce is wanted, add another tablespoon of cornstarch to a little water and stir into the sauce. Place a fish steak and 4 of the onions on each serving plate, and spoon some of the sauce over the top. Pass the remaining sauce. Serve hot with rice or crusty bread.

GULF COAST OYSTERS

The estuary that pours water from the Chattahoochee River and its forks into Apalachicola Bay is one of the most productive in the Western Hemisphere. The water, flowing through a swampy hardwood forest, provides a giant natural filtration system, fills itself with food for oysters, and mixes with bay water to provide the brackish environment that nurtures the hard-shelled creatures. Almost two million pounds of oysters were harvested in 1989, 90 percent of the state's production, and shipped nationwide. Florida, as well as other states, certifies oysters, after meticulous inspection, and seafood shippers urge consumers who eat raw shellfish to ask retailers or restaurateurs if the oysters are certified. Oyster farming, developing in the 1990s, bodes well for the future. Aquaculture allows choice of waters free from pollution and seafood handled in peak condition. The first farmed oysters came to market in 1991, and production is expected to increase rapidly, as more people go into farming. A method for purifying oysters is being tested in Apalachicola. Sterilized seawater is piped into tanks where oysters or clams pump themselves clean within a few hours. The system has not been approved, but is another try at improving the reliability of Florida seafood.

LINDA'S BARBECUED SHRIMP

Peel-your-own shrimp recipes are popular all over the South, but nowhere more than in the Florida Panhandle, where you're never far from the Gulf. Caroline's sister and brother-in-law, Linda and Bill Virgin, worked this one out for easy entertaining. The advantage of this recipe is that the sauce can be made ahead of time; the shrimp are then added to the sauce and cooked in the oven, rather than on the top of the range, freeing the cook to join the party.

The shrimp is served in the shell with the sauce, and guests pile servings onto their plates and do their own shelling. It's messy, but worth it. Toasted Italian, French, or garlic bread is a must for sopping up the sauce. Add a big salad, lots of paper napkins or paper towels, and you have an easy, delicious meal.

1 pound (4 sticks) butter	2 cups ketchup
1 medium onion, chopped	¼ teaspoon liquid crab boil
2 large cloves garlic, minced	(available in seafood markets
1 teaspoon salt	or spice sections of
1 teaspoon freshly ground	supermarkets)
pepper	2 tablespoons prepared
1 teaspoon paprika	mustard
1 teaspoon chili powder	Hot pepper sauce to taste
½ cup firmly packed brown sugar	(optional)
2 tablespoons Worcestershire	5 pounds large shrimp in
sauce	the shell, but headless

Melt the butter in a large saucepan over moderate heat. Add the remaining ingredients except the shrimp and simmer to blend flavors and thicken slightly, about 10 minutes. The sauce can be used immediately or refrigerated until time to cook the dish.

About 1 hour before serving, wash and drain the shrimp. Place them in a Dutch oven or large deep baking pan. Pour the sauce over the shrimp and toss to mix well. Cover, using foil if the pan has no cover. Bake 30 to 45 minutes, stirring occasionally, until the shrimp is pink. Turn off the oven and let the shrimp stand until ready to serve, up to 1 hour.

No alfresco meal is merrier than a fish fry in Florida. It is causal: the food honestly good, the dress comfortable, and the socializing easy. There are lots of excuses for fish fries: business reasons, church events, family reunions, fund raising, or private parties. Whatever the occasion, a fish fry is good plain fun!

The menu includes fried fish and hushpuppies, coleslaw, corn on the cob, baked beans, French fries, grits (usually cheese grits), and watermelon or pies for dessert. Tartar sauce and cocktail sauce are served with the fish. The food is fresh, cooked and eaten on the spot, on the beach, in a park, or backyard.

In the Panhandle, the fish is likely to be mullet or grouper. On the east coast, mullet and snapper fillets are fried. The baby catfish, caught wild in Lake Okeechobee, are a rare treat at fish fries there. Sport anglers in southeast Florida show off grunts and other panfish at their backyard fish fries.

The menu may vary. Around the lake, fried sweet potatoes often go with catfish. Many folk like French fries or potato salad, and fried okra is great with fish and hushpuppies. In south Florida, a big bowl of sliced mangoes or fresh pineapple in season may be the dessert, and sometimes lime pie is served.

Iced tea, lemonade or limeade, and beer are the usual beverages, or vodka drinks, bourbon, or scotch may be poured. Wine and wine coolers might be passed, and many hosts and caterers provide sodas.

SHRIMP STUFFED EGGPLANT

MAKES 4 LUNCHEON SERVINGS.

While eggplant is generally thought of as a veg
etable, this late-season relative of the potato and
tomato is actually a fruit, the origin of which can be traced to India. Eggplant was reportedly introduced to America by the eminent Southern gardener, Thomas Jefferson, and nowhere is it more popular than in Florida.
There cooks are especially fond of frying, or stuffing, then baking it. The
addition of shrimp in this stuffed version makes it special and delicious.

1 large eggplant (1½ pounds)	½ teaspoon dried oregano
2 tablespoons plus 2 teaspoons butter	1 tomato, chopped
	¼ cup water
½ pound large shrimp, shelled and cleaned	1 teaspoon salt
	½ teaspoon freshly ground pepper
1 onion, chopped fine	
½ cup chopped parsley	Hot pepper sauce to taste
½ teaspoon dried leaf thyme	½ cup dry bread crumbs

Preheat the oven to 400 degrees. Cut the eggplant in half lengthwise and
remove the flesh, leaving a shell ½ inch thick. Chop the eggplant flesh
and set aside. Immerse the shells, skin side up, in a bowl of water until
ready to fill. Heat 2 tablespoons of the butter in a large skillet, add the
shrimp, and sauté until pink, 1 to 2 minutes. Remove the shrimp and set
aside. Add the onion, parsley, thyme, and oregano and sauté gently, stirring constantly. Add the chopped eggplant, then the tomato, water, salt,
and pepper. Mix well, cover tightly, and simmer 5 minutes. Cut each
shrimp into thirds and add to the eggplant mixture. Stir in the hot pepper sauce.

Place the eggplant shells, hollow side up, in a lightly oiled shallow baking pan. Sprinkle a thin layer of bread crumbs in the bottom of each shell,
then fill with alternate layers of the eggplant mixture and crumbs, ending
with the crumbs. Dot with the remaining 2 teaspoons of butter. Bake 20 to
25 minutes, or until the crumbs are browned. Serve immediately.

BOURBON MARINATED CHICKEN BREASTS

MAKES 2 SERVINGS.

Southerners love their bourbon, and cooks know it's not just for drinking. Bourbon is well suited for marinades such as this one; when bourbon is combined with soy sauce and mustard, the resulting flavor has a unique kick. The marinade can be made days in advance, and the simple preparation makes this a real Southern Comfort.

The recipe is for two, but multiplying it is no problem; use just enough marinade to cover the chicken. Any extra can be frozen. It is also good for marinating pork, flank steak, and even shrimp.

½ cup bourbon

¼ cup soy sauce

1 tablespoon prepared mustard

2 green onions or scallions,
   including tops, sliced thin

2 teaspoons sugar

Dash Worcestershire sauce

2 boneless chicken breasts
   with skin removed

Mix together all of the ingredients except the chicken, blending until the sugar and mustard are dissolved. Place the chicken in a shallow dish, add the marinade, and turn the chicken to coat well. Cover and marinate in the refrigerator for at least 1 hour, turning the chicken occasionally. Remove the chicken from the marinade. Grill on an outdoor grill over a medium fire, on a kitchen grill, or in an oven broiler. Brush with the marinade several times while cooking, 8 to 10 minutes total grilling time for average-size breast pieces. Test with a sharp knife near the center. If the juices run golden or clear, the chicken is done. If they are tinged with red, grill a minute or two longer.

THANKSGIVING AT THE SAN CARLOS, 1915

The San Carlos Hotel . . . was a principal social center for the city [Pensacola] for half a century. The elegant white marble lobby, the handsome curving grand stairway leading to the mezzanine, and the splendid stained-glass dome over the mezzanine contributed to an aura of elegance and space for fashionable entertaining. . . .

Thanksgiving dinner at the San Carlos in 1915 began with caviar and salted almonds, continued with green turtle soup, planked sea trout, braised sweetbreads, apple fritters with rum sauce, Benedictine punch with a sugar wafer, then a choice of prime ribs or turkey with oyster stuffing, several vegetables, and for dessert, plum pudding (with hard and brandy sauce), hot mince or pumpkin pie, chestnut ice cream, or assorted cake; the last course was creamed neufchatel cheese with bar-le-duc jelly and demi-tasse. Cluster raisins and after-dinner mints rounded out the feast.

from *Florida's Fabled Inns* by Louise K. Frisbie,
Imperial Publishing Co., Bartow, Florida, 1980

CAMPBELL FAMILY CHICKEN

MAKES 4 SERVINGS.

Annie Lee Campbell, who raised her large family in Crestview, in the middle of the Panhandle, put on big Sunday dinners, lavish holiday meals, and daily family dinners as routinely as the sun rose. One Christmas the children and grandchildren collected their favorite recipes in a loose-leaf notebook as a gift for her. One of the recipes was this baked chicken, which the family prefers to fried chicken. They adjusted the sauce to their tastes and thickened it for gravy.

2 tablespoons soy sauce
2 tablespoons packed brown sugar
¼ cup vegetable oil
¼ teaspoon ground ginger
½ cup red or white table wine
½ cup water
1 3-pound broiler-fryer, cut up,
    or 8 meaty pieces (thighs and
    split breasts)

2 tablespoons flour
Salt and freshly ground pepper
    (optional)
3 cups hot cooked rice

Preheat the oven to 375 degrees. Combine the soy sauce, brown sugar, oil, ginger, wine, and water. Stir until the sugar is dissolved. Arrange the chicken in a buttered 9 × 13 × 2-inch baking pan. Pour the sauce over it and turn to coat the chicken on both sides. Bake 20 minutes, turn the chicken, and bake 15 minutes longer, or until the juices run clear or golden when the chicken is slit at a thick joint. Remove the chicken to a platter.

To prepare the gravy, skim as much fat as possible off the pan drippings. Heat 2 tablespoons of the fat in a skillet and stir in the flour. Gradually stir in 1½ cups of the defatted pan drippings. Cook and stir until thickened and smooth. Taste and add salt and pepper if needed. Serve the chicken hot and the gravy with rice.

SMOTHERED QUAIL

MAKES 4 SERVINGS.

Bird hunting is a great sport in this piney woods section of the country, and "smothering" is an old-fashioned way of cooking almost anything. The quail absorbs the flavors and is tenderized by the wine, broth, and by slow cooking with the pan covered.

8 quail
Salt and freshly ground pepper
Flour for dredging
½ cup vegetable oil or butter
1 pound mushrooms, sliced

1 cup sliced green onions or
   scallions
2 cups dry white wine
2 cups chicken broth

Rinse the quail well and pat dry with paper towels. Season with salt and pepper, and dredge in flour, shaking off the excess. Heat the oil in a heavy skillet, add the quail, and brown them well on all sides. Pour off the oil and add the mushrooms, green onions, wine, and chicken broth. Cover and simmer until the birds are tender, 30 to 45 minutes. Serve hot with Pecan Brown Rice (see page 96) or grits.

VENISON EARTH ROAST

Earth roasting is a unique method of cooking venison in the backyard or in the woods. Hunters choose this technique for a different taste of venison. It is fun to do on a fall weekend, and the roast is perfect for entertaining a lot of people. Buried in the ground to roast, the meat is cooked so tender that it practically falls off the bone in shreds. A ham or shoulder is ideal for this, but other cuts of venison or large cuts of beef can be used.

1. To prepare the venison, make 10 to 12 slits in it with a sharp knife and insert slivers of garlic. Sprinkle with salt and pepper.

2. Wrap the seasoned meat in several layers of heavy-duty foil, then place in a heavy cloth bag, such as a laundry bag or pillowcase.

3. Dig a hole in the ground approximately 2 feet deep and wide enough to accommodate the meat with several inches to spare on all sides.

4. Build a fire in the bottom of the hole, preferably using hardwood, and let it burn down to very hot embers.

5. Cover the coals with a layer of sand, about 2 inches thick, so that *no* smoke is coming out.

6. Put the wrapped venison on top of the sand.

7. Place a piece of tin or other metal on top of the meat.

8. Put another layer of sand over the tin, making sure to build up the sides. Cover any escaping smoke (see Note).

9. Leave the venison buried overnight, or for at least 8 hours, then dig it up, unwrap, and serve.

NOTE: If using dirt instead of sand, make a small fire on top of the dirt just long enough to dry it out.

FARM-SUPPER PORK CHOPS

MAKES 6 LARGE SERVINGS.

Thick pork chops barbecued at a park or community center are the pride of farm suppers in the Panhandle. The part-social, part-business suppers put on by grower groups draw families from miles around. Women bring salads, vegetable dishes, and desserts, and the food is "fabulous," say farm wives.

1 cup beef broth
1 bay leaf, crumbled
½ teaspoon dry mustard
½ teaspoon chili powder
Dash hot pepper sauce or
   1 small hot chile pepper,
   minced

1 tablespoon Worcestershire
   sauce
6 butterflied boneless pork
   chops, 1 inch thick

Combine the beef broth, bay leaf, mustard, chili powder, pepper sauce, and Worcestershire in a small saucepan. Bring to a boil, turn heat to low, and simmer 10 minutes. Cool the sauce. Place the chops in a shallow dish or self-sealing bag, pour the sauce over them, and turn the meat in the sauce or close the bag and turn it to coat the chops. Marinate in the refrigerator 1 to 2 hours. Remove the chops from the marinade and place on a rack over hot coals on a grill with a cover. Brush the meat with reserved marinade, cover the grill, and cook 30 minutes, turning the chops and brushing them with marinade every 10 minutes. The chops are perfect when browned on the outside and juicy on the inside. Do not overcook pork, or the meat will be dry and tasteless. Test by slitting a chop at the center with the tip of a knife. If the juices run clear or golden the chops are done. If the juices are pink, cook a few minutes longer. Serve hot with Tomato Salsa (see page 206), applesauce, or other fruit relish.

GREEN BEANS WITH POTATOES

MAKES 4 SERVINGS.

When the first new potatoes are dug in the early summer, string beans are in season; cooking the tender little potatoes with the beans comes naturally. In the past, Floridians and many other Southerners were guilty of cooking green beans so long that they turned almost gray, and always seasoning vegetables with fatty pork. Now most people in Florida have learned to appreciate this updated version. It is lighter; the beans are cooked just crisp-tender and seasoned with garlic, parsley, and olive oil. Very young potatoes dug the morning they are cooked need only a few minutes on the heat. Increase the cooking time accordingly for older potatoes or those dug a few days before.

1 tablespoon olive oil
1 clove garlic, minced
1 tablespoon minced fresh
    parsley or thyme
12 to 16 new potatoes, 1 to
    1½ inches in diameter,
    washed well

½ cup water
1½ pounds green beans,
    tipped and cut in 2-inch
    lengths
Salt and freshly ground
    pepper

Heat the oil in a large saucepan. Add the garlic and sauté until it is aromatic, taking care not to brown it. Add the parsley and potatoes, turn the heat low, and cook 3 to 4 minutes. Add the water and beans. Bring to a boil and cook, uncovered, 5 minutes. Cover the pan and cook over low to medium heat until the beans are crisp-tender and the potatoes tender when pierced with a fork, 7 to 10 minutes for young vegetables. Season to taste with salt and pepper. Serve hot.

SOUL FOOD

Soul food is the heritage of Southern African-Americans. In Colonial and antebellum times, slaves had to make do with the rations parceled out by plantation owners, along with whatever could be hunted, caught, raised, or collected by their own devices. Corn, rice, pork, chicken, sweet potatoes, beans, turnips, and molasses, as well as wild game, fish, and native plants such as greens and field peas, formed the basis of the slave diet.

From these simple ingredients and hard times came the Black cookery that Southerners cherish. Specialties such as cornbread, fried chicken, "hoppin John" (black-eyed peas and rice), turnip, mustard, and collard greens, and sweet potato pie, to name just a few, are well loved in Florida, as they are throughout the South.

COUNTRY BUTTER BEANS

MAKES 4 TO 6 SERVINGS.

Shelled green lima beans about the size of a pinkie fingernail are in farmer's markets, farm stands, and specialty shops for a few weeks in the late spring and summer in north Florida and they are in fancy produce markets in other regions occasionally. Butter beans get their name from the method of cooking them, in boiling water with a good-size lump of butter and a bit of milk, a mixture that accentuates the delicate flavor of the beans. Moist fresh butter beans are a nuisance to shell, but once you've tasted them, you don't mind the trouble. The cooking time varies according to the age and variety of the beans, so test them with a fork after about 25 minutes of cooking. Frozen baby limas look like garden-fresh butter beans and are a perfectly good vegetable. But don't be fooled. The flavor and texture are not the same as freshly harvested butter beans. Southerners spoon a dab of sweet pickle relish or chowchow on the plate with a serving of butter beans.

3 cups (2 to 2½ pounds in the shell) shelled green butter beans	½ teaspoon salt, or to taste
	½ teaspoon sugar
	½ cup milk
Boiling water	1 sprig parsley or fresh thyme
2 tablespoons butter	

Wash the beans, drain, and place in a 1½-quart saucepan. Add boiling water until the beans barely float up from the bottom of the pan. Add the butter, ½ teaspoon salt, and the sugar. Stir, cover, and bring to a boil. Turn the heat to low and simmer 30 minutes, or until the beans are tender when tested with a fork. Add the milk and herb. Simmer 10 minutes longer or until the beans are tender. Taste and add more salt, if wanted. Serve hot with the liquid.

GRILLED WHOLE ONIONS

This is the easiest possible way to cook onions: whole, unpeeled, and soaked in water, then directly on an outdoor grill to "steam" in the skin. When done, the charred outside simply peels back to reveal a moist, tender onion. Have handy some butter, salt, pepper, and condiments so guests can season their own onion. These onions are terrific for cookouts, where the emphasis is on simplicity. They go especially well with beef, chicken, and pork.

1 large yellow or white onion per person	Butter, salt, and freshly ground pepper
Bowl of cold water	

CONDIMENTS OF YOUR CHOICE:

Worcestershire sauce	chopped parsley
hot pepper sauce	chopped dill
lemon pepper	

Put the unpeeled onions into the bowl of water and place a plate on top of them so they will stay submerged. Soak for a half hour so the onions will absorb water and not burn when cooked. Drain and place the onions on a hot grill. Cook for 20 to 30 minutes, depending on the size of the onion, until fork tender. The onions must be rotated to cook on all sides. When done, each guest pulls back the outside skin with a knife and fork, either by cutting the end or through the side. The onion will slip out easily and the charred outside is discarded. Serve with butter and a choice of condiments.

NASSAU GRITS

MAKES 4 TO 5 SERVINGS.

The origin of this Pensacola specialty can be traced back almost seventy years to a local named Henry Richardson, who discovered a dish made with fish and grits while on a fishing trip in the Bahamas. Back home, he introduced the simple dish to his family, who promptly concocted a more flavorful version by substituting ham for the fish and by adding vegetables and bacon. The outcome was christened "Nassau Grits," and became an area favorite, where it can be found on Pensacola restaurant menus.

This recipe comes by way of Richardson's niece, Molly Biggs, who cautions that "you have to use country ham . . . and don't cut out the bacon if you want it to taste like anything." Prepared accordingly, it certainly does taste like something, and its reddish color and rich flavor make it an unconventionally good side dish with meat or fish.

½ pound bacon
1 medium onion, chopped fine
1 small green bell pepper,
    seeded and chopped fine
¾ cup finely ground ham
5 medium tomatoes, preferably
    vine ripened, or a 14½-ounce
    can tomatoes, undrained and
    chopped

1 teaspoon finely chopped
    garlic, ½ teaspoon dried
    oregano, and ½ teaspoon
    dried basil (all optional)
¾ cup uncooked white grits
Salt and freshly ground pepper
    to taste

Fry the bacon until crisp. Drain, then crumble and set aside. Reserve 2 to 3 tablespoons of the bacon drippings. Add the onion and the bell pepper and sauté until tender and the onion is translucent but not browned. Add the ham and stir to mix well. Sauté over low heat for 20 minutes. Add the tomatoes, garlic or herbs, if using, and simmer for 45 minutes to 1 hour. Meanwhile, cook the grits according to the package directions, then stir in the ham mixture. Turn into a large serving bowl and sprinkle the crumbled bacon over the top. Serve immediately or keep warm in a double boiler over low heat.

FISH VARIATION

Omit the ham and substitute ¼ pound fish such as snapper or grouper, cooked and flaked.

BAKED CHEESE GRITS

MAKES 6 SERVINGS.

The South has always relied heavily on corn and corn products, and Florida is no exception. Certainly one of the most primary of all staples here is grits, which is ground dried corn, cooked in water or milk to a creamy consistency. The basic version, served hot off the fire with country ham, eggs, and steaming coffee, is a breakfast tradition, and fried or baked grits, often combined with cheese and other ingredients, appears just as often accompanying fried chicken or pork chops at lunch or dinner. A fish fry wouldn't be complete without this Southern specialty, and in the Panhandle, where such meals reign, cheese grits is an exceedingly popular side dish.

3 cups water
1 cup uncooked grits
2 teaspoons salt
½ cup (1 stick) butter
1 clove garlic, minced
2 teaspoons Worcestershire
   sauce

1 cup shredded sharp Cheddar
   cheese
¼ cup half-and-half
White pepper to taste

Preheat the oven to 350 degrees. In a saucepan, bring the water to a boil. Add the grits slowly, then the salt; turn the heat to a bare simmer. Cook according to the package directions, stirring frequently to prevent sticking to the bottom of the pan. When done, add the butter, stirring until melted. Remove from the heat and add the garlic, Worcestershire, cheese, half-and-half, and pepper. Mix well and turn into a greased 1-quart casserole. Bake uncovered for 15 to 20 minutes until bubbling. Serve hot.

PECAN BROWN RICE

MAKES 4 TO 6 SERVINGS.

This is especially good with game and uses pecans that grow profusely in this section of the state.

2 tablespoons butter
2 tablespoons finely chopped onion
¼ cup chopped mushrooms
1 cup uncooked brown rice
2½ cups chicken broth

1 tablespoon finely chopped parsley
½ cup pecan pieces, toasted (see Note)
Salt and freshly ground pepper

In a saucepan, melt the butter, add the onion and mushrooms, and sauté until they are wilted. Add the rice and stir for 1 to 2 minutes until coated well with butter. Slowly pour in the chicken broth and bring to a boil, then cover and simmer for 45 minutes or until the rice is tender and the liquid is absorbed. Gently stir in the chopped parsley, pecans, and salt and pepper to taste.

NOTE: To toast the pecans, spread the nuts out on a shallow baking pan or cookie sheet and toast in a preheated 325-degree oven for 8 to 10 minutes, turning occasionally, until crisp.

BAKED CORN CAKES

MAKES 6 CORN CAKES.

Little cornbreads such as these were baked by natives on stones over open fires before white men came to Florida; earliest white settlers baked small breads on clean hoe blades outdoors or on a hearth. This bread is slightly refined with a bit of baking powder to lighten it, and a touch of sugar to help it brown.

It is a fast bread, one to bake when a hurried cook has no time to prepare the usual cornbread that goes with vegetables.

2 tablespoons vegetable oil
1 cup white stone-ground corn
  meal
3 tablespoons flour

½ teaspoon salt
¾ cup boiling water
1 teaspoon baking powder

Preheat the oven to 450 degrees. Pour the oil into a 9-inch square baking dish or 10-inch heavy skillet and place in the oven to heat. In a small bowl, combine the corn meal, flour, and salt. Stir in the boiling water slowly and mix well. Let stand while the oven is heating. Stir in the baking powder thoroughly. Drop the batter by tablespoonsful into the hot fat. Let them sizzle a minute or two, then turn the cakes over. Place in the hot oven and bake 10 minutes. Turn with a spatula, return to the oven, and bake 5 to 6 minutes longer. Serve hot.

FLORIDA SPOON BREAD

MAKES 4 SERVINGS.

This spoon bread from Caroline's mother's notebook is an excellent side dish with fried chicken and gravy, ham, or game birds. Cooking grits for the base eliminates the tricky procedure of making lump-free corn meal mush that is the usual foundation for spoon bread. The recipe is scaled down for a small family. It can be doubled for a brunch party, where it will star.

1½ cups water
1 teaspoon salt, or to taste
½ cup old-fashioned or quick grits
½ cup corn meal, preferably
  stone-ground

2 tablespoons butter
2 eggs
½ cup milk
1½ teaspoons baking powder

Bring the water to a boil in a saucepan. Add the salt and stir in the grits gradually. Cover, reduce the heat, and cook according to the label on the grits package. Stir once or twice while cooking. Preheat the oven to 375 degrees. Remove the grits from the heat and stir the corn meal into the hot grits until blended. Stir in the butter, then add the eggs, one at a time, mixing well. Blend in the milk, then the baking powder. Spread the thick batter in a buttered 4- to 5-cup baking dish that can be used as a serving dish. Bake 35 to 40 minutes, until the top is lightly browned, puffed, and a pick inserted in the center comes out clean. Spoon the soft hot bread onto plates and serve with butter or gravy.

BLACKBERRY DUMPLINGS

MAKES 4 SERVINGS.

Berry picking evokes memories of easier, less-hurried times, and you still can see folk filling their buckets on roadsides or in fields in north Florida. On tasting the tangy sweetness of a blackberry dumpling, cobbler, or pie made of wild berries, you understand why youth and many adults can be pried away from summer pastimes for the chore. Dumplings date back to very early settlements and, unlike pies or cobblers, could be cooked over an open fire.

1 pint blackberries	Pinch salt
3 tablespoons sugar, or to taste	¼ cup milk
Juice of 1 lemon	1½ teaspoons butter, melted
½ cup sifted cake flour	Ice cream, whipped cream, or
1½ teaspoons baking powder	milk for topping

In a wide enamelware or stainless steel skillet or saucepan with tight-fitting cover, combine the blackberries, sugar, and lemon juice. Crush the berries lightly with the back of a spoon. Bring to a boil, then simmer 2 or 3 minutes. Taste and add more sugar, if a sweeter dessert is wanted.

While the blackberries are cooking, sift together the cake flour, baking powder, and salt into a small bowl. Stir in the milk, then the melted butter. The blackberry mixture should be juicy. If it has cooked dry, add 2 to 4 tablespoons hot water and bring to a boil before adding the dumplings. Drop the batter by teaspoonsful onto the boiling berries. Cover, turn heat low, and cook 15 minutes. Serve hot or warm with ice cream, whipped cream, or milk.

PEACH ICE CREAM

MAKES ABOUT 2 QUARTS, 6 TO 8 SERVINGS.

A splash of bourbon punches up the flavor of this ice cream, and gives it a light and velvety texture. The liquor can be omitted, but we think it lends a note of elegance. Look for the richest flavored, fully ripened peaches available for a superb summer dessert. In the Panhandle, this means peaches that many people grow as a hobby.

2 cups heavy cream

1 cup milk

⅔ cup sugar

2 cups peeled and sliced ripe
  peaches

1 tablespoon lemon juice

Grated zest of 1 orange

1 tablespoon bourbon or
  amaretto

Additional peach slices and
  spirits (optional)

Heat the cream and milk with the sugar, stirring until the sugar is dissolved, until bubbles form at the edges. Remove from the heat and let stand 1 hour. Combine the peaches, lemon juice, and orange zest in a bowl. Chop half the peaches coarsely in a blender or processor, turning the motor on and off quickly so the fruit is not chopped too fine. Combine the chopped peaches, sliced peach mixture, and bourbon or amaretto. Chill until very cold. Stir the peach mixture into the cream mixture. Freeze, following the manufacturer's directions. Ripen the ice cream in a refrigerator freezer or the ice cream freezer for 8 to 10 hours or overnight, if time allows. Serve garnished with fresh peach slices and splashed with more bourbon or amaretto, if desired.

OLD-FASHIONED POUND CAKE

MAKES 16 TO 18 THIN SLICES.

The old-fashioned quality of this cake is due to the excellence of its ingredients. Most modern cakes use shortcuts, abbreviated quantities, and have added baking powder, resulting in cakes that are fluffy imitations. Make very sure that the butter and sugar are well beaten before adding the eggs. While one might think that it takes an enormous cake pan to hold this much batter, a standard 9- or 10-inch tube pan works perfectly. This recipe comes from Caroline's great-grandmother and has been handed down for good reason.

1 pound (4 sticks) butter, room
   temperature
2¾ cups sugar
10 eggs

4 cups sifted all-purpose flour
2 teaspoons vanilla extract
1 teaspoon lemon extract

Preheat the oven to 325 degrees. Grease a tube pan and dust with flour. In a large mixing bowl or the bowl of an electric mixer, cream the butter until it is very light and fluffy 5 to 10 minutes. Gradually add the sugar, beating well until dissolved and free from lumps. Add the eggs, one at a time, mixing well after each addition. Slowly add the flour, combining thoroughly. Add the flavorings. Pour into the cake pan and spread the batter evenly. Bake for 1½ hours or until the cake is firm and the edges pull away from the sides. If using a tester, it should come out clean. Remove the cake from the oven and cool in the pan for 10 to 15 minutes. Turn out onto a wire rack to cool completely.

DR. GORRIE—THE ICE MAN

$($ ooling the rooms of fever patients in Apalachicola was Dr. John Gorrie's goal when he first experimented with making ice. Apparently it never occurred to him or the people of Apalachicola that ice could keep the oysters from the bay fresh or that iced tea or lemonade might be a pleasure in the hot humid summertimes of the Gulf Coast. Dr. Gorrie was issued a patent on May 6, 1851, for his system for mechanical refrigeration. But he was unable to obtain money to build a plant to manufacture his cooling device for commercial use and he died bitterly disappointed. It was more than a half century before mechanical refrigeration became common and almost a century before air-conditioning changed life in Florida and the South. The Southern Ice Exchange, recognizing his contribution to commercial ice making, erected a monument to Dr. Gorrie in Apalachicola in 1900, and he is one of two Floridians whose statue is in the nation's capitol in Washington.

PEANUT BUTTER SNACK CAKES

MAKES 18 1½-INCH MUFFINS.

Georgia is well known for peanuts, but as crops don't recognize state boundaries, north Florida grows a hefty share as well. In fact, peanuts account for a surprising 18 percent of all Florida field crops. Grown mostly in the Panhandle, they are used primarily for peanut butter and peanut oil. As one might expect, peanuts in one form or another show up in countless recipes and these light, moist snack cakes are a good example.

1 cup sifted cake flour	**⅔ cup peanut butter**
½ teaspoon salt	**2 eggs**
1 teaspoon baking powder	**1 teaspoon vanilla extract**
½ cup (1 stick) butter, softened	**⅔ cup milk**
1½ cups packed brown sugar	

Preheat the oven to 350 degrees. Grease 18 1½-inch muffin tins or fit with paper liners. Combine the flour with the salt and baking powder, then sift again and set aside. Cream together the butter and brown sugar until light and fluffy. Blend in the peanut butter, then beat in the eggs, one at a time, and vanilla. Add the milk alternately with the dry ingredients, beginning and ending with the flour mixture. Spoon the batter into the prepared muffin tins and bake 25 minutes, or until the tops spring back when lightly touched. Cool slightly, then remove from the pan.

LEMON BUTTER COOKIES

MAKES ABOUT 36 COOKIES.

History suggests that lemons were brought to Hispaniola by Columbus, on his second voyage in 1493, and may have been flourishing in St. Augustine as early as 1579. This delicate cookie is an excellent use for the tart juice.

1 cup all-purpose flour	½ cup sugar
1½ teaspoons cornstarch	1 egg yolk
¾ teaspoon baking powder	1 teaspoon lemon juice
¼ teaspoon salt	Grated zest of 1 lemon
½ cup (1 stick) butter, softened	

Preheat the oven to 375 degrees. Sift together the flour, cornstarch, baking powder, and salt, and set aside. With an electric mixer or hand-mixer, cream the butter and sugar together until light and fluffy. Beat in the egg yolk, lemon juice, and the zest. Slowly add the dry ingredients, mixing well after each addition. Drop by teaspoonsful onto lightly greased cookie sheets, leaving about 1¹/2 inches between each cookie. Bake about 10 minutes or until the edges have lightly browned.

ROBERT'S PEANUT BRITTLE

MAKES ABOUT 2 POUNDS.

This candy was a treat for Elizabeth Kelly on wintry evenings when she was growing up in Crestview, Florida. A mother herself and an Episcopal priest now living in North Carolina, she remembers her grandmother cautioning the children to "be careful," as they took the panful of candy to the back porch to cool. Robert, for whom the brittle is named, was an agricultural extension agent in Opaloosa county, a major peanut-growing area.

The recipe as written in Elizabeth's family cookbook reads, "beat it like the mischief" after adding the baking soda, to caution that you must "beat it hard so it won't foam up over the pan."

2 cups sugar	**1 teaspoon butter**
1 cup light corn syrup	**½ teaspoon baking soda**
½ cup hot water	**1 teaspoon vanilla extract**
½ teaspoon salt	
2½ cups shelled raw peanuts,	
with the skins	

Mix the sugar, corn syrup, hot water, and salt in a large saucepan or small stock pot. Stir gently over moderately high heat until the sugar is dissolved, 2 to 3 minutes. Cover and boil slowly for 3 minutes (to melt sugar crystals that form on the sides of the pan). Uncover and boil without stirring until the syrup reaches 250 degrees on a candy thermometer, the firm ball stage. Stir in the peanuts and butter. Continue to cook over moderate heat to 300 degrees on the thermometer, the hard crack stage. Add the baking soda and vanilla. Stir rapidly until the foaming subsides. Immediately turn the hot candy out onto a well-buttered jelly-roll pan, other large flat pan, or a marble counter top. Cool completely. Invert the pan over a tray or large platter and the sheet of candy probably will drop out. If not, whack it smartly on bottom of the pan with the palm of your hand. Break the candy into small pieces with your hands or by rapping it with a mallet or back of a spoon. Store in tightly covered tins or freezer containers. Peanut Brittle is a popular holiday candy in the South; it is especially good cracked and served over ice cream or plain puddings.

THE SPACE COAST, GOLD COAST, AND THE KEYS

APPETIZERS

Bollitos de Frijoles

Florida Conch Salad

Escabeche

Caribbean Ceviche

Date Nut Salad

Papaya Seed Salad Dressing

SOUPS

Cream of Avocado Soup

Guiesso de Maiz (Cuban Corn Soup)

Biscayne Bay Yacht Club Chowder

ENTRÉES

Nassau Breakfast

Grilled Florida Lobster

Shrimp Steamed in Beer

Broiled Yellowtail with Orange Butter

Curried Black-Tip Shark

Grilled Marlin

Sautéed Sea Squab with Grapefruit

Ropa Vieja (Flank Steak and Tomato
   Hash)

Boliche

Cuban-Style Okra and Pork

Curried Lamb Islands-Style

VEGETABLES

Fried Plantains or Bananas

Warm Beet Salad

Peas and Rice

Sue Fisher's Tzimmes

Rosin Potatoes

BREADS

Marie's Banana Bread

Ruby Lord's Sweet Puppies

DESSERTS

Queen of All Puddings

Guava Duff

Miss Etta's Fresh Coconut Cake

Miami Beach Cheesecake

Fresh Strawberry Glaze

Key Lime Pie

Mango Tarte Tatin

Lime Custard Sauce

Classic Mango Chutney

The tastes of the southeastern coast of Florida are as distinctive and diverse as the people who live here, and nowhere are the contrasts greater than along the Gold Coast and south to the Keys. The Cuban food of the Gold Coast is well known, but there is much more. Palm Beach socialites, Cubans in Miami, and Key West "Conchs" have all contributed to the mix, as have thousands of others from the Caribbean, Central America, Europe, and Asia. The cultural mélange defies categorizing in any general way.

Since the 1950s, the space program has brought a new breed with more sophisticated palates to the Melbourne and Cocoa Beach areas. This influx of worldly, well-educated professionals from varied backgrounds has given rise to what marketing people have dubbed "the Canaveral taste."

Leaving the space race behind and traveling through vast citrus groves along the Indian River, one approaches the most developed and diverse section of the state. The Gold Coast, beginning around Vero Beach, is an affluent area straddling the Intracoastal Waterway south through Palm Beach, Boca Raton, and Fort Lauderdale, to Miami, where cultures collide.

It was in 1894 that Henry Flagler brought the railroad and the wealthy Northern social scene to Palm Beach, setting the tone for the aptly named Gold Coast. The opulent hotels of Palm Beach introduced luxury food and imported chefs to Florida, and to this day, fancy continental cuisine is prevalent in the elegant homes and restaurants of the area.

The Hispanic flavor of Miami has become entrenched thirty years after the mass migration of the early 1960s. Cubans had been coming for more than a century, many to work in the cigar factories in Key West and Tampa in the 1880s and '90s, and a trickle of immigration continued until the revolution of 1959 brought a flood tide. With the Cubans came dark-roast coffee to sip *con leche* (made with hot milk) or gulp down strong and black (*café Cubano*). Cuban bakers began turning out their special bread as good as that in Havana, and black beans and rice became a staple for Hispanics and Anglos alike. Now even tourists flock to Calle Ocho, the main street of Miami's Little Havana for specialties like *palomilla* (a thin, grilled, garlic-scented beefsteak with shoestring potatoes and fried plantains), at a tiny café called Lola, or to La Mar for superb seafood. And Cuban sandwiches can be found most anywhere.

Prior to 1959, public fare in Miami Beach was a reflection of its resort emphasis: Jewish and kosher food, along with a polyglot menu of French and Italianate dishes dominated the menus of the glitzy hotels. A notable exception was Joe's Stone Crab in Miami Beach, which sixty-five years after its opening still packs in crowds clamoring for the unique fresh crabs.

Little did the average tourist know that a few miles from Lincoln Road in Miami Beach, the Magic Mile in Fort Lauderdale, or Worth Avenue in Palm Beach, home folk routinely had superb foods, such as sweet mangoes and chutneys, fresh pineapples ripened to perfection, papayas, and other exotic fruits. Few visitors ventured to Fairchild Tropical Garden or the Redlands Fruit and Spice Park, where they might see and sample the tropical fruits. These showcases were miles from hotel rows.

Fishing, a big attraction for the area, provided some of the best eating for resident anglers. They caught and ate red snapper, yellowtail snapper, sea squab, snook, and dolphin fresh from the water. Prized stone crabs caught by sport divers were cooked within hours of capture.

In the 1870s, transplanted Northeasterners came to Coconut Grove, bringing their own style of cooking to the foods that were available locally. Peggy Munroe Catlow, daughter of one of the area's pioneering families, is now in her nineties and remembers her mother making jelly with sea grapes from the backyard, just as she had made it from the wild beach plums in the North. Also, the chowder at the first Washington's Birthday Regatta at the Biscayne Bay Yacht Club, in 1887, was made New England style, with potatoes and milk. B.B.Y.C. members and guests still savor this version at the annual event.

Tories from the Bahamas, who had originally fled Northern states during the American Revolution, came to settle Key West. The descendants of these hardy folk still steam duffs in pudding bags in the traditional British way. Here, too, are special gifts from the sea such as conch and Florida lobster, in addition to the bounty of more familiar fish and seafood. The Keys are also the birthplace of Key lime pie that has become popular all over the country, but can only be called the real McCoy when made with pungent Key limes and condensed milk.

As is true in much of the rest of the state, thousands of people throughout south Florida trace their ancestry to the Carolinas, Georgia, Alabama, and Kentucky. Along with their migration came grits, cornbread, hushpuppies, and other Deep South favorites that are still a part of life here.

The latest additions to the melting pot have been Asian. Chinese, Indonesian, Thai, and Vietnamese immigrants, arriving in the late seventies and the eighties, brought new flavors to the table, making south Florida one of the most international regions in this hemisphere. On farm plots in South Dade county many of these newcomers raise lemon grass and other spices and herbs to sell to their brother and sister refugees, and to supply specialty markets nearby. With so many influences shaping the character and flavor of the area, the Space Coast, the Gold Coast, and the Keys add up to what is perhaps the most interesting section of Florida, and one of the most exciting in the country.

William Cooley, a grower of coontie (arrowroot), was away when his wife and children were massacred in their home at Tarpon Bend on the New River on June 6, 1836. He later petitioned the United States government to replace the property lost, stolen, or destroyed in the attack. The list included:

2 barrels of flour	1 barrel salt
1 barrel pork	21 gallons wine
1 barrel beef	A lot of sugar
1 bag coffee	A lot of butter
4 bags corn	16 barrels arrowroot
1 barrel grits	10 boxes arrowroot
1 barrel rice	

He listed as destroyed:

6 acres planted in sugar cane	Also lots of pigs and fowl
2 acres Bermuda arrowroot	5 sheep etc.
12 acres in corn, potatoes, punkins etc.	A number of valuable fruit trees

from *Fort Lauderdale Recipes,* Historical Society, 1964

BOLLITOS DE FRIJOLES

MAKES ABOUT 2½ DOZEN BOLLITOS.

These black-eyed pea fritters are traditional for the Gasparilla Festival, the Mardi Gras celebration in Tampa, and are a year-round snack with beer, wine, and other drinks in Ybor City and Key West, where they are called bollos.

Skinning the peas is a tedious chore. Adela Gonzmart, daughter of the founder of the Columbia Restaurant, remembers her grandmother in Ybor City rubbing the peas between two boards to loosen the skins, but most home cooks do this by hand, and dislodge clinging skins with their thumbnails. Jean and John Wardlow, who grew up in Key West, used to make a party of skinning the peas. She would soak the peas and put the bowl of peas and water on the kitchen counter, near the bar. Jean and Jack directed guests going to the kitchen for drink refills to rub off a few pea skins en route. Before the guests went home, Jean would fry bollitos and guests would pop the hot crispy fritters into their mouths as fast as she could fry them.

Most recipes call for a pound of black-eyed peas, but we urge you to try a half pound first to see if you really want to tackle more peas for a crowd. A half pound makes plenty of bollitos for a small party or family. Cuban and Spanish families in Florida now use a mix that eliminates the skinning of the peas. Labeled *Bollitos La Gitana,* it can be mail-ordered from La Gitana, 1104 N. Howard Avenue, Tampa, FL 33607, or the Cook's Bazaar, 516 Fleming Street, Key West, FL 33040.

½ pound (1¼ cups) dried black-
    eyed peas
½ teaspoon salt
1 clove garlic, minced
    (optional)

¼ teaspoon hot pepper sauce
    or 1 chile pepper, seeded
    and minced
Peanut or olive oil for deep-
    fat frying

Pick over the peas, removing any dark ones and debris. Place in a large bowl and cover with water by at least 2 inches. Cover the bowl and let the peas soak overnight. Rub the peas between the palms of the hands or place between two small chopping boards or clean pieces of plank and rub vigorously to loosen the skins. Remove as much skin as will come off easily, then cover the peas again with cold water and soak 3 hours. The skins will float to the top. Skim the skins off and rub the peas again to remove the remaining skins. The skins that cling can be lifted off with a thumbnail. A few remaining skins are all right, but too many make coarse-textured bollitos.

Grind the peas in a food processor fitted with a steel blade using on-and-off spurts until smooth or put through a meat grinder fitted with the finest blade three times. Place the ground peas in a bowl and stir in the salt, garlic, and pepper sauce or chile. Beat with a mixer or with a wooden spoon until the batter is thick and creamy. Chill the batter thoroughly. It can be kept covered in the refrigerator for 1 or 2 days.

In a deep-fat fryer or large pan fitted with a frying basket, heat 4 to 5 inches of oil to 375 degrees. Drop the batter from the tip of a teaspoon and fry until golden brown, about 3½ minutes. The bollitos should have space to bob around in the oil, so cook in batches, if necessary. Drain the fritters on paper towels and keep warm on a foil-lined cookie sheet in a 225-degree oven. Spear on wood picks and serve as a snack, with or without Salsa Vinagreta (see page 191) or a Mexican-style salsa.

NOTE: Bollitos may be served as a luncheon dish. Drop the batter by tablespoonsful into hot fat and fry 4 to 5 minutes. Serve hot with tomato sauce or salsa.

Old Spanish Brands

FLORIDA STONE CRABS

Sixty-five years ago, a fishmonger named Joe Weiss "discovered" the fabulous taste of stone crabs, and began serving them with coleslaw and hashed browns at a few tables in his little fish shack near the water in Miami Beach. Joe's Stone Crab has been an institution ever since. The shack has become a commodious restaurant, serving *fresh* stone crab to capacity crowds day in and day out when they are in season.

Florida is the only state that commercially harvests the unique stone crab. It has a flat, oval-shaped body, skinny legs, and two rock-hard claws, one of which is substantially larger than the other. It is this claw that provides the tender sweet meat for appreciative fans like us. The black-tipped claws give way to a mottled and spotted reddish brown body, and a light tan underbelly.

There are two important rules regulating the capture of stone crabs: the minimum size requirement (no crab claw may be taken that does not measure at least 2¾ inches long from elbow to point of lower claw hook), and the law that claws must be removed and the live crab returned to the water. Claws are snapped off with a twisting motion, which, when done correctly, enables the crab to reproduce new ones. Since most of the harvested claws are frozen immediately after being caught, these delectable creatures can be savored year-round.

Stone crabs are traditionally eaten cold with a mustard sauce or drawn butter. They may be served warm, but the meat has a tendency to adhere to the shell, making it difficult to remove when heated.

CONCH—A PERSON OR SEAFOOD

onch is a colloquialism for natives of the Florida Keys. Until recently, a genuine Conch (pronounced *konk)* was born of Bahamian-British ancestry. Today natives with forebears from anywhere call themselves conchs. They are a bit clannish, fiercely independent, but friendly to visitors and newcomers, and proud of their heritage.

Conchs named themselves for one of the toughest seafoods that man ordinarily eats. Conchs, the men and women, attribute great lovemaking power to regular consumption of conch, the seafood. Furthermore, the people believe that eating the shellfish gives them strength and a long life.

Columbus and his men probably were the first Europeans to try eating the white seafood. On the first landfall at San Salvador in 1492, the exploring party found Arawak Indians eating the conch that crawled clumsily on the sandy bottoms of the bays.

FLORIDA CONCH SALAD

MAKES 6 TO 8 SERVINGS.

Key West remained isolated from food and other necessities, except those brought by boat, long after it became a city of some importance. The hardy folk there, called "Conchs," learned the tricks of surviving on native food. This conch salad is one of the best dishes from that life. At its simplest, conch salad requires only the seafood that comes from the lovely pink-lined shell, lime juice, and locally grown bird peppers. However, a conch salad with tomato, bell peppers, and onions is even better tasting and prettier than the basic combination. Key Westers serve it elegantly as an appetizer in stemmed cocktail glasses set on doily-lined plates on special occasions. A bowl of it also is kept in the refrigerator and brought out for impromptu lunches and suppers, or to pile on crackers to pass with drinks.

In south Florida and many cities around the country, cleaned conch can be found in seafood markets, especially those catering to people of Caribbean ancestry. Don't mistake the northern whelk (scungilli) for Florida and Caribbean conch. Scungilli is a stronger flavored cousin, popular in the New York and New England areas but not suitable for this salad.

1 pound cleaned conch meat, coarsely ground or finely diced

2 tomatoes, cut in 8 wedges each

6 green onions or scallions with tops, sliced thin

1 green or red bell pepper, seeded and ribs removed, diced

1 bird pepper (tiny chile) or 1 small dried chile, seeded and minced, or more to taste

¼ cup lime juice (3 Key limes or 1½ Persian limes)

2 tablespoons distilled white or cider vinegar

3 tablespoons olive oil

1 teaspoon Worcestershire sauce

1 teaspoon Old Sour (see page 131) or lime juice plus ¼ teaspoon salt

½ teaspoon salt

¼ teaspoon freshly ground pepper

Combine the conch, tomatoes, green onions, bell pepper, and bird pepper in a large glass or stainless steel bowl. Combine the lime juice, vinegar, olive oil, Worcestershire sauce, Old Sour, salt, and pepper. Mix well, pour over the salad, and toss to mix well. Cover and refrigerate 6 hours, or overnight. Serve icy cold as a salad with greens or in footed cocktail glasses. A few sprigs of watercress or arugula tucked around the salad in cocktail glasses are pretty, or try a Key West enhancement, slender avocado wedges at the sides. Conch salad keeps well in the refrigerator for 2 to 3 days.

ESCABECHE—SEAGOING FARE

Escabeche, marinated cooked fish, is handed down from Cuban fishermen. In years past, the first mackerel caught on an expedition was always made into escabeche (pronounced es-cah-*bay-chay*), so the fish would keep. The fishing party might be out for several days, so the pickling solution kept the fish edible until the men sailed back into port.

The Voltzes were introduced to escabeche in the 1950s at a party on a sleek yacht out of Havana tied up at the Miami Marina. The marinated mackerel, in a jar set in a place carved out for it on the bar in the yacht's main cabin, was the winning hors d'oeuvre of the evening. A steward ladled a chunk of fish with olives and vegetables onto a small plate for each guest, along with a small fork. Cuban crackers, somewhat like water biscuits, were served with it. Miamians went wild for the escabeche.

ESCABECHE

MAKES 6 MAIN-DISH SERVINGS OR 12 TO 14 APPETIZERS.

This Caribbean-style pickled fish is served at room temperature as a snack, on salad greens as an appetizer or luncheon salad, or hot with yellow rice as a main dish. The king mackerel is a larger cousin of the Spanish mackerel, and is cut into steaks of a half pound or more each.

2½ pounds king mackerel steaks
1 cup olive oil
¼ cup vegetable oil
1 large clove garlic, sliced thin

2 bay leaves, crumbled
1 green bell pepper, seeded and
  cut in thin rings
2 medium onions, sliced thin

2 canned pimientos, sliced thin

1 5¼-ounce jar stuffed green
   olives, drained

Salt and freshly ground
   pepper

¾ cup distilled white vinegar

1 to 2 tablespoons minced
   parsley

Cut away the dark portions of the fish and, if desired, pull off the skin, though the skin helps the fish hold its shape while cooking and pickling. Heat ¼ cup of the olive oil and the vegetable oil in a large skillet. Add the garlic and bay leaves, then the fish in one layer. Cook the fish in batches, if necessary. Sauté it 5 to 6 minutes on each side, until lightly browned, taking care not to overcook it. Place it on a platter, and sauté the remaining fish. Remove the remaining fish and add the green pepper and sliced onions to the skillet; cook and stir until the onions are tender.

Layer the fish steaks in a casserole with a cover or a large wide-mouth glass jar, adding the green pepper, onions, pimientos, and olives to each layer. Sprinkle lightly with salt and pepper, keeping in mind that olives are briny. We use about ½ teaspoon salt total. After all the fish and vegetables are placed in the jar, beat together the vinegar and remaining ¾ cup olive oil. Pour over the fish, cover, and refrigerate at least 4 hours. Escabeche can be aged in the refrigerator up to 10 days, but it is tangy and richly flavored in 2 to 4 days. Pull off the skin of the steaks, if wished. Sprinkle the fish with parsley and serve chilled or at room temperature. The dressing is drippy, so put the fish on small plates to serve.

CARIBBEAN CEVICHE

MAKES 4 SALAD SERVINGS, 24 TO 36 APPETIZER
SERVINGS.

Lime juice "cooks" the fish for this Caribbean-style appetizer or salad. Choose extremely fresh saltwater fish such as belly flounder that produces a beautifully white, sea fresh–flavored ceviche. Freshwater fish can be unsafe for no-heat cooking. Other saltwater species that are suitable for this dish include pompano, snapper, tuna, and amberjack. If in doubt, ask a reliable seafood dealer. Jamaicans, Dominicans, and Haitians brought the idea of adding coconut to ceviche to Florida. It contributes a rich texture and mellows the flavors. Sliced kumquats, a common dooryard fruit in Florida and available in Northern markets in the winter, are a piquant addition, or try tomato pieces, grapefruit sections, seeded mandarins or tangerines. The ceviche is piled on Cuban crackers (*galletas*), thinly sliced French bread, or any first-rate crackers.

Juice of 5 Persian limes (¾ cup)
1 teaspoon salt
⅛ to ¼ teaspoon Pickapeppa or
    other hot pepper sauce
1 pound belly flounder, skinned
    and cut in ¼-inch dice or thin
    strips
¾ cup shredded coconut, fresh
    or frozen unsweetened (see
    page 159)

16 small kumquats, seeded
    and sliced, or small cherry
    tomatoes, cut in quarters
Cuban crackers, water biscuits,
    or sliced French bread for
    serving

Combine the lime juice, salt, and pepper sauce in a deep bowl. Add the fish, and mix well with the marinade. Cover the bowl and marinate the fish in the refrigerator 3 to 6 hours. Or, if preferred, put the fish and liquid in a self-sealed bag to marinate. Drain the fish and discard the marinade. Toss the fish with the coconut. Add the kumquats or tomatoes, mix lightly, and refrigerate until ready to serve. Arrange on a platter, and garnish with additional kumquats or tomatoes, if wished. Pass with crackers or bread. To serve as a salad, spoon onto Boston or limestone lettuce and garnish with a fresh slice of fruit or sprig of lettuce or watercress.

DATE NUT SALAD

MAKES 4 SERVINGS.

The Palm Beach area has long been renowned for its socializing, and light salads are especially favored by "ladies who lunch." The oranges in this one make it refreshing in the warm climate, while the ham and cheese give it substance.

SALAD

2 large oranges

1½ cups (6 ounces) diced baked ham

1½ cups (6 ounces) diced muenster cheese

1 cup finely chopped celery

1 cup chopped pitted dates

1 jar (2 ounces) sliced pimiento, drained

½ cup toasted pecans or walnuts (see page 96)

lettuce greens

DRESSING

½ cup vegetable oil

¼ cup tarragon vinegar

2 tablespoons finely chopped parsley

1 tablespoon grated orange zest

Slice off both ends of each orange and peel, cutting deep enough to remove all of the white membrane. Cut along the dividing membrane of the orange to the center, removing each section. Set aside. In a medium bowl combine the ham, cheese, celery, dates, pimiento, and nuts. Combine all of the dressing ingredients and beat together well or shake in a tightly closed jar until blended. Add enough dressing to the salad to moisten and toss lightly. (Any leftover dressing can be reserved for other salads or passed at the table.) Line a serving platter with lettuce leaves. Place some shredded lettuce evenly in the center, then mound the salad on the top. Arrange the orange sections around the edge of the platter.

PAPAYA SEED SALAD DRESSING

MAKES ⅔ CUP, ENOUGH FOR 6 TO 8 SALADS.

Floridians many years ago discovered the peppery bite of papaya seeds. They are eaten spar-
ingly with fruit on the half shell for breakfast or used as a seasoning for
salad dressings. This lightly sweetened dressing is good with a salad of
the papaya slices, avocado, orange cartwheels, and a few red onion rings
on greens.

¼ cup salad oil	1 tablespoon minced onion
¼ cup rice vinegar	1 teaspoon papaya seeds,
2 teaspoons sugar	rinsed and dried on paper
1 teaspoon salt	toweling
¼ teaspoon dry mustard	

Combine the oil, vinegar, sugar, salt, and dry mustard in a small bowl or
jar with a tight-fitting lid. Beat together with a small whisk until the sugar
and seasonings are dissolved or cover the jar and shake vigorously. Add
the onion and papaya seeds. Whisk or shake again before adding to a
salad. Store any leftover dressing in a covered jar in the refrigerator.

THE FLORIDA GREEN GIANT

Your grandmother called them alliga-
tor pears, and some Floridians still mean avocados when they talk of "pears."
It was weird to the railroad workers who came at the turn of the century.
Homesteaders' wives and children in South Dade county still recall the thrill
or despair at first tasting an avocado. It grew on a tree, got soft and dropped
when it was ripe, but was nothing like a peach.

Some say it got the name "alligator pear" because of the pebbly skin,
like an alligator's, and others say that it is the fruit grows in areas where

alligators are found. This does not hold true for the avocados grown in California.

There are dozens of avocado varieties and sub-varieties grown in Florida. Some are the size of a football and others not much larger than an egg. Those in markets have smooth green skin and are less fatty and slightly lower in calories than the California fruit, but more richly flavored. The flesh is creamy and smooth, and in the Caribbean it is mashed and spread on bread as a substitute for butter.

An avocado ripens well if plucked mature but still hard, but never refrigerate it before it is soft. It is best used the day it is ready, though it can be refrigerated overnight before cutting it. To test an avocado, cup it in your hands and press it gently. It will yield slightly if it is ripe. Or poke a toothpick in the stem end; the pick will slide in easily if the avocado is ripe.

To slice the fruit, cut it in half lengthwise and whack the seed smartly with the flat side of the knife. The seed should pop out, or it can be lifted out easily. Pull the skin off or peel it off in thin strips with a paring knife.

The ideal salad to Floridians is an avocado half sprinkled with lime or lemon juice or Old Sour (see page 131) and oil. It is combined with fruits for other salads, is tossed with greens, or mashed and served as a snack spread. Avocado darkens quickly if exposed to air; coating it with lime or other citrus juice deters discoloration.

Avocado is not often heated, as it tends to turn bitter. But a popular use is to fill half with chili, creamed chicken, or crab.

CREAM OF AVOCADO SOUP

MAKES 4 TO 6 SERVINGS.

This delicate soup has been a standard meal starter since the age of the great resort hotels, from the 1880s to the 1920s. Visitors had it at the Roney Plaza in Miami Beach, the Royal Palm in Miami, the Breakers in Palm Beach (where an avocado soup is still offered), and in restaurants and clubs all over the state. The flavor of a perfectly ripened avocado dominates the velvety soup. Lemon juice, dry sherry, and green onion season the soup, made creamy by the avocado itself, with chicken stock as the base. Young chefs sometimes zip up the mixture with fresh gingerroot, chile pepper, or hot sauce, and some versions have orange or pineapple juice as the base. We prefer the pure avocado flavor of this one.

2 medium Florida avocados or
   3 smaller ones
¼ cup lemon or lime juice
2 strips lemon or lime zest
2 tablespoons dry sherry
2 large green onions or scallions
   with tops, coarsely sliced
4 cups cool chicken broth

½ teaspoon salt
¼ teaspoon freshly ground
   pepper
Sour cream or sour half-and-
   half for garnish
Minced green onion tops or red
   bell pepper for garnish

Peel the avocados, following the directions on page 121, and slice. Place in a blender or food processor with the lemon juice and zest. Process until well mixed, then gradually work in the sherry and green onions. Place the chicken broth in a bowl or large pitcher, and stir in the avocado mixture, salt, and pepper until smooth and creamy. If too thick, stir in more chicken broth. Serve at once in chilled bowls, or cover closely with plastic wrap and refrigerate up to 6 hours. Garnish each serving with a dollop of sour cream and minced green onion or red bell pepper.

BRADLEY'S PALM BEACH DINING AND GAMING PALACE

Only the wealthy or socially elite, approved for "membership" by the Colonel himself, frequented Bradley's Beach Club. A world-famed gambling place, it operated on Royal Poinciana Way for forty years, beginning in the heyday of the Breakers and Royal Poinciana hotels. Gentlemen wore white tie and tails or tuxedos in the evening and alcoholic beverages were banned except in the dining room. The club was known for superb food and service as well as for the games. (Gambling was illegal in Florida, but for clubs catering to tourists enforcement was lenient.)

Colonel Bradley insisted on decorous behavior by his patrons, but tolerated the high jinks that accompanied the introduction of green turtle soup to the menu. His Swiss chef, Conrad Schmitt, had live turtles on chains paraded through the clubhouse before they went to the soup pot.

C. W. Barron, founder of *Barron's Weekly*, esteemed the cuisine at Bradley's so highly that he arrived prepared, with tuxedos in five sizes. For the first week of dining at Bradley's he wore the smallest. As he indulged and his waistline expanded, he worked up to the largest suit; when he left he headed for Saratoga Springs for a weight-reducing regimen.

GUIESSO DE MAIZ
CUBAN CORN SOUP-STEW

MAKES 6 SIDE-DISH SERVINGS OR 8 TO 10
FIRST-COURSE SOUP SERVINGS.

We prefer freshly cut corn for this hearty soup-stew, but Key West folk who like this dish as a soup or with rice as an accompaniment to fish, poultry, or meat say canned or frozen corn is an adequate substitute when high-quality green sweet corn is out of season.

¼ pound smoked bacon, diced

1 ham shank, about 1 pound

3 ounces chorizo, sliced or crumbled

2 cups chopped peeled tomato or 1 16-ounce can whole tomatoes with juice, cut up

1 small onion, chopped

1 small green bell pepper, chopped

2 cloves garlic, minced

3 cups water or more, if needed

6 ears corn, cut off cob and scraped

1½ teaspoons salt

¼ teaspoon freshly ground pepper

2 hard-cooked eggs, sliced or chopped fine

In a large soup kettle, combine the bacon, ham shank, chorizo, tomato, onion, green pepper, and garlic. Add the water, cover, bring to a boil, and simmer 45 minutes to 1 hour, until the meat on the ham hock is tender. Remove the ham shank from the soup, cut the meat from the bone, dice it and return it to the soup. Discard the bone and fat. Add more water if a soup is wanted; do not add water if serving this as a side dish. Add the corn, salt, and pepper. Cook 5 minutes longer. Serve hot over rice as an accompaniment to meat or seafood, or ladle into warm bowls and serve as soup. Garnish with hard-cooked egg.

BISCAYNE BAY YACHT CLUB CHOWDER

MAKES 4 SERVINGS.

Charlie Frow, who used to keep the Cape Florida lighthouse in the 1870s, brought his family across the bay to live in Coconut Grove and became the handyman at Biscayne Bay Yacht Club after the clubhouse was erected. At the time, no food was served in the club, so Charlie was asked to make the chowder for the first Washington's Birthday Regatta in 1887. He got the recipe from Charlie Peacock at the nearby Peacock Inn, he said. The original called for canned milk and tomato soup, as the fresh counterparts were almost nonexistent, since foods came by boat from Key West. We've substituted fresh milk and tomatoes and the chowder contains potatoes and salt pork in the New England manner. It closely resembles the one at B.B.Y.C. Saturday chowder lunches today, and the Washington's Birthday Regatta still is observed by parties who sail across the bay for chowder and socializing.

¼ pound salt pork, diced

1 large onion, chopped

2 tablespoons diced green or
  red bell pepper

1 cup chopped fresh or drained
  canned tomato

2 cups Shrimp Broth (page 25)
  or chicken broth

1 teaspoon salt, or to taste

½ bay leaf, crumbled

Pinch dried thyme, crumbled

Pinch mace

Dash white pepper or hot
  pepper sauce

2 potatoes (¾ pound), peeled
  and cubed

1½ to 2 pounds boned and
  skinned grouper, cubed*

1½ cups milk

2 teaspoons butter

1 cup light or heavy cream
  (optional)

*If grouper is not available, use snapper, drum, or other white-fleshed fish.

In a large saucepan, cook the salt pork until crisp. Add the onion and bell pepper, and sauté until the onion is tender but not browned. Stir in the tomato and sauté a minute or two. Add the broth, salt, bay leaf, thyme, mace, and pepper. Bring to a boil, and add the potatoes. Cover and boil slowly until the potatoes are tender but not mushy, 15 to 18 minutes. Lay the fish on the potatoes in the broth, cover, and simmer 10 minutes, or until the fish is opaque when tested with a fork. Add the milk and butter. Heat but do not boil. Taste and add more salt and pepper, if needed. Add the cream, if wanted to thin the chowder. Warm the chowder, ladle into heated bowls, and serve with oyster crackers.

THE PEACOCK INN AND CAMP BISCAYNE

The Peacock Inn on the Bay in Coconut Grove was the first public lodging house within miles of what was to become Miami Beach and the world's most famous hotel strip. The inn was operated by a British couple, Charles and Isabella Peacock, from 1882 to 1900. The guests, including Europeans as well as those from Northern cities, found the food "surpassing," writes Helen Muir in *Miami U.S.A.*

Few details of the meals or afternoon teas at the inn were recorded, but cooks had to make do with the limited resources of the settlement. Wild turkeys, other birds, and game were brought by Indians from the Everglades. A superabundance of fish was at the inn's doorstep. There were flour, sugar, and coffee from the trading post at the mouth of the Miami River, and coconuts from an earlier planting, sapodilla, mangoes, avocados, and bananas were growing nearby. Beef was available occasionally when a rancher from Titusville drove his cattle to Lemon City, twenty miles north of Coconut Grove, butchered it, and sold it to anybody who sailed up to fetch it. Most people raised a few chickens for meat and eggs. Sea turtles were kept in kraals at the water's edge to sell or butcher for eating, and the eggs were highly prized for baking. Today sea turtles are on the endangered species list, and neither the eggs nor meat can be taken. Canned goods, sometimes barrels of flour, and other staples were salvaged from wrecks. In 1889, collecting the debris from the "wine wreck" was a source of amusement for several weeks. A cargo of Bordeaux wines bound for Cuba was broken up in a hurricane, and the wines gradually floated to shore from the Keys to Lake Worth. With the inn's reputation for fine meals, doubtless the Peacocks took advantage of wreck food and drink, wild food, and trading post staples.

When the Peacocks retired, Ralph Munroe, a boat designer and civic leader, spearheaded a move to provide food and lodging for visitors. He and his partners built Camp Biscayne, a cluster of cottages and a dining room among the palms. The atmosphere was simpler and the costs lower than those of the Royal Palm Hotel at the mouth of the Miami River. The meals, supervised at first by Munroe's sister-in-law, Josephine Wirth, drew praise, too. However, with rising costs in World War I, holding to the rate of five dollars a day became impossible. Camp Biscayne was closed ten years before hotels began to rise on Miami Beach, and fifty years prior to the glitzy hostelries on Coconut Grove's Bayshore Drive.

NASSAU BREAKFAST

MAKES 4 SERVINGS.

The name for this dish in the Keys is fish steam. A stew, whether it is of beef, pork, chicken, or fish, is a steam in Keys lingo. Before sea turtles were declared off limits to protect them from extinction, a turtle steam was a highly prized regional specialty. The first fish steam, called a Nassau Breakfast, that the Voltz family had was prepared by a fishing yacht mate, descended from Africans working the cane fields in the Bahamas. Vera Johnson, a friend and household helper for years, was flattered when asked to show the family how to cook the dish. Vera carefully layered the onions, limes, and fish, and peppered and salted them liberally, as her mother had taught her while growing up in Key West. She then simmered the fish gently just until it had lost its translucent look, warning, "You don't cook it too long, it'll be tough!" The fish, onions, and juice are ladled onto mounds of hot cooked grits, buttered and seasoned with more lime juice or Old Sour, and hot sauce. We like the fish and grits served in soup bowls, allowing space for the rich juices, which we eat with soup spoons.

1 large or 2 medium yellow
   onions, peeled and sliced thin
2 or 3 Key or Persian limes,
   unpeeled and sliced thin
2 cups water, or as needed
1½ pounds grouper fillets or
   2 pounds pan fish, cleaned
   and heads removed*
3 tablespoons butter or
   margarine

1 teaspoon salt
¼ teaspoon freshly ground
   pepper
3 cups hot cooked grits
Fresh lime wedges, hot sauce,
   and Old Sour (page 131)
   for garnish

*Grunts, which can be caught before breakfast any day in the Keys, schoolboy snapper, or freshwater sunfish are excellent in a fish steam. If grouper is not available, snapper or rock cod fillets may be used.

Layer the onions and sliced limes in a large deep skillet or sauté pan, add water to barely cover the onion and lime slices, cover, and simmer 20 minutes. Cut the fillets into 4 servings. Layer the fish into the hot broth, using a spoon or tongs to slip onion and lime slices over and under it. Add boiling water, if needed, to not quite cover the fish and put a teaspoon of butter or margarine on each piece of fish. Season with the salt and pepper. Cover and simmer 8 to 10 minutes, just until the thickest part of the fillets or whole fish flakes when tested with a fork. Spoon the juices over the fish once or twice while cooking.

The fish and juices can be served from the pot or a large tureen. Spoon a mound of grits onto each plate or soup plate. Ladle fish, pan juices, onion, and the cooked lime slices over it. Each diner butters his serving of fish and grits and adds fresh lime juice, hot sauce, and Old Sour to taste.

GRILLED FLORIDA LOBSTER

MAKES 4 SERVINGS.

Spiny lobster, still called crawfish by old-timers, was renamed Florida lobster many years ago, and some lovers of this species and the New England variety think the comparison unfortunate. Each is excellent food, delicious in its distinctive way. The New England lobster is sweeter flavored and softer textured. The Florida lobster has no claws, only skinny feelers not worth eating. The meaty tail is firm textured and tastes strongly of the sea. Scuba divers often bring home their limit of Florida lobster, six per person, and cook them pristine-fresh this way. If you don't have fresh lobster, use frozen shellfish. Even fresh-cooked lobster tails can be used, but grill them just long enough to brown them lightly.

1 cup (2 sticks) butter	¼ teaspoon paprika
¼ cup lime or lemon juice	1 tablespoon minced chives
¼ teaspoon salt	4 spiny lobster tails, thawed,
¼ teaspoon freshly ground	if frozen
pepper	

Combine the butter, lemon juice, salt, pepper, paprika, and chives in a small saucepan. Heat at the edge of a grill until the butter melts. Mix well, and keep warm at the edge of the grill.

Using scissors, clip away the thin membrane on the underside of the lobster tails. Grasp each tail with both hands and snap it backwards toward the shell to crack it, or insert a wooden skewer the full length of the lobster tail. This will keep the tail from curling while cooking.

Place the lobsters, shell sides down, on the grill over a medium-hot fire that has burned down to glowing coals covered with gray ash. Grill for 5 minutes, brushing two or three times with the butter sauce. Turn the flesh side down and grill 5 minutes longer, until the fish is opaque. Serve each diner a lobster tail with a small cup of the hot butter sauce. To remove the meat, loosen it from the small end with a fork. Dip pieces into the sauce.

OLD SOUR

This homemade table sauce is splashed on seafood, salads, fresh vegetables, and, some say, any food, except dessert. In the past, a bottle of the condiment was a fixture on almost every dinner table in the Keys: It remains the most-used seasoning there.

Years ago, a used Old Crow whiskey bottle was the container, the theory being that the brown glass kept the salty sauce in best condition. Other people said the glass color was immaterial, and kept the lime juice concoction in clear glass cruets.

Old Sour came about naturally. The ingredients, salt and freshly squeezed lime juice, were handy when the Key West salt ponds were operating at the turn of the century. And anybody can make it! This is how: Strain 2 cups lime juice through muslin or doubled cheesecloth in a funnel into a clean bottle. Add a tablespoonful of salt, shake the bottle well, and tie a square of clean cloth over the top of the bottle. Let the sauce age in a dark cupboard for 6 or 8 weeks. It should have an acid-salty flavor with a bite on the tongue. Cork the bottle, and the sauce keeps indefinitely.

"Conchs" put the bottle of Old Sour on the table or a cupboard shelf, and think the older it gets the better. Some new residents refrigerate Old Sour, but natives scoff at such niceties. The purpose of the concoction was to preserve Key limes in season for use when ripe fruit was scarce. The sauce turns brownish as it ages, but is usable as long as the flavor is tangy and salty, and well-aged Old Sour becomes more mellow.

Some folk drop a fresh or dried hot pepper and/or a peeled clove of garlic into the Old Sour before it is aged. The fresh pepper or garlic should be tied on a thread and fished out after a couple of days to prevent pieces of mushy vegetable floating in the sauce.

SHRIMP STEAMED IN BEER

MAKES 4 TO 6 SERVINGS.

Big bowls of shrimp in beer used to be set on the bars in south Florida until rising costs priced it off the barkeeps' freebie list.

This home-style version survives around picnic tables in backyards. A big pot of hot shrimp and another of a warm butter sauce are set on the table; diners ladle out the shrimp, shell, and eat them. Ketchup, Old Sour (page 131), fresh lime or lemon juice, or hot sauce is added to the butter sauce to taste. Coleslaw or tossed green salad and hearty slices of garlic bread are served with the shrimp.

3 pounds shrimp in the shell
3 12-ounce bottles or cans beer
  (can be flat)
1 teaspoon dried leaf thyme or
  1 tablespoon minced fresh
1 tablespoon dry mustard
2 bay leaves

2 cloves garlic, peeled and
  slivered
1 teaspoon salt
½ teaspoon freshly ground
  pepper
1 tablespoon minced parsley
1 tablespoon minced chives

Wash and drain the shrimp. If you wish, cut off the "legs" with scissors, though many like them left intact. In a large sauté pan or Dutch oven, combine the beer, thyme, dry mustard, bay leaves, garlic, salt, pepper, parsley, and chives. Bring to a boil, add the shrimp, and cook just until the shellfish turns a bright pink, about 1 minute. Remove the bay leaves and serve from the pot or transfer the shrimp to a large bowl. Offer the Butter Sauce or condiments as desired.

BUTTER SAUCE FOR SHRIMP IN BEER

Makes 4 to 6 servings.

½ cup (1 stick) butter
¼ cup lime or lemon juice
2 tablespoons minced parsley

2 tablespoons minced chives
Few drops hot pepper sauce

Melt the butter and stir in the remaining ingredients.

LOBSTER CHILAU—A GALLEY FEAST

A weekend sail or cruise to the Bahamas calls for something more than peanut butter sandwiches. A super boating dish is Lobster Chilau, an adaptation of the Cuban-Keys enchilada, a hearty seafood stew on rice. Potatoes are cooked in the chilau, making it a meal in a pot in deference to the tiny galley stoves.

A chilau (pronounced *chee*-lau) takes some planning. Lobsters are speared by some of the party or obtained from local fishermen. The galley chef brings other ingredients aboard. A jar with a tight lid holds the pre-measured seasonings: 2 bay leaves, 2 cloves of garlic, minced fine, and ¼ teaspoon each freshly ground black pepper, dry thyme or oregano, and crushed red pepper (cayenne). Also needed are ¼ pound of salt pork, a large onion, 3 or 4 potatoes, and two 16-ounce cans of tomatoes.

To prepare the chilau, start a potful of clean seawater heating. Dice the salt pork, chop the onion, and peel and cube the potatoes. Brown the salt pork lightly in a large pot, add the onion, and sauté it until barely tender. Add the potatoes, 1½ cups of the hot seawater, and the premeasured seasonings; bring to a boil, turn the heat low, and simmer the stew until the potatoes are tender, 15 or maybe 20 minutes on a balky galley stove. Shell and cut the lobster meat in 1-inch cubes. Add it to the stew along with the tomatoes. Heat almost to boiling, and ladle into large soup bowls. Three or four persons will devour this amount at sea; at home it makes 6 average servings. Serve crusty bread to sop up the juices and tossed green salad with this soup-stew.

Chilau is not just for boating. It is traditional for Christmas eve in many homes. When freshwater is used in place of seawater, salt is needed. The crushed red pepper is not added with the other seasonings, but with the tomatoes and lobster, as the strength of the spice tends to dissipate in cooking. Other seafood can be substituted for the lobster; shrimp, crab, or chunks of any firm white-fleshed fish.

BROILED YELLOWTAIL WITH ORANGE BUTTER

MAKES 4 SERVINGS.

The delicate flavor and texture of this very special fish of south Florida, the Bahamas, and the Caribbean is lost if seasonings are too powerful. The orange juice marinade and a few fennel seeds gently complement the flavor, but some fans of this fish would eliminate the fennel.

ORANGE BUTTER

4 tablespoons (½ stick) butter, softened
Finely shredded zest of 1 orange

2 tablespoons orange juice
¼ teaspoon fennel seed (optional)

THE FISH

2 pounds yellowtail fillets
Juice of ½ orange (2 to 3 tablespoons)

2 tablespoons peanut or vegetable oil

½ teaspoon fennel seed	4 thin slices orange with
(optional)	the peel
4 thin slices onion	

Several hours or days before cooking the fish, whip the butter with a small mixer or spoon until fluffy. Gradually work in the orange zest and juice and the fennel seed, if using. Shape into small balls or flat circles and refrigerate up to 3 days or freeze up to a month.

To prepare the fish, pat the fillets dry with a paper towel and cut into 4 portions. Combine the orange juice, oil, and fennel seed, if wanted, mixing well. Place the fish in a deep bowl or self-sealing plastic bag. Pour the sauce over it, and marinate in the refrigerator for 1 to 3 hours.

Preheat the broiler. Remove the fish from the marinade, draining well, and reserving the marinade for later use. Arrange the fish in a broiler pan lined with foil that is oiled lightly. Brush the fish with the marinade and broil 4 to 5 inches from the heat 6 to 9 minutes, just until the flesh is almost flaky but very moist when tested near the center of a fillet with a fork. Brush again with the marinade and place an onion slice and orange slice on each fillet. Broil 1 to 2 minutes longer, until the fish feels firm but not hard when pressed with the back of a fork. Arrange on a warm platter or individual serving plates, pour the pan juices over the fish, and top each serving with a round or ball of orange butter.

THE MAGNIFICENT CARIBBEAN YELLOWTAIL

Ask a native of the Florida Keys which fish is best and he is apt to say without batting an eye, "Yellowtail!" and tell you of his favorite way of preparing it. It is a fish with rare delicacy, yet a definite sea-fresh flavor. Yellowtail is a member of the snapper family and tastes like a red snapper, with finer texture. The flesh of yellowtail is softer, leading to rapid deterioration, so it is rarely shipped. The fresher the better is the cardinal rule with this fish.

Yellowtail used to be known as a breakfast fish. Fishermen would peddle the previous night's catch early in the morning, walking the streets of Key West shouting, "Yallertail, Yallertail for sale," and there is hardly a better hearty breakfast than a small yellowtail split, brushed with butter, and broiled. Today it is more often sautéed or grilled.

A whole yellowtail is easily recognized by the streak of yellow running from the head to the tail. Depend on a reliable dealer to ensure that fillets are the real thing. Don't be tricked. The Pacific yellowtail, a member of the jack family, is oily and strong flavored, falling far short of a genuine Caribbean or Southern Atlantic yellowtail.

CURRIED BLACK-TIP SHARK

MAKES 4 SERVINGS.

Floridians, like seafood lovers everywhere, are beginning to appreciate fresh shark. Shark, dolphin fish (mahimahi), and other thick firm-textured fish steaks often are poached in curry sauce in the Keys. The people there like richly spiced curry, but the amount is adjustable for those who favor a milder flavor.

1 tablespoon vegetable oil	¼ teaspoon freshly ground
1 medium onion, diced	pepper
2 tablespoons curry powder, or to	1½ pounds black-tip or other
taste	shark steaks
2½ cups chopped peeled fresh or	2 cups hot cooked rice
drained canned tomatoes	Three or more garnishes
1 teaspoon salt, or to taste	(see Note)

Heat the oil in a large skillet. Add the onion and cook until it is tender but not browned. Stir in the curry powder and sauté for 30 seconds. Add the tomatoes, salt, and pepper. Bring to a boil and gently lower the fish into the sauce. Cover the pan, lower the heat, and simmer slowly for 12 minutes, or until the fish is opaque when tested with a fork near the center bone. Baste with the hot sauce two or three times while cooking. Serve the fish and the sauce with the rice, and pass condiments to be added as desired.

NOTE: In Key West, condiments are optional, but mango chutney (homemade or purchased) and shredded fresh coconut are top choices. Other possibilities include sliced banana fried in butter or oil, salted peanuts or almonds, chopped green onion or Florida sweet onion tops, chopped red or green bell pepper, and papaya cubes or starfruit (carambola) slices in lime juice lightly sweetened with honey.

FLORIDA'S HOMEGROWN BON VIVANT

In the 1950s magazine writers, reporters, and photographers from New York and other cities often stopped over at the Voltzes' home in Miami en route to assignments in south Florida, the Caribbean, or South or Central America. The cooking enthusiasts among them would hardly park their briefcases or camera bags before asking, "Do you know Charles Baker?" We did. He lived a half mile down Douglas Road. The visitors, if they cooked, leaned to the show-off recipes that were Charles H. Baker Jr.'s forte.

"Bake," as friends called him, was the reigning master of exotic cookery at that time on the strength of his two books, *The Gentleman's Companion* and *The South American Gentleman's Companion*.

He grew up in rural Florida, near Zellwood, and could describe graphically the tastes of country cooking and outdoor culinary adventures as long as he lived. After writing a novel, and articles for *The Saturday Evening Post* and other magazines, he landed a job as the food and beverage writer for *Town and Country* magazine. In this post, he tasted and sipped his way around the world, but he never lost his appreciation of Florida food, like conch salad, rosin potatoes, and broiled mackerel masked in hollandaise sauce, as well as exotic foods from around the world.

"Bake" died in the 1980s and his books are long out of print, but for fun and insight into what was exotic in the 1940s, borrow the books from a good library. Not only did adventurous Florida cooks indulge in the fantastic dishes he wrote of, so did New Yorkers, San Franciscans, and a host of other folk who loved culinary challenges.

GRILLED MARLIN

MAKES 4 TO 5 SERVINGS.

Bobby Dykes, a sportfisherman and hunter who lived in Miami in the 1950s and 1960s, loved to share his catches. On a Monday, he would phone and say, "Come by Thursday for smoked marlin. I caught a two hundred–pounder yesterday." He cold-smoked the fish, so it took two to three days to get it just right. He would grin proudly as he parceled out his prize catch.

To protect marlin in Florida, selling it is forbidden. Old-time sportsmen invariably smoked marlin, if they used it for food at all, so we never had fresh-caught marlin until we found it in fish markets and on restaurant menus in other states. Marlin is a meaty fish, similar to fresh tuna in texture, with superb flavor. But don't overcook it, or it will become dry. This version is juicy and tender, and well seasoned with the marinade. And if you don't have marlin, tuna or salmon is good in this recipe.

1½ pounds marlin fillet
½ cup lime juice
1 tablespoon minced fresh
   ginger
1 tablespoon soy sauce

¼ cup peanut or vegetable oil
½ teaspoon freshly ground
   pepper
Lime wedges for garnish

Place the fish in a shallow glass dish. Combine the lime juice, ginger, soy sauce, oil, and pepper in a small bowl or measuring cup. Pour the marinade over the fish. Cover and marinate in the refrigerator at least 30 minutes, preferably 2 to 3 hours. Oil the grill well or spritz it with nonstick cooking spray. Let the fire burn down to glowing coals covered with ash, and space the coals slightly to maintain moderate heat. If using a gas grill, turn the heat low. Drain the fish, reserving the marinade. Place the fish on the grill 5 to 6 inches above the coals. Cook until seared. Using a wide spatula, carefully turn the fish and sear the other side. Baste with the reserved marinade and continue to grill until opaque, 10 to 12 minutes for fillets 1 inch thick. Place on a warm platter and garnish with lime wedges.

SEA SQUAB

Sea squab is a fancy term for a puffer, aka blowfish, blowtoad, and other inelegant sobriquets. The Voltzes first had it when they pulled a blowfish from Biscayne Bay years ago. Their fishing mentor urged, "Don't throw it back. They're the best mouthful you'll ever eat." After they had cleaned and sautéed the fish, they agreed: The flavor is sweet and mild, enhanced by a light coating of corn meal and flour; a garnish or sauce should be low key, perhaps just a squeeze of lime juice.

Sea squab used to get top billing on restaurant menus and it still is served in other states, but Florida game laws prohibit its sale.

Sea squab is the benign cousin of fugu, the highly prized Japanese fish that is deadly if not properly cleaned. The East Coast blowfish is safe, but fish cutters take great care to remove every shred of the liver and other innards.

When a blowfish is pulled from the water, it is inflated to about three times its size, the inspiration for some of its names. Children scream excitedly, while Dad gingerly dehooks the fish (it has two sharp fang-like teeth). Along with the innards, the tough skin, liver, and air bladder that is inflated when the puffer senses danger are discarded. Only the tail portion, two fillets of meat divided by a main bone, is eaten. The tail fin is left on, so each sea squab looks like a plump white chicken drumstick. Each tail fin portion weighs about an ounce, so you need three or four for an average-size entrée serving.

SAUTÉED SEA SQUAB WITH GRAPEFRUIT

MAKES 4 SERVINGS.

Don't overpower this dainty fish with breading. Just dip it lightly in the flour and corn meal mixture.

½ cup milk

⅓ cup all-purpose flour

⅓ cup corn meal

¾ teaspoon salt

¼ teaspoon freshly ground pepper

12 sea squab tail sections, about 1½ pounds, cleaned and dressed

2 to 3 tablespoons corn or vegetable oil

2 tablespoons butter

1 teaspoon minced fresh marjoram or ¼ teaspoon dried

1 shallot, diced

1 grapefruit, peeled with white membrane and pith removed, and sectioned

Fresh marjoram sprigs

Pour the milk into a wide bowl. Mix the flour, corn meal, ½ teaspoon of the salt, and the pepper together on a plate. Dip each sea squab in milk, then in the flour mixture to coat it well. Heat the oil in a large skillet until a piece of fish sizzles in it. Add the fish in a single layer. Sauté 3 to 4 minutes, until golden and the flesh is slightly firm. Turn and lightly brown the other side, adding oil as needed. Remove the fish to a hot platter and keep warm. Cook the remaining fish. Pour off the drippings and wipe out the skillet with a paper towel. Melt the butter in the skillet and add the minced marjoram and shallot. Sauté 2 to 3 minutes. Add the grapefruit with its juice and heat 2 minutes. Add the remaining ¼ teaspoon salt. Spoon some of the sauce and fruit onto the fish and pour the remainder around it. Garnish with the marjoram sprigs. Serve immediately.

ROPA VIEJA
FLANK STEAK AND TOMATO HASH

MAKES 4 SERVINGS.

The literal translation for the name of this dish is "old clothes" or "rags," Hispanic folk say, laughing. The original may have been made with left-over meat, but the stringy texture of boiled flank steak is preferred. The humble name does not do justice to the lusty flavor and rich red color of the hash on white rice. The combination may be garnished with fried plantains or bananas or it may be circled with olives and slices of Cuban bread, fried golden in olive oil.

1 to 1 ¼ pounds flank steak	¼ cup olive oil
2 to 3 cups water	½ green bell pepper, seeded
4 bay leaves	and chopped
1 teaspoon dried leaf oregano	2 large cloves garlic, minced
2 teaspoons salt, or to taste	¼ teaspoon ground cumin
1 small fresh tomato or	1 10-ounce can tomato
canned whole tomato,	purée
drained and seeded	1 tablespoon red wine
2 small onions	vinegar
2 ribs celery, cut in 4-inch pieces	2 cups hot cooked rice

Place the meat in a large skillet; add water to cover, 1 bay leaf, the oregano, 1½ teaspoons salt, the tomato, 1 whole onion (it is not necessary to peel it), and the celery. Cover, bring to a boil, turn the heat to low but keep the water boiling (meat should be stringy for this hash), and cook until the meat is tender and falling apart in strings, about 1½ hours. Cool the meat in the broth, remove it, and refrigerate the meat and broth separately.

Tear apart the meat into shreds or shred it with a sharp knife by cutting it with the grain. Heat the olive oil in a large skillet. Dice the remaining onion and add to the oil with the green pepper. Sauté until the onion is translucent. Add the garlic and sauté until aromatic, but do not let it brown. Add the meat and cook and stir until hot. Add ½ cup of the reserved broth, the 3 bay leaves, crumbled, with the veins removed, and the cumin. Cook and stir until the liquid is absorbed. Add the tomato purée, vinegar, and remaining ½ teaspoon salt. Cook and stir until thoroughly heated, taste, and add salt, if needed. Serve hot with white rice and garnish with Fried Plantains or Bananas (see page 146) or with pimiento-stuffed green olives and slabs of fried Cuban bread.

AN UNBELIEVABLE ARABIAN NIGHT

Opa-Locka was founded on the edge of the Everglades north of Miami by aviation pioneer Glenn H. Curtiss in 1926. Minarets and other fantastic buildings sprang up overnight and by January 1927 an Arabian Nights Festival was put on. Mrs. Frank S. Bush, a great-granddaughter of Queen Victoria and social leader in the young community, was known for her Sunday evening "at homes." To celebrate the Arabian Nights Festival, she served "cous-cous a la Opa-Locka," which she described as "probably Irish stew with a Moroccan accent." The recipe, provided by her son, the poet-historian Frank S. Fitzgerald-Bush, in truth does contain lamb cut up for stewing, onions, green and red bell peppers, celery, lots of green peas, and carrots. The mixture is stewed together and served over rice. Mrs. Bush explained that the traditional base for cous-cous is wheaten, but that it is difficult to cook.

from *Biscayne Bights and Breezes,*
compiled by the Villagers, Inc., Miami, 1987

BOLICHE

MAKES 6 TO 8 SERVINGS.

Beef eye-of-the-round is labeled "boliche meat" (pronounced bo-*lee*-chay) in markets in Ybor City, Key West, Little Havana in Miami, and other Cuban areas. The name comes from the Spanish word for ball, the shape of meat when it is stuffed and tied. A meat man cuts a hole lengthwise through the roast to hold the filling. Home-cooks may cut a slit down the side of the roast or skip the stuffing and braise the chorizo and aromatics in the pot with the beef for a meaty sauce.

1 beef eye-of-the-round, 4 to 4½ pounds	3 tablespoons olive oil (can use half canola oil)
1 large or 2 small cloves garlic	1 medium onion, chopped
Salt and freshly ground pepper to taste	½ cup beef stock or dry red wine
3 ounces chorizo (2 small), skinned and crumbled	2 ribs celery, sliced
1½ cups chopped peeled tomatoes or drained canned tomatoes	2 carrots, peeled and cut in chunks
¼ cup minced pimiento-stuffed green olives	2 bay leaves, crumbled
	1 teaspoon ground cumin

Have your butcher cut a hole lengthwise in the meat almost through to the wider end. Or slit the roast lengthwise to provide space for stuffing. Cut half of the garlic in slivers and slit the roast at intervals, pushing in the garlic pieces. Sprinkle the meat lightly inside and out with salt and pepper. Mince the remaining garlic and mix it with the chorizo, ½ cup of the tomato, and the olives. Stuff the mixture into the beef, close the opening with skewers and lace with string.

Heat the oil in a large, heavy Dutch oven or sauté pan. Add the meat and brown it on all sides. For a lean sauce, pour off and discard the drippings, though many cooks prefer a richer sauce, and do not discard the fat. Add the onion to the pot and sauté until translucent. Add the remaining 1 cup tomato, the stock or wine, celery, carrots, bay leaves, and cumin. Sprinkle lightly with salt and pepper. Simmer 1½ to 2 hours, until the meat is cooked through. Remove to a platter, cover with foil, and let it rest 20 minutes before carving. Slice crosswise to serve. Taste the sauce and add salt and pepper, if needed. Pass the sauce with the meat. Black beans and white rice may be served with Boliche, and it is good with the rice only. Sliced cold Boliche makes wonderful sandwiches.

CUBAN-STYLE OKRA AND PORK

MAKES 4 SERVINGS.

The Black Heritage Cookbook, a collection of home-cooks' recipes published by the South Dade Regional Library near Miami, credits this dish to the foodways of Caribbean Indians, the Spanish, and Africans of Cuba. The savory combination usually is served over rice with fried plantains or green bananas on the side.

¾ **pound okra**	**1 clove garlic, minced**
Juice of 2 limes or lemons	**1 cup diced peeled tomato or**
½ **pound boneless pork loin,**	**drained canned tomato**
cut in small strips	**1 teaspoon salt, or to taste**
1 tablespoon olive oil	¼ **teaspoon freshly ground**
1 large green or red bell	**pepper**
pepper, seeded and diced	**2 cups hot cooked rice**
1 small onion, diced	

Wash the okra, slice ½ inch thick, and place in a deep bowl or a self-sealing bag. Add the lime or lemon juice, cover or close the bag, and let the okra marinate while browning the pork.

In a large skillet or sauté pan, cook the pork in the hot oil until lightly browned, turning with a spatula to brown evenly. Add the bell pepper, onion, and garlic; stir well and cook a minute or two. Add the tomato, salt, pepper, and the okra with the juice. Stir well, cover, and simmer for 15 to 20 minutes, until the okra is tender. Taste and add more salt and pepper, if needed. Serve hot over the rice.

CURRIED LAMB ISLANDS-STYLE

MAKES 4 TO 6 SERVINGS.

In Jamaica, the Bahamas, and other islands, barbecued kid is feast-day food. A few markets in south Florida offer kid and more mature goat at special seasons, but most people who have come from the islands substitute lamb for goat, spicing the lamb with a hot curry blend containing allspice for its softening effect. The flavor is similar to the spiced goat. Everybody likes this zesty barbecue, but if it rains the lamb can be broiled in the kitchen. For authentic Caribbean taste, don't stint on the spice.

1 small or half a large leg of
 lamb, boned and butterflied
 (4½ to 5 pounds before boning,
 2½ pounds boned)
1 tablespoon curry powder
1 teaspoon ground allspice

½ teaspoon salt
½ teaspoon freshly ground
 pepper
½ teaspoon ground red pepper
 (cayenne, optional)

Open the lamb like a book to form a flat roast. Wipe it with a damp cloth, then rub with the curry powder, allspice, salt, pepper, and ground red pepper. Place in a large plastic bag or shallow dish. Close the bag or cover the dish and refrigerate at least 2 hours. You can marinate this several hours, if you like, with no bad results.

Preheat the grill or let the fire burn down until coals are covered with gray ash. Oil the grids or spritz with nonstick spray. Place the lamb on the grill and cook over a moderate fire until browned, about 5 minutes. Turn and brown the other side, about 4 or 5 minutes. Turn the heat low or spread the coals to lower the heat. Continue to grill the lamb until it is done as desired, about 35 minutes for meat that is well done in thinner spots, rare in thick places, and medium in some parts. We like it at this stage, to suit different tastes. Insert an instant-reading thermometer in a thick section. It will register 120 degrees at rare, since meat cooks more after it is removed from the grill. Let the meat stand 10 to 15 minutes before carving. Serve with Bahamian Peas and Rice (see page 149) or white rice and Fried Plantains (recipe follows).

FRIED PLANTAINS OR BANANAS

MAKES 4 TO 6 SIDE-DISH SERVINGS.

Hispanic markets in the Miami area offer many varieties of plantains and bananas, from the tiny finger bananas, so fragile that they are not shipped, to sturdy plantains and red bananas. The sweet small bananas are reserved for eating as a snack or in special desserts, but other members of this prolific family are fried or used in many other ways. They are best deep-fried, as here, but can be cooked in a lightly oiled skillet or ¼ inch hot fat. Bananas or plantains may be floured before cooking, or sugared afterward. To go with meat, the fried plantains or bananas are salted lightly. They accompany meat as often as potatoes, and sometimes are served in addition to potatoes.

**Peanut or vegetable oil for
   deep frying**
**2 firm-ripe plantains or large
   green-ripe bananas (about
   1½ pounds)**

Salt to taste

In a deep-fat fryer or large pot fitted with a frying basket, pour oil to a depth of 3 to 4 inches and heat to 375 degrees. Meanwhile, prepare the fruit. Peel the hard green plantain this way: Cut off the ends, then cut crosswise in halves. Slit the skin lengthwise about four times at the prominent ribs, then push the hard flesh out of the skin. Peel ripe plantains and firm bananas in the usual way. Cut the fruit diagonally in ½-inch slices. Place a few slices in a frying basket and fry 4 to 5 minutes, until golden brown. Drain on paper towels and salt lightly. Continue frying in small batches until all the fruit is fried. Serve hot or at room temperature.

FLATTENED FRIED PLANTAINS

Each large plantain makes 3 servings.

Peel the fruit as for Fried Plantains, slice ½ inch thick, and fry in deep fat heated to 375 degrees 4 to 5 minutes, until softened and lightly browned. Remove from the fat, drain, and cool the fruit a few minutes. Place the slices flat sides down on waxed or brown paper, cover with another sheet of paper, and with a rolling pin roll firmly but gently so as not to tear the fruit; flatten the slices. Plantains can be prepared to this point a few hours before serving. Fry the flattened slices again in deep fat heated to 375 degrees until browned, 2 or 3 minutes. Drain on paper towel; season with salt and serve hot.

WARM BEET SALAD

MAKES 4 SERVINGS.

Fat little beets with crisp fresh green tops make an enticing sight stacked in orderly bunches in farm markets, and are irresistible. This dish combines the sweet and sour seasoning typical of Yankee and East European cookery, with a unique use of the greens, a Southern favorite. Serve it with ham or smoked meats, as you might offer warm potato salad, and it is an exciting side dish to a roasted holiday bird.

2 bunches beets with fresh greens
   (8 to 10 medium beets)
1 tablespoon butter
3 tablespoons sugar
3 tablespoons finely diced or
   grated onion

1 tablespoon vinegar
1 orange, juice and slivered
   zest
½ teaspoon salt, or to taste

Cut the tops off the beets, leaving 1 inch of the stems, and boil the beets in water until tender, but not soft, about 45 minutes. Cool the beets until they can be handled, peel, and slice them into a saucepan. Stir in the butter and sugar until the butter is melted. Add the onion, vinegar, orange juice and zest, and the salt. Cover and simmer 10 minutes, stirring once or twice. Meanwhile, wash the beet tops, trim off the thick stems, and shred the greens finely with a knife. Add the greens to the beets, mix well, and simmer 3 to 4 minutes longer, until the greens are wilted. Turn into a bowl, toss lightly to distribute the beetroot through the greens, and serve hot or warm. Pepper vinegar may be sprinkled over the beets at the table by those who want it.

LAKE WORTH'S FIRST CHRISTMAS

One of the first homesteaders on the island that became Palm Beach, Charles Moore, and his family had all the settlers around Lake Worth, eight persons, for a Christmas dinner in 1873. The menu consisted of big possum, sweet potatoes, biscuits with cane syrup, and prickly pear pie. Later in the 1870s other permanent settlers came from the Midwest, fleeing blizzards for what they had read was a wonderland of opportunity.

Adapting to the tropical planting schedules was difficult for the Midwesterners, and cleaning the jungle growth for planting was a huge job. Nevertheless, the transplanted farmers grew sweet potatoes and pumpkins, and later, tomatoes, peppers, and eggplant. Citrus did well, but pineapple and sugarcane failed. Game was plentiful, with settlers bagging bear, deer, possums, and wild turkey, and occasionally Seminoles appeared with meat to barter. Fresh- and saltwater fish were bountiful and turtles provided both meat and eggs.

PEAS AND RICE

MAKES 4 TO 6 SERVINGS.

The people of every island country eat a version of rice with legumes, and pigeon peas are the choice of Bahamians. The combination is celebrated in the calypso ditty "Mamma ain't got no peas, no rice." Cooked fresh pigeon peas are best for this recipe, and canned green pigeon peas, found in most markets catering to Caribbean and Bahamian people, are second choice. The cooked or canned dried pigeon peas are acceptable. Wild marjoram, native to the Bahamas, is the usual seasoning for peas and rice. In south Florida, dried or fresh thyme is a good substitute.

Peas and Rice (continued)

2 ounces salt pork

1 tablespoon olive oil

1 small onion, chopped

1 rib celery, diced

1 small or ½ large green bell pepper, seeded, deveined, and diced

1 teaspoon dried leaf thyme

1 teaspoon salt

¼ teaspoon freshly ground pepper

2 cups diced peeled tomato or 1 16-ounce can, drained and chopped

2 cups cooked green pigeon peas, drained (1-pound can or 1½ pounds fresh before shelling)

1 cup water

1 cup long-grain rice

Slice the salt pork into thin strips and sauté in olive oil until browned. Add the onion, celery, and green pepper. Cook until the onion is tender but not browned. Add the thyme, salt, pepper, and tomato. Simmer and stir for a minute or two. Stir in the peas. Add the water, bring to a boil, add the rice, cover, and steam over low heat until the liquid is absorbed, about 20 minutes. If the rice is not done, add ¼ cupful of hot water, cover, and steam 10 minutes longer. Taste and add salt and pepper, if needed. Serve hot with curried lamb or other meats, or serve as a main dish.

PIGEON PEA–PICKING

Pigeon pea shrubs once grew wild in ditches and along fence rows in south Florida. The Voltz family knew the wonderful taste of the green peas as compared with the dried or canned ones, and so they jumped at the chance when a farmer friend invited them to pick the peas on the shrubs near her house, west of Miami. It is an odious task. The leaves and pea husks exude a sticky substance that makes the peas cling to you and coats your fingers with black goo.

But the peas are worth it, lively and lighter than the starchy dried ones. Shelling the pigeon peas is an ordeal, too. Cutting a thin slice off the convex edges of the shells makes it easier to open them. Rinse the peas and cook them in a small amount of water until they are tender, about 25 minutes. Drain them and use in recipes such as peas and rice, or reheat them with butter or a warm oil and garlic dressing.

Housing developments and malls have taken over the spots where pigeon peas once grew, but occasionally you will find the fresh ones in the people's market in Coconut Grove on Saturdays or in specialty produce markets.

SUE FISHER'S TZIMMES

MAKES 4 TO 6 SERVINGS.

Sue Fisher's mother, Pearl Dubois, brought her treasured recipe for this Jewish specialty from New York when the family moved to Miami in 1950. Sue has used the recipe, revising it and reworking it each year as she prepared it for Rosh Hashanah. Today it is lighter (no meat), it uses fresh ingredients, always available in Florida, and the children, now grown, like it so much that she serves it for Thanksgiving and other family dinners. Vegetarian tzimmes complements roast chicken or turkey perfectly, to her mind.

1½ pounds sweet potatoes,
    peeled and cubed
1 large or 2 small carrots,
    peeled and sliced
½ fresh pineapple, shredded
    coarsely with a knife (see
    Note)
¾ cup water

⅛ teaspoon cinnamon
Salt and freshly ground
    pepper to taste
¼ cup honey
12 pitted prunes
⅛ teaspoon vanilla extract
Juice of ½ lemon

Combine the sweet potatoes, carrots, pineapple, water, cinnamon, salt, and pepper in a large saucepan. Simmer, covered, 30 minutes, or until the sweet potatoes and carrots are tender. Stir the mixture two or three times while cooking to prevent sticking. Add the honey, mix well, and put the prunes over the vegetables. Cover and simmer 10 minutes longer. Add the vanilla and, if needed, more salt and pepper. Squeeze the lemon over the tzimmes, turn into a bowl, and serve hot.

NOTE: One 8½-ounce can crushed pineapple in juice can be substituted for the fresh pineapple.

ROSIN POTATOES

Rosin potatoes were a favorite food in the turpentine camps of north Florida until the 1930s and 1940s. Food historians suspect that a potato intended for roasting in the coals fell into a pot of boiling rosin (a step in refining the pine sap), and the result was a cooked potato with super flavor and a texture unlike any potato. The workers from then on cooked their potatoes in the rosin for lunches.

Novices at eating rosin potatoes don't know what to expect. Those in the know think there is no better potato. The flesh pops out of the potato skin fluffy, steaming, and with only a faint aroma of pine; most of the rosin is sopped up by a wrapping of newspapers on the hot potatoes.

What used to be a workers' lunch is a big deal with the fearless barbecue chefs of south Florida who love challenges.

The pot and rosin can be bought or ordered from some hardware, building supply, or outdoor equipment stores in this part of Florida. You will need:

**A large cast-iron pot and a lid
   to cover it
Rosin (in pellets or a hunk of
   it), to fill the pot ¾ full when
   melted
1 to 2 large russet or sweet
   potatoes for each person**

**Butter, sour cream, salt,
   pepper in a mill, minced
   chives, and other toppings
Newspapers**

Place the pot over a fire.* Add the rosin and melt it, keeping the pot only three quarters full so it won't spatter out. Dip some of it out, if necessary. When the rosin is bubbling gently, with tongs add the potatoes. Cook as many as will move easily in the boiling rosin. The potatoes immediately sink; in 25 to 30 minutes they rise to the top. Remove sweet potatoes at this point; white potatoes become fluffier and more tender if allowed to bob in the boiling rosin for 5 to 10 minutes longer. Take them out with tongs or a ladle, being careful not to puncture the skins.

Wrap each potato in 2 to 3 thicknesses of newspaper, twisting the ends. The rosin will stick to the paper as it cools, a matter of a few minutes. To open the potato, cut through the paper and skin, pull back the edges, and pass the toppings. Some cooks have tried foil for wrapping the potatoes, but the foil transfers the heat, burning your fingers, and will not sop up the rosin.

Rosin is reusable. After it has cooled, cover the pot of rosin and store it in a garden shed or garage. Reheat the pot and rosin for the next rosin potato feast.

*Some rosin potato mavens use an electric hot plate under the footed pots as the heat source.

MARIE'S BANANA BREAD

MAKES 2 COFFEE-CAN LOAVES OR ONE
9 x 5 x 3-INCH LOAF.

The rustle of banana leaves as the trade winds blow gently in the evening is one of the coolest sounds of south Florida. The shrubs in the Voltz garden in Coconut Grove provided the rustle, but the occasional bunch of bananas they gave was a mixed blessing. The fruit is ripe one day, and overripe two days later, it seems. A favorite way to save bananas, after giving away as many of them as friends and neighbors will take, is baking them in bread to be frozen. This recipe, from Jeanne's mother, Marie Sewell Appleton, is the best of the many we've tried, unusually rich with banana, tender, golden brown, and a grand snack or party sandwich, spread with butter or cream cheese.

Marie's Banana Bread (continued)

1¾ cups all-purpose flour

1 teaspoon baking soda

¼ teaspoon salt

3 large, very ripe bananas

½ cup (1 stick) butter,
softened

1 cup sugar

2 large eggs

½ cup chopped walnuts

Butter and lightly flour two 10-ounce coffee cans or one 9×5×3-inch loaf pan. Preheat the oven to 350 degrees. Mix the flour, baking soda, and salt together on a plate or piece of waxed paper; set aside. In a shallow bowl or another plate, mash the peeled bananas with a fork until almost smooth; a few soft lumps of fruit should remain. In a mixing bowl, cream together the butter and sugar until fluffy. Beat in the eggs, then mix in the bananas. Stir in the dry ingredients in three or four additions. Fold in the walnuts. Turn into the pan or cans, filling no more than half full. Bake 1 hour, or until a skewer inserted in the center comes out clean. Cool in the pan or cans 15 minutes. Open the bottoms of the coffee cans and loosen the bread with a sharp knife or loosen the bread around the edges of the loaf pan with a thin-bladed spatula. Turn out and cool on a rack. Wrap in foil and refrigerate overnight before slicing. Slice thin and serve with butter, cream cheese or mascarpone cheese, an Italian-style creamy cheese, or for novelty, softened American or imported blue cheese.

RUBY LORD'S SWEET PUPPIES

MAKES AT LEAST 24 SWEET PUPPIES.

Ruby Lord, "Hush Puppy Queen" of the Grant Seafood Festival, near Melbourne, originated sweet puppies for volunteers to enjoy with coffee before starting to cook for the thousands of visitors each February. One of the country's largest seafood festivals, it is held the third weekend of the month when clams and oysters are harvested from the Indian River. Rock shrimp, frog legs, clam chowder, deviled crabs, and fish dinners are served, and a fresh market sells seafood to take home. Sweet puppies look like hushpuppies and taste like doughnuts, with just enough sugar in them to satisfy a sweet tooth. At the Grant Festival a hushpuppy machine is used to shape the batter, but dropping them off a teaspoon works well, too.

1½ cups self-rising flour	½ to ¾ cup buttermilk
¾ cups sugar	Vegetable oil for deep frying
3 teaspoons baking powder	Confectioners' sugar or
1 egg	cinnamon sugar
1½ teaspoons vanilla extract	

Sift the dry ingredients together into a mixing bowl. Add the egg, then the vanilla, blending well. Add ½ cup of the buttermilk to moisten so that the batter holds together. Add more, if necessary. In a heavy skillet, heat 2 to 3 inches of oil over medium heat and drop the batter from a teaspoon into the hot oil. Cook until well browned on all sides, about 3 to 4 minutes. Remove the fritters with a slotted spoon and drain on paper towels. While warm, sprinkle with confectioners' sugar or a combination of cinnamon and granulated sugar. Serve immediately.

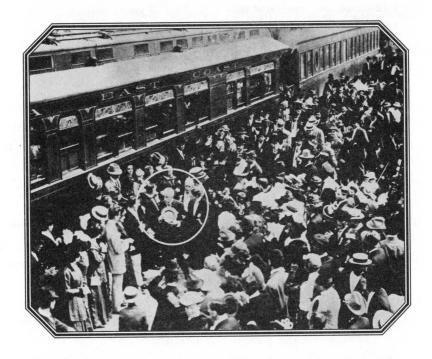

QUEEN OF ALL PUDDINGS

MAKES 6 SERVINGS.

The Key West version of this recipe that was popular all over the country in the early part of this century employs guava paste in place of fruit jam. The base is dry Cuban bread, a household staple until recent years, as fresh bread would be bought three or four times a day, each time a new batch came from the bakery ovens. As in many Key West recipes, canned milk is used, since fresh milk was scarce until trucks began to bring it down the highway in the 1930s. Daughters and granddaughters stick to the old ways, recognizing the creaminess and slightly caramelized flavor that the processed milk gives to a custard. This interpretation of the old recipe is made with one can of milk and an equal quantity of fresh milk.

**2 cups dry Cuban bread cubes,
    crumbled Cuban crackers, or
    dry French-type bread**

1 12-ounce can evaporated milk

**1 can (1½ cups) fresh milk
    (measured in milk can)**

4 eggs

**¼ cup plus 5 tablespoons
    sugar**

½ teaspoon cinnamon

**Slice of guava paste,
    2½ × 2 × 1 inches**

**1 to 2 tablespoons rum or
    apple juice**

Preheat the oven to 350 degrees. Lightly butter an 11½ × 7½-inch baking dish. Don't use a deep dish or the pudding takes twice as long to bake. Place the bread in a large bowl and pour the evaporated and fresh milks over it. Soak 10 to 15 minutes, until the bread is saturated. Push down any floating bread into the milk with a spoon. Separate 3 of the eggs and add the remaining whole egg to the yolks. Set aside the egg whites at room temperature for the meringue. Add the ¼ cup of the sugar and the cinnamon to the egg yolk mixture. Mix, then stir into the bread and milk mixture. Pour into the prepared baking dish. Bake 30 minutes.

Cut the guava paste in 4 or 5 pieces and place in a small saucepan with the rum or apple juice. Stir over low heat until it is melted and smooth, adding more liquid if necessary to make a syrupy paste. Spread the guava mixture on the pudding and return to the oven.

Beat the egg whites until soft peaks form, then gradually beat in the remaining 5 tablespoons of sugar. Beat until the whites are stiff and the sugar dissolved. Spread the meringue over the pudding, swirling it with a spatula and sealing it to the rim of the baking dish. Return the pudding to the oven and bake 15 minutes, or until lightly browned. Cool to lukewarm or room temperature to serve. The pudding is best if eaten the day it is prepared.

GUAVA DUFF

MAKES 6 TO 8 SERVINGS.

The steamed puddings of Key West are handed down from the British and Bahamian settlers who came in the late eighteenth century. The puddings are called by an old British name, duffs, but are made with fresh tropical fruits. The most popular flavor is guava, though duffs are made of mashed ripe papaya, peaches, or freshly made chunky applesauce. Some cooks steam them the old-fashioned way in bags, but this recipe is cooked in a pudding mold, standard equipment in Conch kitchens and local cookware shops. Lacking a pudding mold, coffee cans can hold the dessert for cooking.

1 cup guava pulp (see Note)	1 cup all-purpose flour
½ cup (1 stick) butter, softened	1 teaspoon baking powder
1 cup sugar	½ teaspoon cinnamon
2 eggs	¼ teaspoon salt
1 tablespoon lime or lemon juice	Lightly sweetened whipped cream flavored with rum, or
2 tablespoons dark rum	vanilla ice cream and rum

While preparing the batter, slowly bring to a boil 3 or 4 inches water in a pot with a tight-fitting cover and large enough to hold the pudding mold with room for water to circulate freely. Butter well a 5-cup pudding mold or two clean 12-ounce coffee cans.

Cream together the butter and sugar until fluffy. Beat in the eggs, one at a time, then stir in the lime or lemon juice and rum. Stir in the flour, baking powder, cinnamon, and salt. Blend in the guava pulp. Spoon into the prepared pudding mold or cans, and cover tightly, using foil tied with a string for the cans. Place in the boiling water to reach two-thirds up the side of the mold or cans. Cover and steam 2 hours. Add more boiling water as needed to keep the water level at least half the depth of the molds. Cool the pudding in the mold 5 minutes, then loosen the sides with a thin-bladed knife, and turn the pudding out on a plate. Cool it until warm or cool it thoroughly and reheat it to serve by wrapping it in foil and reheating it in a moderate oven. Top with rum-flavored whipped cream or a scoop of ice cream and splash of rum on each serving.

NOTE: To prepare the guava pulp, wash and cut 4 to 6 guavas in half, scoop out the seedy portions from the centers, and slice the guavas into an enamel or stainless steel saucepan. Add ½ cup water and simmer covered until tender, about 10 minutes. Drain well and purée the guavas in a food processor. Set aside.

COCONUTS—SEE HOW THEY GROW

Coconut palms grow in almost every yard in south Florida, and the huge nuts that drop off them, myth says 365 of them a year for each of the gracefully curved trees, are food, fantasy, and playthings for children. Play telephones, tiny doll beds and bassinets, or dollhouse furniture are made of the sawed-off coconut shells by dads and children. Luke, the Voltzes' son, knew how a coconut was husked and shelled before he was three. He and Mr. Peterson, the gardener, checked the fringe of palms at the seawall on the bay each morning, picking up the nuts that had fallen the night before.

It was years before the little boy was strong enough to husk and shell coconuts himself, but he oversaw Mr. Peterson seriously. The man would whack the stem end of the husk onto an iron fence post to split it; others open the husk on a sharp rock or with a machete. The gardener then cracked the shell with a hammer; a child's way is to hurl the nut hard onto a concrete walk.

The coconut meat was divided between the little boy and his sister, Jeanne, who chomped on it as they played in the tropical garden. The other coconuts went to people in the bayside colony who treasured them for cooking.

If you buy a coconut, there is an easier way of shelling it. Punch holes in the "eyes" with an ice pick or clean Phillips screwdriver. Invert the nut over a glass and drain out the water, shaking and turning the nut as necessary to drain it well. (Water is the correct term for this liquid; coconut milk is made from grated fresh coconut steeped in water or fresh milk, and it is much used in Southeast Asian cookery.) Drink the water or use it in cooking, though the flavor is bland.

Place the coconut on a shallow pan lined with foil and roast it in a 350-degree oven for 30 minutes. The nut usually cracks, but whack it with a hammer until the shell is cracked in several places. Remove the meat from the shell, prying out any bits that cling with a small knife. Peel the thin brown skin off the snowy flesh, brushing away any brown fibers.

Shred the meat, using an old-fashioned three-sided shredder, a Mouli shredder, mandoline, or food processor with the shredder blade in place. Use the coconut immediately, refrigerate it for a few days, or freeze it for a few weeks.

Frozen unsweetened shredded coconut is available in the South, but a purist uses it only if no fresh coconuts are available. It is better for most Florida dishes than the sweetened dried coconut that is commonly available.

MISS ETTA'S FRESH COCONUT CAKE

MAKES 20 TO 24 SERVINGS.

When President Truman made Key West his winter vacation headquarters, townsfolk asked Miss Etta Patterson to bake her famed coconut cake for him. Newsmen, hot for a fresh angle on the President, reported on the gorgeous three-layer cake in detail. Jeanne's editor at The Miami *Herald* sent her to Key West for Miss Etta's recipe. Miss Etta, then in her sixties, was a genuine "Conch," descended from several generations of Bahamians. She lived in the house in which she had been born, where she gathered the coconuts for the cake from the palms in the garden. She confided that you have to use lots of frosting and two coconuts for an impressive cake.

3 cups sifted cake flour (sift just
    before measuring)
3 teaspoons baking powder
¼ teaspoon salt
1 cup (2 sticks) butter,
    softened

2 cups sugar
4 eggs, at room temperature
1½ teaspoons vanilla extract
1 cup milk

MISS ETTA'S COCONUT FROSTING

2 fresh coconuts, shredded (see
    page 159)
1 cup water
½ teaspoon white or cider
    vinegar
2 cups sugar
4 egg whites, at room
    temperature

20 regular-size marshmallows,
    cut in pieces with scissors
    dipped in water from time
    to time
1 teaspoon vanilla extract

Butter 3 9-inch layer cake pans and line the bottoms with parchment or waxed paper cut to fit; butter the paper. Preheat the oven to 350 degrees. Sift together the flour, baking powder, and salt. In a large bowl, cream the butter until fluffy. Add the sugar gradually, beating until creamy. Beat in the eggs, one at a time, then the vanilla extract. Add the flour mixture alternately with the milk in four or five portions, beginning and ending with the flour, folding gently with a spoon or on the lowest speed of a mixer.

Turn the batter into the prepared pans. Stagger the pans on two oven racks set near the middle, so that no pan is directly over another and the pans do not touch each other or the oven wall. Bake 25 to 30 minutes, until a pick inserted in the center comes out moist but with no batter clinging. Cool in the pans 10 minutes. Turn out onto wire racks and cool completely.

Place overlapping waxed paper strips around the edge of a cake plate and center one layer over the waxed paper, letting edges of the paper extend to catch the excess frosting and coconut. Place the shredded coconut on a plate or waxed paper sheet to have it handy while frosting the cake.

To prepare the frosting, combine the water and vinegar in a heavy saucepan. Bring to a boil, stir in the sugar until dissolved, cover, and boil for 2 minutes to melt the crystals on the sides of the pan; uncover and boil without stirring over moderate heat until the syrup spins a 4-inch thread when poured from a spoon (238 degrees on a candy thermometer). In a large bowl, beat the egg whites until stiff but not dry. Pour the hot syrup in a thin stream over the egg whites, beating constantly. Add the marshmallows, a few pieces at a time, while beating in the syrup, until all are used. Add the vanilla and continue to beat until cool and thick enough to spread. Frost and stack the layers, pressing in as much coconut as will cling easily before stacking. Frost the top and sides and press the remaining coconut on the top and around the cake. Let the cake stand 2 to 3 hours before slicing. Cut in thin wedges, as the cake is tall and rich.

MIAMI BEACH CHEESECAKE

MAKES 12 TO 16 SERVINGS.

To many, indulging in cheesecake is as much a part of a Miami Beach vacation as sun and surf. Large wedges of cheesecake generally are fluffy textured; rich dense ones like this are cut in slender triangles. A tropical fruit glaze gives a chef an opportunity to be innovative, but customers prefer New York–style toppings, blueberry and strawberry, two to one over newfangled novelties.

CRUST

6 ounces zwieback	2 tablespoons sugar
Pinch cinnamon or nutmeg	5 tablespoons butter, melted

FILLING

2 8-ounce plus 1 3-ounce package cream cheese, at room temperature	2 tablespoons lemon juice
	¼ teaspoon vanilla extract
¾ cup sugar	3 eggs, room temperature
1 tablespoon cornstarch	2 tablespoons sour cream or
1½ teaspoons grated lemon zest	heavy sweet cream
	Strawberry Glaze (recipe follows)

Crush the zwieback into fine crumbs with a rolling pin or in a blender. Mix the crumbs, spice, and sugar in a bowl. Add the butter, a little at a time, and work it in with a spoon or your fingers. Use only enough butter to moisten the crumbs throughout. Butter the sides of an 8½- or 9-

inch springform pan. Press the crumbly mixture to the bottom and halfway up the sides of the pan. Chill while preparing the filling.

Preheat the oven to 300 degrees. In a medium-size bowl, beat the cream cheese until fluffy. Beat in the sugar, a few tablespoons at a time. Add the cornstarch with the last addition of sugar, then the lemon zest and juice, and vanilla; blend until smooth. Add the eggs, one at a time, beating well after each addition. Stir in the sour cream. Pour the filling into the prepared crust. Wrap foil around the bottom of the pan to prevent butter melting onto the oven floor. Bake 1 hour and 25 minutes, or until the top looks dull and dry except for a shiny spot in the center. Turn off the heat and cool the cake in the oven at least 1 hour. The cake may develop a crack, but it will be hidden with glaze. Cool the cake on a wire rack, then chill 2 hours. Top with the Strawberry Glaze or another of your choice.

Dip a sharp knife in hot water to cut cheesecake in wedges.

FRESH STRAWBERRY GLAZE

MAKES 1 CUP, ENOUGH FOR THE TOP OF AN 8- TO 9-INCH CAKE.

Peaches, nectarines, mangoes, or other fruit and berries such as blueberries and blackberries are good in this glaze. The fruit should be sliced and the berries crushed, with a few whole ones left for garnish.

1 pint strawberries

3 tablespoons sugar, or to taste

1 tablespoon lemon juice

Wash and cap the berries. Save the prettiest berries to slice or use whole as garnish. Place ½ cup of the remaining berries in a bowl. Add the sugar and let stand until the mixture becomes juicy. Mash with a fork or large spoon, adding the lemon juice. Taste and add more sugar, if needed. Slice the remaining berries, leaving some for garnish, and stir into the crushed berry sauce. Spoon over the cake, pushing the sliced berries into place for an attractive top.

Florida Keys folk are purists about their Key lime pie: It must contain pure Key lime juice, not the Persian limes that are commercially grown; sweetened condensed milk is obligatory, and the filling is never tinted green with food coloring, but is a natural creamy yellow color.

Sweetened condensed milk was a staple on the Keys before fresh milk was trucked in after the Overseas Highway was opened in the 1930s, and Key limes were on trees in almost every dooryard. As late as 1940, mothers fed their children lime pie and other canned-milk specialties for the health benefits, when fresh milk was hard to come by.

Actually, there are certain "legal" variations on the famous delicacy—for example, folding the meringue into the egg-yolk, lime-juice, and condensed-milk mixture for a lighter filling; then topping the pie with whipped cream. Some cooks prefer whipped cream topping, saving the egg whites for another use.

Through the years, some have baked the filled pie briefly for a firmer texture and others have chosen to pile the meringue onto unbaked filling.

Second- and third-generation Key lime pie makers say their grandmothers baked a flaky pastry shell for the pie; today many use a graham-cracker crumb crust, and prefer it. A chocolate-wafer crumb crust is not authentic, but is a pleasing contrast to the sweet-acid tang of the lime filling.

We have described the pie that would be approved by the folk hanging on to old-time rules of lime pie. Don't be surprised to find examples made with pudding mix, gelatin, and other unauthorized ingredients. Don't be fooled by shortcut lime pies, served in too many restaurants and homes; but dozens of pastry chefs and amateurs serve excellent lime pies in south Florida. Taste around and you'll find them.

KEY LIME PIE

MAKES 6 TO 8 SERVINGS.

It doesn't matter how many eggs you use in this recipe, and when eggs were scarce Key West housewives made the pie with as few as two eggs. Key limes now are shipped from Haiti and other islands to markets in almost all parts of the country in the late summer. But if they are not available, bottled Key lime juice, available in specialty food stores in most of the country, can be used. If you must use Persian lime juice (the large seedless commercial lime), add ½ teaspoon of the grated zest along with the lime juice.

Today since uncooked eggs are thought to be a health hazard, we pondered how we could make this pie perfectly safe. Jack Donnelly, the chef at the St. Petersburg Yacht Club, explained his method. "We bake the filling for fifteen minutes," he said. This was part of some old-time recipes, so it meets traditional standards. Following Jack's advice, we tested this version, and it is a fantastic Key lime pie with a high-standing meringue, and no doubts of safety. Bottled Key lime juice can be ordered from Florida Key West Inc., 3521 Central Avenue, Fort Myers, FL 33901.

1 baked 9-inch pastry shell or graham-cracker crumb crust	½ cup Key lime juice
3 to 4 eggs, separated	Pinch cream of tartar or ½ teaspoon lime juice
1 14-ounce can sweetened condensed milk (not evaporated)	6 to 8 tablespoons sugar

Cool the pastry crust or refrigerate the graham-cracker crumb crust. Preheat the oven to 350 degrees. In a mixing bowl, beat the egg yolks slightly, then stir in the condensed milk and lime juice. Stir until the mixture is thickened, 2 or 3 minutes. Pour into the pie shell. Bake 15 minutes. While the pie bakes beat the egg whites until foamy throughout. Add the cream of tartar or ½ teaspoon lime juice and continue beating until soft peaks form. Add 6 tablespoons sugar for 3 egg whites, 8 for 4 egg whites, 2 tablespoons at a time, and continue to beat until stiff. Swirl the meringue over the hot pie filling, sealing it to the edges of the crust all around, and bake 15 minutes, until the meringue is tipped with brown. Cool before serving, but the pie is best served two or three hours after the meringue is baked.

BOATERS' LIME PIE

Boating cooks from Pensacola to the Keys know lime pie without eggs. The pie is less likely to spoil on a cruise than the traditional one with eggs, the ingredients are easy to take along, and the pie a snap to put together. Many eaters don't miss the eggs at all.

For a packaged or frozen 8-inch graham-cracker crust, use a 14-ounce can of sweetened condensed milk (not evaporated), ⅓ to ½ cup lime juice, and for better flavor, the grated zest of 1 lime. Combine the condensed milk and ⅓ cup lime juice in a bowl and stir it to blend well. The acid in the lime juice thickens the milk immediately. Stir in the zest, then taste the filling. If you like a sharper flavor, add 2 or 3 tablespoons more lime juice. Spread the filling in the crumb shell, cover it, and refrigerate it 8 hours, or until firm in the center. For a 9-inch homemade crumb shell, you may like a thicker filling. Simply double the recipe of the basic lime and milk mixture. For a change, the pie filling can be served as a creamy dessert, in small bowls with plain cookies or graham crackers.

MANGO TARTE TATIN

MAKES 6 TO 8 SERVINGS.

The exotic fruits of Florida have inspired thousands of good home-cooks to create brilliant variations on tried and true cookery themes. In recent years, new chefs have taken this route. This luxurious tart from the Foundlings, a women's club on Lincoln Road in Miami Beach, is the invention of Chef Dewey Losasso, formerly at the Mayfair in Coconut Grove. It is as buttery and rich as the French original made with apples, but the mangoes give an aromatic sweetness to the tart. Dewey bakes the tart in a 12-inch, straight-sided tart pan, but a cast-iron skillet works as well. His baking method is unique—a half hour covered, then uncovered until the sugar is caramelized (an hour or more). The tart is served warm with whipped cream or a lime-scented custard sauce.

¾ cup sugar
2 medium firm-ripe mangoes
½ pound (2 sticks) butter,
 cut in cubes
1 sheet frozen puff pastry,
 thawed, but cold, or 1 recipe
 Butter Pastry (see page 54)

Whipped cream or Lime
 Custard Sauce (recipe
 follows)

Preheat the oven to 350 degrees. Spread the sugar evenly in a 12-inch straight-sided tart pan or 12-inch iron skillet. Peel and cut the mangoes in ½-inch slices and arrange overlapping over the sugar. Dot the butter over the fruit. Roll out the pastry very thin and trim to a circle 2 to 3 inches larger than the diameter of the pan. Carefully lift onto the filling and tuck the edges down around the fruit. Cut several slits in the crust to allow the steam to escape. Cover the tart with foil and bake 30 to 45 minutes, until the filling is bubbling and the crust crisp. Uncover, lower the oven heat to 325 degrees, and bake 1½ to 2 hours longer, until the juices are thick, with a light caramel color, and the mangoes are tender. Place the pan on a wire rack and cool for 10 to 15 minutes. Invert a cake plate over the tart and quickly turn the pan over to unmold the tart onto the plate without losing juices. Rearrange the fruit for looks and serve warm. Cut in wedges and top with whipped cream or place wedges in pools of Lime Custard Sauce on dessert plates. Leftover tart may be reheated in a conventional oven (a microwave toughens the pastry). Place the tart on a baking pan, cover with foil, and heat in a preheated 350-degree oven for 8 to 10 minutes.

LIME CUSTARD SAUCE

MAKES 2 CUPS, 6 TO 8 SAUCE SERVINGS.

The faint aroma of lime in this sauce complements the Mango Tarte Tatin to perfection, and is an exquisite accent to fresh fruit compotes, plain cakes, and puddings. The lime flavor is intensified if the sauce is allowed to ripen in the refrigerator overnight.

1½ cups milk	4 egg yolks
Zest of 1 large Persian or	¼ cup sugar
2 Key limes, in thin strips	Pinch salt
or grated	

Combine the milk with the lime zest in the top of a double boiler. Scald over direct heat. Beat the egg yolks with the sugar and salt, stir half the hot milk mixture into the egg yolks, then stir the yolk mixture into the remaining milk. Cook and stir over boiling water until the custard coats a spoon. Remove from the heat and place the pan in cold water to stop the cooking promptly. Pour the custard into a jar or bowl, cover, and refrigerate overnight to ripen the flavor. Serve cold as a sauce on tarte tatin and other desserts.

THE RESTAURANT SCENE

Florida, once a wasteland when it came to dining out, is suddenly on the map as perhaps the most interesting restaurant scene in the United States today. In the 1980s dozens of chefs who had been trained in the European and northern United States traditions came, saw, and tasted the riches that explorers since Ponce de León have found. Now they are conquering the restaurant world in south Florida and the East Coast, and their influence is felt from Pensacola to Key West. A new restaurant opening in Tampa or Sarasota is as exciting as the ribbon cutting of a new tourist attraction used to be.

And the world is taking notice. There is hardly an important food writer who has not reported the good things that these new chefs are doing around Miami, Fort Lauderdale, Key West, and environs. In May 1992, the IACP (International Association of Cooking Professionals) had its annual conference in Miami, and all the talk centered on the exciting new restaurants— who had eaten what and where. A New York editor had what he called the "best meal in years" at A Mano, Norman Van Aken's place in the Art Deco section of Miami Beach. Another at Mark's Place in North Bay Village went mad for the taste of a pineapple salsa with cilantro. Linda Gassenheimer, trained at the London Cordon Bleu and a food columnist for The Miami *Herald*, compares the food of Allen Susser at Chef Allen's in north Dade county to that of the top chefs of Europe when she was a culinary teacher in London and frequent diner on the continent before moving to Miami.

The new breed of chefs borrows spirit and inspiration from the contemporary-style menus of the best restaurants in California, New York, Chicago, and other cities. They work with fruits, vegetables, fish, and seafoods that many barely knew about before they shopped around Florida, and they introduce their customers to such delicacies as calamondin-marinated fish, mango tart, papaya-seed dressings, and mango and pepper salsas. They borrow from the Caribbean in such combinations as pork with black bean or fresh citrus sauces; the fish may be adorned with tarragon blossoms; and they take great pains to serve fresh hearts of palm, scarce even here where it grows wild. They use peppers and chiles with a fine hand that capitalizes on the nuances of flavors in partnership with stinging heat.

The yellowtail snapper, little known outside south Florida, is on finest restaurant menus, as is the elite grouper, scamp. Dolphin fish (no relative of the playful porpoise) is featured by these young cooks for its meaty goodness.

The kind of person who visits or is settling down in this part of Florida today has a lot to do with the success of these young culinary artists. There is the new international business community and a burgeoning world of artists as well as all those highly educated workers at Cape Canaveral and the luxury-seeking vacationers. All of these people know fine food when they taste it, and they patronize the upscale chefs frequently and enthusiastically.

Is it any wonder that the influential life-style and food magazines cover the Florida restaurant scene energetically? And tourist-style restaurants are joining the revolution, serving such newly chic foods as warm chicken salad and steamed shrimp and fish to travelers with more taste than money.

One recognizes immediately a bright new flavor everywhere. It is as though the wonders that Mother Nature bestowed on Florida and the rich heritage of cultures that co-exist here were inspiring culinary talent to create a genuine New World cusisine.

CLASSIC MANGO CHUTNEY

MAKES 6 TO 7 HALF-PINT JARS.

Fairchild Tropical Garden, a living museum of native and imported plants from around the world, is a peaceful tourist stop and a favorite excursion for local people. The park is located in a natural hammock a few miles south of Miami. The annual fund-raising ramble, usually the first weekend in December, is like a huge lawn party among palms, orchids, gingers, and other subtropical flora. Visitors come early to shop and rummage for elegant cast-offs, plants, holiday decorations made of palm spathes and other plant materials, and dozens of jars of tropical fruit chutneys, relishes, jams, and jellies made by volunteers. Chutneys such as this one are cherished. Since mangoes are available in most of the country now, the condiment can be a culinary adventure for a dedicated cook anywhere. Tamarind pulp is found in shops that stock East Indian and Pakistani foods, but the chutney will still taste richly of the Orient, if the tamarind is not available.

2½ cups cider vinegar

1 pound light brown sugar

2 tablespoons salt

2 jalapeños, chopped fine, or 1½ teaspoons crushed red pepper (cayenne), or more to taste

3 large onions (1¼ pounds), chopped

2 cloves garlic, minced

1 tablespoon minced fresh ginger or 3 ounces preserved ginger, chopped fine

½ cup lime or lemon juice

1½ teaspoons whole mustard seeds

1½ teaspoons celery seeds

1½ teaspoons finely broken cinnamon stick

1½ teaspoons whole allspice

½ teaspoon whole cloves

1 cup (½ 12-ounce box) raisins

1 cup (½ 12-ounce box) dry currants

3½ pounds chopped, peeled mango (7 cups) (see Note 1)

½ cup tamarind pulp (see Note 2)

To make the chutney, in a large stainless steel or enamelware pot, combine the vinegar, brown sugar, salt, and jalapeños. Bring to a boil, stirring until the sugar is dissolved. Add the remaining ingredients, mix well, and bring to a boil again. Cover, remove from the heat, and let the chutney stand overnight. The next day, stir the chutney together, bring it to a boil, and simmer 2 to 3 hours, until the mango pieces are tender, but not mushy. Cook over low heat and stir often to prevent scorching. Spoon the chutney into hot, sterilized ½-pint jars, seal immediately, and refrigerate. For longtime storage in a cupboard, the chutney should be processed 10 minutes in a boiling water bath, using manufacturer's instructions for sealing the jars.

NOTE 1: Mangoes should be half green and hard and half firm-ripe. Peel and chop them roughly into the syrup before adding the other ingredients.

NOTE 2: Tamarind paste available commercially works well in a chutney. Break off a quarter of a one-pound block of the paste, and chop it into pieces. In an enamelware or stainless steel saucepan, combine the tamarind pieces with hot water to cover, bring to a boil, and simmer 2 or 3 minutes. Drain the mixture in a sieve and press the pulp to extract water. To use fresh tamarind, gather beans that have brittle brown husks: Crack open the husks and pull or scrape out the pulp and seeds with a spoon. Place the pulp and seeds in water to cover in a glass or stainless steel bowl. Let stand overnight; the next morning pour into a stainless steel or enamelware saucepan and simmer until the seeds can be removed. Discard the seeds and drain the pulp to use in chutney or other recipes. Leftover reconstituted tamarind pulp can be refrigerated and stirred into ice water with sugar to taste to make tamarindade.

THE BIG BEND AND THE SUN COAST.

APPETIZERS

Crab Meat–Stuffed Eggs

Naples Hotel Cocktail Cheese

Orange Herring

Green Bean and Walnut Pâté

Hearts of Palm Salad

Strawberry and Spinach Salad

Ybor City Calabaza Salad

Salsa Vinagreta (Sauce Vinaigrette)

Louis Pappas' Greek Salad

SOUPS

Garlic Soup

Caldo Gallego (Spanish Bean and
    Collard Green Soup)

The Heron's Clam Chowder

ENTRÉES

Fried Shrimp with Coconut

Land's End Stew

Naples Deviled Crab

Broiled Scallops with Fresh Tomato
    Salsa

Grouper Russian-Style

Smoked Mullet

Arroz con Pollo (Yellow Rice with
    Chicken)

Cacerola Cubana de Arroz y
    Calabaza (Chicken and Rice
    Casserole with Squash and Sausage)

Pastitsio

Cuban-Style Roast Pork

Chorizo

Greek Leg of Lamb

VEGETABLES

Coliflor Vinagreta (Cauliflower
    Vinaigrette with Capers)

Black Beans and White Rice

Orange Red Pepper Brown Rice

BREADS

Home-Baked Cuban Bread

Indian Fry Bread

Sweet Potato or Pumpkin Fry Bread

Indian Burger

Grapefruit Biscuits

DESSERTS

Tarpon Springs–Style Rice Pudding

Rum Spanish Flan with Caramelized
    Oranges

Banana Bites

Mrs. Harvey's White Fruitcake

Fresh Strawberry Pie

Passover Lemon Pie

Almond Matzo Pie Crust

Naples Chocolate Cheese Pie

The Gulf Coast sweeps eastward from Apalachicola around the Big Bend, passing St. Theresa, a playground for beach lovers from Tallahassee, and fishing villages such as Panacea, little changed from a century ago. The oyster shacks at St. Marks are worth a stop. The shucker opens the shellfish so fast, you've eaten a couple of dozen before you know it. At Steinhatchee, around the Bend, third- and fourth-generation fishermen work the waters for mullet and grouper.

The Gulf Coast of Florida was settled by white Americans, many staying after the Indian Wars almost two centuries ago and others coming from Southern states. They ate what little they could raise, hunt, or fish, and wild plants, including hearts of palm.

A few miles south of the Suwannee River is Cedar Key, a fishing village and artists' colony. The Island Hotel here was famous for fine food in the antebellum era and again in the 1940s to 1960s. Here the traveler had fresh local foods, stone crabs, blue crabs, fin fish of the Gulf, and a famous hearts of palm salad. The Island Hotel still serves sandwiches and salads, and other restaurants carry on the food traditions of the town.

The town was named for the cedars that three major pencil factories milled there; when the trees were depleted, the pencil makers moved out. The village has survived numerous other booms and busts since then; a recent hurricane took the pier, where fishermen landed their major cash catch, mullet. The pier has been replaced, mullet fishing is back, and other fish, crabs, and clams are packed here.

Cedar Key, like a well-worn fisherman's shirt, may look a bit frayed, but a short walk along Front Street, and a stop to eat in a seafood restaurant or raw bar, will explain the easygoing charm the town holds for the people who live here and the thousands who visit.

Moving down the coast, you pass Crystal River, where soft-shell crabs are big business, and towns where retirees and permanent residents live quietly. A few miles south, New Port Richey looks like an affluent suburb of a big city, with its large homes and well-tended lawns, but this is retirement Florida style. The picnics brought to the town park when residents watch the sun set over the Gulf are noted for superb home-cooked delectables, from chilled soups in thermoses to cookies and cakes. Arleen Arnold, a consumer services expert with large appliance and food companies before coming here, said that retirement provides time for cooking, and the picnics become culinary showcases.

Heading to Tarpon Springs, one finds Florida's largest Greek community, and an intriguing look at the "Sun Coast." Here the flavor is distinctly Mediterranean, with traditional foods such as spicy lamb, Greek salads rich with feta cheese, black olives, and anchovies, and honey-glazed pastries.

Sponge fishing, once a major industry, has dwindled to almost nothing due to red tide kill and competition from synthetic sponges. But boats still bring in a few, for benefit of the tourists who wander along the harbor, browsing for souvenirs and sampling Greek dishes. St. Nicholas Church is a center of activity, attracting hundreds at Easter and Epiphany.

Tampa lies just twenty-five miles south of Tarpon Springs, but they are worlds apart. Tampa is a business city, with tall contemporary structures of glass and steel, and the dress code is suits and ties. While Tampa, like Tarpon Springs, has a prominent Greek community, the primary ethnic influence is Hispanic; Ybor City, a section of the city once populated by cigar workers and their families, is now an historic district. Floridians and tourists patronize area favorites like the Columbia Restaurant for *paella,* chicken and yellow rice, and garbanzo bean soup, and the Silver Ring Cafe, famous for its Cuban sandwiches. Tampans have fresh crab cakes at La Tropicana Cafe, and buy loaves of Cuban bread from bakeries such as La Segunda Central.

Tampa's awakening came in 1884, when the first Plant train steamed into town, sparking agricultural and industrial growth. Henry B. Plant was to Tampa and west Florida what his former partner, Henry M. Flagler, was to the east coast of Florida.

Agricultural interests are still strong in the area, but shipping and other industry has flourished, as well. With it has come a move toward more updated American and continental fare, which co-exists with the Latin and traditional Southern cookery that prevailed in the past.

Across Gandy Bridge in St. Petersburg, smoked mullet and mackerel attract fish lovers to Ted Peters Famous Smoked Fish. Until a few years ago, smoked-fish shacks dotted the roads to the beach, and weekend drivers would count on stopping for smoked fish for hors d'oeuvres. Most of the shacks have gone out of business, but the Peters place carries on the tradition.

Since its founding in 1888, St. Petersburg has attracted Northerners, as tourists or residents. The taste has been more Northeastern and Midwestern United States than the Southern tongue of Florida before Sputnik. Grits and greens were available, but James L. Appleton, an Alabamian living there in the 1960s, complained of the "Yankee watermelons" and "Kansas City bacon" that he found in markets. The taste was not there for fragrant melons ripened to Southern standards or salty, smoked bacon.

Going south by water or driving west from Bradenton, you come to Cortez. It is a tiny town perched at the north end of Sarasota Bay, colonized by fishermen from North Carolina in 1880. They isolated themselves purposely, to protect their simple life and livelihood—fishing. Now the descendants of the town's founders fear that they can't hold the line against the dollars of high-rise-condo builders. But at this writing, townfolk still fish for a living, as they wish.

Down the coast, Sarasota began in the 1880s when a Scottish syndicate purchased 60,000 acres, and one of the first golf courses in the nation was built. Soon players by the dozen came to learn the new game.

From the start, Sarasota attracted wealthy folk. Mrs. Potter Palmer came from Chicago before World War I, and John Ringling brought his circus, then built a thirty-room Florentine mansion, now an art museum that sets the pace for the town. Many tourists and residents are not so wealthy as Mrs. Palmer, but just as social, centering their days around lunch at their clubs and evenings at concerts and museum events. Sophisticated restaurants surround St. Armands Circle on Longboat Key, across the causeway. Hispanic restaurateurs, come from Tampa, and other old-timers whose families have operated restaurants for years, are prominent here. Residents who cook at home have access to locally grown produce including tomatoes from Ruskin and such delights as ambrosia melons (a sweet, aromatic muskmelon).

Quiet beaches and year-round warm temperatures lure people to the succession of small towns that dot the coastline to the south. Game fishermen gravitate to Boca Grande chasing tarpon, and Sanibel and Captiva islands, across the causeway from Fort Myers, are world famous for shell collecting. In Captiva, fish is grilled over buttonwood, and a lightly blackened fish that is called Sanibel-style cooking is found on menus. Seafood markets tout local snapper and mackerel, but the freshest catch often can be found dockside.

Naples, the most southerly major resort on the Gulf, has the established air of Palm Beach with a somewhat quieter attitude. The shops are chic and expensive, as are many of the restaurants. But a tourist on a budget can breakfast or lunch at sweet little tea shops or other modest places. Many tourists and residents cook at home. Wynn's Family Market on Fifth Avenue caters to these home-cooks, including those who dash in at mealtimes for carry-out foods.

For a look at what once was a lonely outpost, fifteen miles southeast of Naples, take the road to Marco Island, a picturesque village that used to be a haven for Floridians wanting to fish far from the hubbub of resorts. The solitude is gone, with condos and motels abounding. But eating here means the freshest stone crabs and mullet, and one or two places cook game fish. Many, such as snook, cannot be sold under Florida law, but a lucky angler can have a prized catch cooked for him and his friends. Mounds of clam shells, covering several acres, have been found by archeologists here, attesting to the diet of natives six or seven centuries ago, and native clams are coming back slowly.

Another few miles to the east, take a turn off the Tamiami Trail to Everglades City, at the edge of Everglades National Park. The tiny town is a few miles from Chokoloskee, a rough and ready fishing village where, legend says, fugitives have hung out for years. Everglades City and Chokoloskee lie amid the Ten Thousand Islands, a tangle of mangrove that protects the tiny settlements from storms and unwanted interference by outsiders. Everglades City was a Seminole trading post and is now a fishing village with restaurants selling the freshest frog's legs, stone crabs, shrimp, alligator tail, and mullet, all fried. And home folk talk and generally eat in a Cracker mode, as their grandparents and great-grandparents did.

From Cracker cooking of the Big Bend and the natural wonderland of the Ten Thousand Islands, to the refined foods of the Sun Coast cities and the flavors of Hispanic and Greek settlers, this is a deliciously rich mélange of tastes.

CRAB MEAT–STUFFED EGGS

MAKES 12 EGG HALVES.

The warm Gulf water lures droves of sun worshipers, and picnicking is naturally popular. The abundance of good, fresh crab meat in this coastal area provides a special resource for these stuffed eggs. "Deviled" eggs have been packed in picnic baskets for generations, and with today's insulated coolers, they can stay fresh all day even in the hot Florida sun.

½ cup crab meat

6 hard-cooked eggs

¼ cup finely chopped celery

2 tablespoons finely chopped green bell pepper

2 teaspoons lemon juice

2 tablespoons sour cream

2 tablespoons mayonnaise

¼ teaspoon curry powder

⅛ teaspoon salt

⅛ teaspoon pepper or to taste

Minced parsley for garnish (optional)

Flake the crab meat and discard any bits of shell or cartilage. Shell the eggs and cut each in half lengthwise. To prepare the filling, transfer the yolks to a mixing bowl and mash them well with a fork until free from lumps. Add the crab meat and the remaining ingredients, blending well with the yolks. Using a pastry bag or a spoon, fill the egg-white halves, mounding the stuffing slightly on the top. Garnish with a sprinkle of curry powder or finely chopped parsley. Cover with plastic wrap and refrigerate for several hours or overnight.

FOR YOUR HEALTH'S SAKE EAT MORE ORANGES AND GRAPEFRUIT

TABLE D'HOTE DINNER

Guests will please write on check, list of items desired

Florida Shrimp Cocktail

Hearts of Florida Celery   Spiced Cucumber Rings

Peanut Soup, Aux Croutons

Baked Florida Shad with Roe
Milk Fed Chicken, Fried, Southern Style
Grilled Lamb Chops with Banana Fritters
Roast Young Capon with Tokay Jelly

Golden Bantam Corn in Cream   Green Peas

Florida Broccoli, Hollandaise

Hot Tea Biscuits   Corn Sticks

Hearts of Lettuce, Thousand Island Dressing

Strawberry Shortcake with Whipped Cream

Ice Cream   Cake

Apple Pie a la Mode

Coffee   Tea   Milk
Sanka   Kaffee Hag

$1.50

SUGGESTIONS A LA CARTE

Florida Shrimp Cocktail 40
Peanut Soup, Aux Croutons, Cup 25; Tureen 35
Baked Florida Shad with Roe 80
Fried Oysters with Bacon, Chili Sauce 75
Grilled Lamb Chops with Banana Fritters 1.00
Milk Fed Chicken, Fried, Southern Style, Corn Fritters 1.00
Calf's Liver, Saute, with Bacon and Broccoli Hollandaise 90
Roast Young Capon with Tokay Jelly, Green Peas 90
Golden Bantam Corn in Cream 30
Florida Broccoli, Hollandaise 35   Green Peas 35
Hearts of Lettuce, Thousand Island Dressing 35
Strawberry Shortcake with Whipped Cream 40
Apple Pie 25; a la Mode 40
Florida Grapefruit 20

A LA CARTE

Relishes

Chilled Florida Celery	20	Spiced Cucumber Rings	25
Queen Olives	25	Pin-Money Pickles	25
Tomato Juice Cocktail	25		

Soup

Chicken, Cup 25; Tureen 35   Tomato, Cup 25; Tureen 35
Consomme, Hot or Cold, Cup 25

Fish and Oysters

Broiled or Fried Fresh Fish 80
Oysters, Fried, Chili Sauce 65; Stewed with Milk 55; with Cream 65

Grilled, etc.

Sirloin Steak	1.50	Ham and Eggs	80
Extra Sirloin Steak	2.50	Bacon and Eggs	80
Lamb Chops, each	50	Broiled or Fried Ham	80

Vegetables

| Potatoes—Hashed Browned, Lyonnaise or French Fried | 30 | Baked Beans, Hot or Cold | 35 |
| Boiled or Mashed | 30 | Asparagus, Drawn Butter | 40 |

Sandwiches

| Ham | 30 | Club | 85 |
| Tongue | 30 | Chicken (Toasted) | 40 |

Cold Meats, Salads, etc.

Boneless French Sardines	50	Sliced Chicken	90
Assorted Cold Meats, Potato Salad	1.00	Chicken Salad	85
Ham 80; with Potato Salad	90	Sliced Tomatoes	30
Head Lettuce, Choice of Dressing	35	Lettuce and Tomato	35

Bread

Assorted	15	Corn Sticks	15
Milk Toast	40	Toast	20
Hot Tea Biscuits	20	Cream Toast	60
Hot Rolls	15	Crackers	10
Boston Brown	20	Yeast Cake with Crackers	10

Fruits, Desserts, etc.

Sliced Pineapple	30	Prunes with Cream	30
Preserved Figs with Cream	40	Orange Blossom Honey	25
Florida Guava Jelly	25	Florida Papaya Marmalade	25
Preserved Strawberries	25	Florida Kumquat Marmalade	25
Cake	10	Florida Orange Marmalade	25
Ice Cream	25		

Cheese with Crackers

Cream with Guava Jelly	45	Swiss Gruyere	35
Imported Roquefort	40	Imperial	30
Imported Camembert	40		

Beverages

After Dinner Coffee	15	Instant Postum, Pot	25
Iced Tea or Coffee	25	Cocoa, Pot	25
Coffee with Cream, Pot for One	25	Malted Milk	15
Green, English Breakfast, Oolong or Orange Pekoe Tea, Pot	25	Milk, Individual Bottle	15
		Buttermilk, Individual Bottle	20
Kaffee Hag or Sanka, Pot	25		

Guests will please write orders on check furnished by the Steward and pay only the total indicated thereon.
Suggestions for the betterment of the service will be appreciated.
An extra charge of 25c per capita will be made for all meals served to adults outside of the dining car.

C. E. BELL, Superintendent Dining Cars, Washington, D. C.

THE DINING CAR CARRIES A STOCK OF CONFECTIONERY, MAGAZINES AND TOBACCO PRODUCTS FOR THE CONVENIENCE OF THE TRAVELER

COASTAL CRAB BOIL

One of the most popular coastal beach activities in Florida is crabbing for blue crabs, then boiling, cracking, and eating the fresh lumps of crab meat. Crabbers are easy to spot; at dusk or later, they walk along the beaches at the water's edge with flashlights and long-handled crab nets, scooping up the crabs as waves wash them in, dumping them ashore in the surf. You have to be fast to catch them before they scurry back into the water, then shake them out of the net into a pail. Usually there are accompanying squeals when feisty crabs run in the direction of barefoot crabbers.

The next best thing to catching your own crabs is purchasing live ones from the market. Be sure to select ones that are lively, avoiding any that are sluggish or not moving. Also, they should have a fresh seafood smell and no strong, stale odor.

For a crab boil, allow 3 to 4 crabs per person. Fill a deep pot with water (saltwater if you're at the beach), and bring to a boil. Many opt for adding commercial crab seasoning, available in food markets and seafood shops. Drop in the live crabs, head first. When the water returns to a full boil, cook for 5 to 10 minutes, until the crab shells have turned bright red. Remove the crabs and put them under cold water or into the kitchen sink or a big pot filled with ice or cold water to stop the cooking process.

To serve, put the cooked crabs on a large platter in the middle of the table, or cover the table with newspaper and put them directly on the paper. Supply nut or lobster crackers, cocktail forks, plenty of paper napkins or paper towels, and a container for the discarded shells. Warm clarified butter and lemon wedges are popular accompaniments.

Holding the crab body firmly, pull back the flap (apron) and break off from the under part of the shell. Then grasp both sides of the shell and pull to separate. Remove the gills ("dead man's fingers"), and wash out the intestines or wipe out with paper towels. Break off the claws, then break the body of the crab, revealing the meat pockets.

NAPLES HOTEL COCKTAIL CHEESE

MAKES ABOUT 2 CUPS, 12 TO 16 APPETIZER SERVINGS.

Cheddar cheese has long been one of America's favorite flavors. At the old Naples Hotel, built in the late 1800s, the chef's cheese spread was served to succeeding generations of visitors and guests. The original recipe called for fine, aged cheddar and, oddly, a bit of green food coloring. We have resurrected the spread and eliminated the coloring. We have also added flour to help the cheese melt smoothly. The result is a tangy warm cheese spread with a past as distinguished as the old hotel itself.

6 tablespoons butter
4 teaspoons flour
4 cups (1 pound) shredded
   aged Cheddar cheese
½ cup light cream
⅓ cup dry sherry
2 tablespoons minced parsley

2 tablespoons minced chives
1 teaspoon minced fresh
   tarragon leaves or ¼ to
   ½ teaspoon dried
½ teaspoon powdered thyme
1 teaspoon crushed anise seed

Place the butter in the top of a double boiler over boiling water and melt. Toss the flour lightly with the cheese and set aside. Add the cream and sherry to the butter, stirring well to blend, then add the cheese by handfuls, blending after each addition, but stirring as little as possible. When the cheese has melted, add the parsley, chives, tarragon, thyme, and anise seed. Serve lukewarm with water biscuits or crackers of your choice.

CUBA LIBRE

hen the Spanish-American War broke out in 1898, Tampa became the port of embarkation for troops en route to Cuba, and the Tampa Bay Hotel housed the general staff of the Expeditionary Force awaiting transport. Legend has it that a group of young army officers drinking in the hotel's rathskeller discovered that Cuban rum, mixed with a new soft drink called Coca-Cola, made a potent and popular cocktail—one that prompted the soldiers to shout, "Cuba libre!"

ORANGE HERRING

MAKES 12 APPETIZER OR 6 SALAD SERVINGS.

Sue Sutker is in great demand as a cooking teacher, television food personality, and producer of celebrity chef benefits in Tampa. One of her pet volunteer jobs is as chairman of benefit luncheons at Congregation Schaari Zadek. For food of her European forebears adapted to Florida, try her unique version of marinated herring!

1 large jar herring in wine sauce	1 6-ounce can orange juice
½ small red onion, sliced thin	concentrate, thawed
and separated into rings	Slivered zest of 1 orange
¼ cup distilled white vinegar	1 orange, sliced thin and the
¼ cup sugar	slices cut in half

Drain the sauce off the herring and rinse the fish, discarding the onion and spices in the jar. Place the herring in a deep bowl. Add the onion rings and mix lightly. Stir together the vinegar and sugar until the sugar is dissolved, then stir in the undiluted orange concentrate and zest. Mix with the fish. Refrigerate, covered, for several hours. Place the fish on a serving plate and garnish with the orange pieces; or serve on greens as a first-course salad.

LUSCIOUS LITCHIS

The Chinese have treasured litchis as food for two thousand years, but Floridians came to know them first for their lovely trees, then later as fruit. Driving through Fort Myers and other coastal towns and cities, one sees dozens of the handsome trees with coppery foliage and bunches of fruit, looking like oversized strawberries.

Litchi lovers regard it as the most exotic fruit in the world. Its flesh is white and translucent, juicy and sweet, with a haunting perfume. It is eaten as is for dessert, and sometimes is combined with other fruits in salads or desserts.

Today fresh litchis are found in Chinatowns in New York and San Francisco in the summer; they are from China or Taiwan, though in the 1950s a small group of growers in southwest Florida shipped fresh litchis.

A fresh litchi (also called lychee or lichee) is egg-shaped, though a bit smaller than an egg, and is clad in a brittle red or reddish-brown shell. The shell is pulled off easily after nicking it with the tip of a paring knife or your fingernail.

Litchis are among the few fruits that can be frozen in the shell, thawed, peeled, and served as if it were fresh.

Litchis may be ordered from Norman Brothers Produce, 7621 S.W. 87th Avenue, Miami, FL 33173.

GREEN BEAN AND WALNUT PÂTÉ

MAKES 1½ CUPS, OR APPETIZER SERVINGS FOR 6 TO 8.

Syd Cline is one of the stalwarts pitching in at the annual spring food festival at Temple Shalom in Naples, highlighting delicacies from cherished family recipes of participating cooks. Syd, a longtime vegetarian, urges his wife, Julia, to offer this version of "chopped liver." It looks like home-chopped chicken liver, and some don't even notice that it is meatless. In any case, it is a light, oniony spread for thin rye bread.

1 cup finely chopped onion
2 tablespoons vegetable oil
½ cup cooked cut green beans, drained
¼ cup toasted walnuts (see Note)
2 hard-cooked eggs, cut in quarters

⅓ cup mayonnaise, or to taste
⅛ teaspoon ground nutmeg
½ teaspoon salt
⅛ teaspoon freshly ground pepper
Thinly sliced rye bread or crackers

Sauté the onion in oil until lightly browned, but take care not to burn it. Combine the beans, walnuts, and onion mixture in a food processor and chop fine, using on-and-off spurts. Add the eggs, a quarter at a time, through the feed tube and continue to chop until blended with tiny flecks of egg white remaining. Turn the mixture into a bowl. Add the mayonnaise and seasonings. Mix well, and add more mayonnaise if needed to moisten. Pack lightly into a small bowl, pressing a thin spatula into the top at six or eight places like spokes as decoration. Cover and chill. Serve as a spread with rye bread or crackers.

NOTE: To toast walnuts, spread in a shallow pan. Place in a preheated 325-degree oven until light brown, about 8 minutes. Shake pan once or twice while toasting the nuts.

HEARTS OF PALM SALAD

MAKES 6 SERVINGS.

Fresh hearts of palm can be cut anytime during the year on one's land or by persons licensed to harvest them, but farm stands and an occasional small store carry them mainly in the cool months. The humidity and heat discourage cutters going out in the summer, and the palm hearts lose their freshness faster in humid weather. Anytime you get fresh hearts of palms is a treat, and there is no substitute. But this dressing is good on the canned palm hearts and other crisp vegetables.

1 small clove garlic
½ teaspoon salt
⅛ teaspoon freshly ground pepper
½ teaspoon sugar
2 tablespoons rice or white wine
   vinegar
3 tablespoons olive oil
2 tablespoons corn or canola
   oil

1 tablespoon minced parsley
   or fresh tarragon
3 cups thinly sliced fresh
   hearts of palm (see Note)
1 green onion or scallion
   with top, sliced thin
½ cup diced red bell pepper
Garden lettuce leaves or
   watercress

Mash the garlic, salt, and pepper together until the garlic is almost creamy, using a mortar in a pestle or the back of a wooden spoon in a small bowl. Stir in the sugar, then the vinegar until the sugar is dissolved. Add the olive and corn oils, beating them until blended, then stir in the parsley or tarragon. Combine the hearts of palm, green onion, and red pepper. Add about half the dressing and toss until the palm hearts and vegetables are well coated. Spoon the salad onto the lettuce or salad plates and garnish generously with watercress. Pass the remaining dressing on the side.

NOTE: To cut the palm heart, slice it thinly in rounds, working up from the butt end. Cut the slices in halves crosswise, then separate them. Place in a bowl of cold water acidulated with the juice of half a lemon.

HEARTS OF PALM ICE CREAM DRESSING

Talk about fresh hearts of palm with a group of Floridians, and at least one will remark, "I still make it with the ice cream dressing." It was created by Bessie Gibbs, who with her husband came to Cedar Key in the late 1940s, fleeing the hustle of New York City. They owned and operated the Island Hotel (now an historical landmark), where customers came from all over Florida to eat Bessie's famous food. Her unusual dressing for hearts of palm salad is made of equal parts softened vanilla ice cream and mayonnaise, one-eighth as much peanut butter (2 tablespoons to each cup of ice cream), and a drop of green food coloring. The dressing is poured over a salad of chopped lettuce and sliced hearts of palm, then sprinkled with pineapple chunks, chopped dates, and candied ginger. Bessie died in the 1970s, but her salad is still famous in Cedar Key, where variations of it are served in restaurants and homes. The dressing is sweet, but has a surprising affinity for the bland, crispy hearts of palm and lettuce that accompany it.

STRAWBERRY AND SPINACH SALAD

MAKES 6 TO 8 SERVINGS.

This richly colored salad is a jewel of the harvest season in Plant City, the strawberry capital of Florida. Our version of poppy seed dressing is considerably toned down from the dressings of the turn of the century, so that the sweet-tart strawberry flavor comes forth in contrast to the bland spinach.

1 pound tender young spinach
1 pint ripe strawberries

About ½ cup Poppy Seed
Dressing (recipe follows)

Wash and dry the spinach in a salad spinner, then wrap it in kitchen towels to sop up the last drops of water. Wash and cap the strawberries, and slice them into a small bowl. Refrigerate the spinach and berries until just before serving. Shred the spinach, discarding the stems. Place the spinach and berries in a large bowl. Add 3 tablespoons of the dressing and toss well to coat the greens and berries. Add enough dressing to coat the greens well and toss.

POPPY SEED DRESSING

Makes 1 cup.

¼ cup sugar
¼ cup rice vinegar
1 teaspoon grated onion
½ teaspoon dry mustard

¼ teaspoon salt
1½ tablespoons poppy seed
½ cup safflower or corn
   oil

Combine the sugar and vinegar in a small saucepan and stir over low heat until the sugar is dissolved. Remove from the heat and add the onion, mustard, and salt. Beat in the oil until well blended and stir in the poppy seed. Pour the dressing into a jar, cover tightly, and refrigerate until ready to serve.

YBOR CITY CALABAZA SALAD

MAKES 4 SERVINGS.

Calabaza, the "Cuban pumpkin," tastes of home to Floridians of island ancestry. Adela Gonzmart, whose family came from Cuba in the early part of this century and operates the Columbia Restaurant in Ybor City, often serves *calabaza* dressed with a Spanish-style *vinagreta* to her family. A similar salad made of chayote, another Hispanic squash, is less colorful and milder flavored, but a pleasing variation on this theme. The chayote is cubed and boiled barely tender. *Calabaza* and chayote are found in Hispanic markets and most supermarkets in Florida and in specialty produce markets everywhere. Adela advises using butternut or acorn squash, if *calabaza* is not available.

1½ to 2 pounds *calabaza*,
   butternut or acorn squash
Salt and freshly ground
   pepper
Boston, butter, or garden
   lettuce leaves

Salsa Vinagreta (recipe
   follows)
1 tablespoon minced parsley
2 hard-cooked eggs, sliced

Seed the *calabaza*, cut the flesh in 1½-inch cubes, and peel it. The rind is tough, so use a sharp heavy knife or cleaver. Bring ½ inch water to a boil in a large saucepan. Add the squash cubes and cook until barely tender, about 15 minutes. Test the pieces with a fork after 10 minutes and remove the tender cubes from the pot, leaving remaining squash to continue cooking until ready. Drain the squash well, add salt and pepper to taste, and cool uncovered to preserve the color.

Line 4 salad plates or a platter with the lettuce. Pile squash in the center of the greens, and drizzle just enough dressing over it to moisten lightly. Too much vinegar causes the squash to turn dark. Sprinkle the salads with parsley and arrange egg slices around the edges. Serve at once so that the squash does not fade.

SALSA VINAGRETA
SAUCE VINAIGRETTE

MAKES A SCANT 1 CUP, 4 SERVINGS.

This is a staple in Hispanic kitchens of south Florida, Ybor City, or anywhere. Although we like it freshly made, a double or triple recipe can be prepared and kept in the refrigerator for salads and drizzling over vegetables. Chopped hard-cooked egg may be added to the sauce, but we prefer the freshly chopped egg over the salad. Notice the Spanish seasoning principle—not much salt, but lots of garlic and capers, salty within themselves.

½ cup mild olive oil

¼ cup balsamic or other wine
    vinegar

½ teaspoon salt

½ teaspoon freshly ground
    pepper

2 tablespoons minced parsley

1 green onion, scallion, or
    ½ small yellow onion, minced

1 large clove garlic, minced

3 tablespoons drained small
    capers

Combine the oil, vinegar, salt, and pepper in a small bowl; beat well. Add the remaining ingredients and beat until blended. Cover and let stand at room temperature. Pour over the salad or toss with greens.

LOUIS PAPPAS' GREEK SALAD

MAKES 4 SERVINGS.

The famous Greek Salad of the Louis Pappas restaurant in Tarpon Springs was once shown on the cover of *Gourmet* magazine in the 1940s. And it is a sight to behold, standing tall on the platter. The base is potato salad and greens. Sprigs of roka (arugula), tomato wedges, avocado slices, cucumber spears, bell pepper rings, beet slices, cooked shrimp, and green onion wands are built up around the base to form a small turret, and the whole is garnished with anchovy fillets, small slabs of feta cheese, Greek black olives, and radishes. Today the restaurant offers the salad chopped (easier to eat, say some). Other restaurants and home-cooks say Greek salad can be as simple as crisp greens with a few black olives and crumbles of feta cheese, and an olive oil dressing. This is how to prepare the original salad, and the way you still can have it in the restaurant, if you choose. A salad for four makes a magnificant show piece.

POTATO SALAD

6 medium new potatoes

2 medium yellow onions, chopped

½ cup thinly sliced green onions
or scallions

¼ cup minced parsley

¼ cup white vinegar

Salt and freshly ground
pepper

GREEK SALAD

1 large bunch garden lettuce or
mixture of lettuce

12 roka (arugula) sprigs

2 tomatoes, cut in 6 wedges
each

1 cucumber, peeled and cut
lengthwise in 8 spears

1 medium avocado, peeled,
seeded, and cut in thin
lengthwise slices

4 ounces feta cheese, cut
in fingers or slices

1 green bell pepper, cut in
8 rings

4 slices cooked or canned beets

4 cooked large shrimp, shelled
and cleaned

4 anchovy fillets

12 Kalamata or other black
olives

12 Salonika peppers	⅓ cup olive oil
4 radishes, cut into roses	¼ cup vegetable oil
4 whole green onions or	½ teaspoon dried oregano
scallions	leaves or 2 to 3 teaspoons
½ cup white vinegar	minced fresh oregano

To prepare the potato salad, boil the potatoes in their jackets until tender but not soft, about 25 minutes. Drain, cool, and peel them. Slice the potatoes into a bowl. Add the chopped yellow onions, green onions, and parsley to the potatoes. Beat together the vinegar and olive oil. Season with the salt and pepper. Toss with the potato mixture, taste, and add more salt and pepper, if needed.

To construct the salad, line a large platter with the outside lettuce leaves, and mound the potato salad in the center. Shred the remaining lettuce, pile it loosely on the potato salad, and scatter the roka on top. Place the tomato wedges, interspersed with cucumber spears, standing up around the outer edge of the salad. Arrange the avocado slices around the outside, the feta cheese, then the green pepper rings over all. Place the beet slices on top, evenly spaced, and a shrimp on each slice of beet. Scatter the anchovy fillets, the olives, Salonika peppers, radishes, and green onions around the salad. At this point, it can be covered with plastic wrap and chilled for up to an hour. Just before serving sprinkle with the vinegar and the two oils, blended together. Scatter the oregano over the salad and serve at once. Greek Salad with toasted Greek bread is more than enough for lunch or supper for most people.

GARLIC SOUP

MAKES 1 SERVING.

This quick hot soup (if you have chicken broth on hand) is a tried-and-true hangover cure, said the Cuban-Florida friend who gave us the recipe. We also like it as a comforting supper for one or two on a chilly evening. We are giving the method for a single serving, the simplest way to prepare it.

1¼ cups chicken broth
2 teaspoons olive oil
1 small clove garlic or ½ large, peeled and crushed
1 slice Cuban or French bread
1 egg

Salt and freshly ground pepper to taste
1 teaspoon minced parsley
2 teaspoons grated hard queso blanco (see Note) or Parmesan cheese

Bring the chicken broth to a boil. In a small skillet, heat the oil. Add the garlic and sauté until golden and aromatic. Place the bread in a large soup bowl, pour the oil and garlic over it, add the boiling chicken broth, and immediately break the egg into the soup. It will cook in 2 to 3 minutes. Add salt and pepper, and sprinkle with the parsley and cheese.

NOTE: There are dozens of quesos blancos, or white cheeses, which is exactly how the name translates. Some are soft, some fresh, but many aged. Queso blanco generally is mild flavored, though some of the aged ones can be quite tangy. They are found in markets in Florida and in most cities with colonies of residents of Caribbean, Cuban, or Mexican ancestry. Try the cheeses, and choose the one that suits your taste.

GARLIC GALORE

Garlic runs a close third to salt and pepper in popularity as a seasoning in Florida; much of it is dehydrated garlic, garlic powder, or salt. Home-cooks who know the trials of cooking in the warm, humid climate of Florida understand why. Before air-conditioning, moldy garlic, onions, and potatoes were a constant annoyance, and as cooking has become sporadic in many homes women and men go back to their mothers' ploys: garlic powder, dried flakes, or salt in tightly closed containers. We converted most recipes that used garlic powder or salt to fresh garlic.

For those who like the durability of the dried products, the flavor is best developed by soaking the granulated garlic in a little water for 2 or 3 minutes, or moistening the powder before adding it to food. Another solution is to freeze the fresh garlic cloves soon after purchase. The Epicure Market in Miami Beach, catering to sometime cooks in apartments in the nearby Art Deco section, sells garlic by the clove. It is displayed in a jar atop a produce case, and like fresh meat or chicken, a clove of garlic can be bought fresh daily, or as needed.

CALDO GALLEGO
SPANISH BEAN AND COLLARD GREEN SOUP

MAKES 8 TO 10 SERVINGS.

In Ybor City in the early 1900s, this filling soup and Cuban bread were the lifeblood of cigar workers who tried to eat daily for a few cents in order to save so they could bring over fiancées or wives and families from Cuba or Spain. The Columbia Restaurant, which began as a modest soup bar to feed single men, grew to be a mammoth restaurant, as did others. This version of *caldo gallego* is from Cathy Fernandez, who was taught it by the women of her husband's family, who came from Galicia early in the cigar-maker migration.

Buy the freshest and tenderest greens available for this soup—they will make all the difference. You can halve the recipe, but the soup keeps well in the refrigerator or freezer, so we think it worth making a big potful.

1 pound dried great northern
   beans (see Note 1)
Water
4 ounces salt pork, diced
1 large onion, diced
3 cloves garlic, minced
Ham hock, about 1¼ pounds
1 quart chicken broth
1 large bay leaf
Salt to taste
¼ teaspoon freshly ground
   pepper

1 bunch (½ pound) tender
   turnip or collard greens
2 large potatoes, peeled and
   cubed
3½ ounces chorizo sausages,
   sliced or crumbled
   (page 219)
4 to 5 strands saffron, toasted
   (see Note 2), a pinch of bijol,
   or yellow food coloring

Cover the dried beans generously with cold water and soak overnight. Drain, add fresh water to cover by 1 inch, and simmer, covered, until the beans are tender, 1 to 1½ hours. Add hot water while cooking, if needed to keep the beans covered. When done, the beans should be tender and the liquid thick. Boil rapidly, uncovered, to thicken the liquid, if necessary.

In a large pot, sauté the salt pork until almost crisp. Add the onion and garlic and sauté until tender. Add the beans and their liquid, the ham hock, chicken broth, bay leaf, salt, and pepper. Bring to a boil, skimming off the scum that rises to the top. Cover and simmer until the ham is tender, about 1 hour. Discard the bay leaf. Remove the ham hock and, when cool enough to handle, cut off the meat in pieces and return to the soup. Discard the bone. Add more water or chicken broth, if wanted.

Shred the greens and add to the soup along with the potatoes and chorizo. Dip a large spoonful of hot broth from the soup, crumble the saffron into it, and steam over the boiling mixture until it is colored golden. Stir the saffron mixture into the pot. Cover and simmer 15 minutes, or until the potatoes are tender. Serve hot in warmed soup bowls.

NOTE 1: Two 16-ounce cans garbanzo beans can be used in place of the dried beans. Drain the beans, rinse them, and combine with the sautéed salt pork, onion, and garlic, adding water as needed to make a thick soup.

NOTE 2: To toast saffron: Place the paper packet of saffron, found in Spanish markets, or place the strands on a square of foil or parchment on a small baking pan in a preheated 350-degree oven (toaster oven is okay) and heat 5 to 7 minutes, until the saffron is slightly darkened.

THE HERON'S CLAM CHOWDER

MAKES 4 TO 6 SERVINGS.

When Janice Coupe and her family fell in love with Cedar Key and bought an antebellum house on the main street, they cast about for ways to care for an old house needing attention and money. They thought of a small restaurant. The whole family pitched in and restored the house and opened the restaurant, and called it the Heron.

After tasting the Heron's New England–style chowder, billed "fresh clam," we asked Mrs. Coupe where she got clams. "At the packing house," she said, surprised that we did not know. She buys shelled clams and grinds them in a food chopper. This is a home-size version of her recipe.

¼ pound salt pork, diced	4 tablespoons (½ stick) butter
1 cup chopped onions	1 teaspoon salt, or to taste
1 cup diced celery	⅛ teaspoon white pepper
4 cups diced peeled potatoes	½ teaspoon dried leaf thyme
Water	½ teaspoon dried rosemary
4 cups minced clams, fresh	leaves
preferred	Dash hot pepper sauce
2 tablespoons flour	1 cup light cream or
1 can (12 ounces) evaporated milk	half-and-half, or as needed

Sauté the salt pork until crisp in a large Dutch oven. Skim out the pork bits with a slotted spoon and set aside. Add the onions and celery to the drippings, mix well, then add the potatoes and ½ cup water or enough to almost cover the vegetables. Cover and simmer 18 to 20 minutes, until the potatoes and other vegetables are soft. Add the clams and bring to a boil. Blend the flour with ½ cup water until smooth. Add to the soup and cook, stirring, until smooth and thickened, about 2 minutes. Stir in the evaporated milk, butter, salt, pepper, thyme, rosemary, pepper sauce, and the reserved pork bits. Heat, but do not boil. Taste and add more salt, pepper, or other seasonings, if needed. Ladle into warmed soup bowls and add light cream or half-and-half to thin as wished. Serve hot.

FLORIDA CLAMS

Floridians have rediscovered fresh clams. For years, the mollusks were considered a New England food, something that in Florida was food for pelicans and seagulls, or came in cans. Yet clams were living on Florida shores before Europeans came, and were dug up and eaten by Native Americans. In the 1950s and 1960s, severe red-tide blooms killed tons of clams, and few people ate them, anyway, then.

Scientists brought the red tide under control, and today people dine on fresh clams in restaurants everywhere in the state and buy them to prepare at home. The new demand for clams is a facet of an oft-noted upgrading of the Florida palate by well-educated transplants attracted by high-tech industry.

Market development of clams goes on. A plant in Cedar Key, where crab fingers and freshly picked meat were packed in the 1950s and 1960s, today processes clams. A Merritt Island packer introduced fresh clam strips in 1991, and in 1990 a processor on the west coast of Florida tested refrigerated minced fresh clams in cups in commercial kitchens. The chefs voted the product excellent for chowders and clam cakes, and both forms of clams could be in widespread distribution soon.

Meanwhile, intrepid beach folk dig for clams in the sand and chefs and home-cooks serve them in ways that Floridians barely knew a few years ago.

FLORIDA SHRIMP

Tons of shrimp are caught off the coasts of Florida annually, and the boats bring in several varieties for local consumption and for shipping around the country. White and brown shrimp are the most common, and except for shell color, are hard to distinguish from one another. Pink shrimp, another major type, was first discovered near the Dry Tortugas. Some shrimp lovers consider them the most flavorful of all. Rock shrimp, as the name implies, have a very hard shell that is difficult to remove, but the taste and texture are good. (See page 28 for more on rock shrimp.) Royal red shrimp are less common. They are a deep-water shrimp, making them expensive to fish, and you are apt to pay a little more for them. The flesh of royal reds is softer than the others, requiring careful handling and lighter cooking.

Shrimp customarily is frozen aboard the boat within hours of catching, but Floridians can buy it fresh at the docks from short-run shrimpers. Larger boats stay out for several days and cover long distances to bring in huge quantities for shipping to commercial markets.

The modern shrimping industry was born in Fernandina Beach about 1915, when shrimpers switched from in-shore to off-shore hunting for the shellfish. Shrimping has faded in the Amelia Island–Fernandina area, but nets for worldwide use are still woven there, and a few boats still operate.

FRIED SHRIMP WITH COCONUT

Many would name fried shrimp Florida's favorite food, and by any standards, it is exceedingly popular. This version is gussied up by adding coconut or almonds to the batter. Fried shrimp is served with lime or lemon wedges and often a spicy sauce, such as Dat'l Do It.

1½ pounds large shrimp

3 eggs

4 tablespoons all-purpose flour

½ teaspoon salt

¾ to 1 cup shredded fresh (see
    page 159) or frozen unsweet-
    ened coconut or toasted chopped
    almonds

Peanut or vegetable oil for
    frying

Shell and clean the shrimp, leaving the tails intact. To make the shrimp look larger, butterfly them. Cut almost through the center of each shrimp and press it open with your fingers. Dry the shellfish thoroughly, then set aside. Beat the eggs with the flour and salt until smooth. If time allows, let the batter stand 30 minutes before dipping the shrimp. Pour oil to a depth of 2½ to 3 inches in a deep-fat fryer or large saucepan and heat to 365 degrees. Dip the shrimp, one by one, in the batter, drain off the excess, then lightly roll it in the coconut or almonds. Place carefully in the oil, cooking in batches so the shrimp are not crowded. Fry 2 minutes, or until crisp and golden. Drain on paper towels and serve hot.

LAND'S END STEW

MAKES 10 SERVINGS.

Land's End Stew is a Florida relation of Frogmore Stew and other Low Country shrimp or crab boils from the Carolinas and Georgia. It is a hearty meal-in-a-pot, great for outdoor cooking over an open fire or portable gas burner. After cooking, the seafood, sausage, corn on the cob, and sometimes potatoes, are scooped from the liquid onto plates, and eaten with both hands; a messy but satisfying feast. It is also served drained and piled onto newspapers and eaten without plates. This recipe is a favorite of Jeff Stokes, whose family has lived in Florida for generations. A young lawyer in Tampa, he earned a reputation as a good cook, preparing dishes such as this for crowds of friends.

6 quarts water

2 lemons, cut in half and
  seeded

⅔ cup seafood seasoning
  (commercial)

4 tablespoons salt

½ teaspoon ground red pepper
  (cayenne)

4 bay leaves

3 pounds Italian sausage,
  sweet or hot, cut in 2- to
  3-inch links

12 ears corn, shucked and
  broken in half

4 pounds large shrimp,
  unpeeled

In a very large pot bring the water, lemons, seafood seasoning, salt, cayenne pepper, and bay leaves to a boil and cook for 5 minutes. Add the sausage and cook for 10 minutes. Add the corn and cook 5 minutes, then add the shrimp. Bring back to a boil for 1 minute, no longer. Remove from the heat and let stand 5 minutes before serving.

FROGMORE STEW

In Fernandina Beach, at the northeastern corner of the state, this stew is named for the town in South Carolina, where it became famous. Here Polish sausage or kielbasa is cut in 2½-inch links and used in place of the Italian sausage above. Just before serving, a stick of butter and lots of black pepper are added for seasoning.

NAPLES DEVILED CRAB

MAKES 4 TO 6 SERVINGS.

Plenty of fresh crab meat, zesty seasonings, and butter—seafood's flavor-maker—are the secrets of superior deviled crab. It is everywhere, from street vendors in Ybor City to elegant restaurants. Few examples are as pure and loaded with crab as this one from Jacque Elmore, who operated the Fish House in Naples until her death in the 1970s.

1 pound fresh crab meat (claw or
    lump meat)
2 hard-cooked eggs, diced
½ cup fine dry bread crumbs
¾ cup (2 ribs) diced celery
½ cup (1 stick) butter
1 teaspoon prepared Dijon-
    style mustard

⅛ teaspoon hot pepper sauce
1 tablespoon lime or lemon
    juice
½ teaspoon salt
¼ teaspoon freshly ground
    pepper
Lime or lemon wedges

Pick over the crab meat, removing any bits of shell and cartilage. In a large bowl, combine the crab meat, eggs, crumbs, and celery. Melt the butter. Add the mustard, pepper sauce, lime juice, salt, and pepper to the butter. Pour over the crab mixture and toss lightly. Spoon into cleaned crab shells or large scallop baking shells. Deviled crab also can be baked in a shallow baking dish. Refrigerate until shortly before baking, or bake immediately in a preheated 375-degree oven 10 to 12 minutes, or until heated through. Serve 2 crab shells or 1 scallop shell of the deviled crab per person as an entrée. Serve with lime or lemon wedges.

HENRY B. PLANT'S GREAT HOTELS

Henry Plant was born a Connecticut Yankee, but this self-made entrepreneur, who began his career as a deckhand on a steamer, eventually made his name and fortune in the South. He worked in Georgia as the Southern representative of a New York shipping company, and during the Civil War was in charge of express shipments for the Confederacy. Following the war, he was able to capitalize on his status in the South, and find Northern investors to aid in his development of the Plant System, based in Tampa, which became an extensive network of steamship and rail lines.

With the coming of the railroad, Tampa developed into a boomtown, prompting Plant to build several hotels in the area to accommodate the great influx of people and provide business for his railroad. One was the Port Tampa Inn built over the water on stilts, where guests could fish from their windows. Another was the grand Hotel Belleview in nearby Clearwater (now the Belleview Mido), built in 1896, said to be the largest occupied wooden structure in the world. But the most magnificent of all was the Tampa Bay Hotel (now part of the University of Tampa). Opened in 1891, the exotic, Moorish-style structure with its thirteen domes and minarets towering above the hotel, covered six acres and was lavishly furnished with European antiques. A staff of three hundred catered to guests at the 511-room hotel with services that included hair styling, a drugstore, billiards, casino, mineral baths, hunting excursions, dances, teas, rickshaws to transport guests around the grounds and throughout the long hotel corridors, and, most importantly, a restaurant that earned a national reputation for fine food served on Wedgwood china.

The Tampa Bay Hotel's opening ball took place on February 5, 1891. Over two thousand guests arrived by rail, ship, and carriage. They danced to a New York orchestra, drank champagne, and had an elegant dinner, prepared by chefs brought in from all over the country.

BROILED SCALLOPS WITH FRESH TOMATO SALSA

MAKES 4 SERVINGS.

The three major American scallops—sea, bay, and calico—are landed in Florida, and all are excellent. Given a choice, we prefer bay scallops for broiling. This combination of broiled scallops with fresh tomato salsa is fast and easy for busy young working women and men to prepare.

TOMATO SALSA

3 medium tomatoes (12 ounces), peeled, seeded, and diced

1 small onion, minced

1 small jalapeño, seeded and diced

½ teaspoon salt

¼ teaspoon freshly ground pepper

½ teaspoon sugar

½ Persian lime

SCALLOPS

1¼ pounds bay or sea scallops

4 tablespoons (½ stick) butter

1 clove garlic, minced

2 tablespoons minced parsley or cilantro or 1 teaspoon paprika

In the morning or the evening before serving, combine the tomatoes, onion, jalapeño, salt, pepper, and sugar in a small bowl. Mix well. Squeeze the lime juice into the sauce and place the squeezed shell on the sauce. Cover and refrigerate the salsa several hours or overnight. To serve, remove the lime shell.

Butter or spritz a shallow baking pan with butter-flavored nonstick cooking spray. Place the scallops with their juice in the pan. Combine the butter and garlic in a small saucepan and heat until the butter is melted. Stir, then mix lightly with the scallops to coat them well. Broil 4 inches from the source of heat 2 to 3 minutes. Stir gently to turn and coat the scallops with pan juices. Broil 1 to 2 minutes longer, until firm, but not hard, when pressed with a finger or back of a fork.

Spoon the salsa onto a platter or a pool of it onto each plate and place the hot broiled scallops on it. Sprinkle with the parsley, cilantro, or paprika.

SCALLOPING IN CEDAR KEY

The grassy flats off Cedar Key, which juts out into the Gulf one hundred miles north of Tampa Bay, offer some of the best scallop hunting in Florida. The fresh waters pouring into the Gulf from the Suwannee River, a few miles north, and the Waccasassa, to the south, converge to temper the salinity of the Gulf to the specific needs of scallops. In the summer when the tides are high, boats anchored over the flats and tiny specks of scallopers around them are easily sighted from the pier.

To go scalloping with a "Shorty" Hodges or other native fishermen is rare adventure. The captain will advise wearing pants and sneakers so old that you don't mind discarding, since you must trudge through the water.

The run out takes a half hour or so. When the anchor is dropped the scallopers scramble down the boat ladder onto the grassy flat. They slosh to the dinghy, tied behind the boat and filled with an assortment of croker sacks (large burlap bags), galvanized tubs, and buckets. Each person gets a tub, bucket, or croker sack, tied to his belt, to hold the scallops. The tubs float, the buckets are buoyed up by the water, but the sacks are a dead weight, growing heavier as they are weighted down.

To capture a scallop you first have to spot a red object in the sea grass, which is the coral roe showing from the slightly parted shell. In an instant you have to clasp the shell from what you hope is behind. If you grab it from the front, the scallop is likely to snap the shell shut on your finger. You toss the scallop into the sack, tub, or bucket; when the container is filled or too heavy to tow, you slog back to the dinghy trailing twenty-five feet behind the boat and dump the load into it. The dinghy is filled until water almost laps over the gunwale; then, the scallops are piled onto the boat deck.

The party chugs back into the dock, the hunters weary but anticipating a feast. Commercial fishermen, as a rule, shell the mollusks on the way in, discarding the coral. In Europe, the roe is considered a choice morsel. To save it, cut the roe along with the main muscle (the white part), and lift them from the shell together. The coral is cooked quickly with the white meat, or can be poached separately and served as a pretty and delicious garnish to the shellfish.

GROUPER RUSSIAN-STYLE

MAKES 4 SERVINGS.

This fish with a fresh-flavored lemon, egg, and parsley sauce can be found on the menus of Cuban restaurants in Ybor City. It is a refreshing alternative to the heavy tomato, bell pepper, onion, and garlic sauces in other Spanish fish dishes. Snapper, flounder, or any white-meated fish is excellent prepared this way, but grouper is the first choice.

½ cup all-purpose flour

1 egg, beaten

1 teaspoon plus 2 tablespoons
   vegetable oil

2 tablespoons water

½ teaspoon salt

⅛ teaspoon freshly ground
   pepper

¾ cup fresh bread crumbs

4 fillets grouper, flounder,
   or snapper

3 tablespoons butter

1 tablespoon minced parsley

2 tablespoons lemon juice

1 hard-cooked egg, chopped
   fine

Lemon wedges for garnish

Spread the flour on a plate or waxed paper. Beat together the egg, the 1 teaspoon oil, the water, salt, and pepper. Place the crumbs on another plate. Coat the fish fillet with the flour, shaking off the excess; dip it into the egg mixture and let the excess drain off, then coat evenly with the bread crumbs. Brush a heavy skillet or grill with oil, heat, and add the fish in a single layer. Cook over high heat 30 seconds, or until browned, adding oil as needed; turn carefully and cook the second side over medium-high heat 1 minute, or until golden brown. Lower the heat, and cook the fish 3 to 4 minutes longer, until the flesh is opaque but moist when tested with a fork. Remove to a warm platter, and keep warm while cooking the remaining fish, if it is necessary to cook it in batches.

To make the sauce, melt the butter in a small skillet over low heat. Add the parsley and sauté a half minute or so. Add the lemon juice and blend well. Stir in the chopped egg. Pour the sauce over the fish, and garnish with lemon wedges.

FISH FARMING FOR TABLE DELICACIES

Aquaculture in Florida is in its infancy, but chefs already are serving freshwater crawfish, catfish, hybrid striped bass, eels, and tilapia, produced on fish farms. Many markets in the state carry the commercially grown seafood and alligator that are raised for eating.

Production is expected to grow in the 1990s, thanks to the good growing conditions in central and south Florida. Among the species farmed are:

Freshwater crawfish: The red-shelled fish that is beloved in Louisiana has lived wild in Florida for eons, but until it was farmed, was little used for food.

Channel catfish: Another native that has been commercialized, catfish are raised in ponds and fed a ration that gives them firm-textured light meat; they are dressed and packed immediately after netting.

Tilapia: Farmed at the time of the Pharaohs in Egypt, tilapia today are tank-grown in Israel and Taiwan. One species, the Nile perch or blue tilapia, was introduced in Florida in 1963, but the commercial species is the red tilapia. It has a buttery flavor, flaky white meat, and is excellent for broiling, baking, frying, or poaching.

Hybrid striped bass: A cross between the striped and white basses, this bass has a firm texture and flavor similar to freshwater bass. The fillets can be fried, broiled, or grilled.

Eels: Elvers swimming from the Sargasso Sea up freshwater streams to mature are captured by farmers to grow in ponds and tanks; they reach a larger size and have especially delicate meat when raised under controlled conditions. Eels can be smoked, baked, or grilled.

Alligator: Anybody who has eaten alligator talks about it as a feat of bravery, but farm-raised alligator is as easy to buy as going to a fishmarket in most of Florida. Several alligator farms supply restaurants, as well as markets. The tender parts can be fried, sautéed, or grilled and tougher parts are smoked and ground for use in spreads or alligator patties.

SMOKED MULLET

MAKES 4 SERVINGS.

Smoked fish was on the native diet when the Spanish arrived in 1513; nearly five centuries later, Floridians revel in it. Crowds line up at rush hour for tables at Ted Peters Smoked Fish in St. Petersburg, a family-owned cafe since it opened in 1951. Locally netted mullet is the favorite here, but shipped-in salmon is smoked and tourists prefer it. Mackerel also is smoked commercially and sportfishermen smoke marlin and swordfish. Any fish that can be cut into steaks or fillets that don't fall apart on the grill is suitable for smoking. Traditional trimmings for smoked fish are sliced tomato, onion, and pickle. Some cooks add potato salad and coleslaw to the plate.

4 mullets, 1 to 1¼ pounds each
Salt
¼ cup ketchup
¼ cup cider vinegar
¼ cup lime or lemon juice
2 tablespoons prepared
    horseradish
1 tablespoon oil
½ teaspoon hot pepper sauce,
    or to taste
Tomato, sweet onion, and dill
    pickles
Lime or lemon wedges

Do not skin the fish. Have it split almost through and the main bone cut out. The head may be cut off, but the fish will be juicier if the head is left on for cooking. Open the fish like a book, rub lightly with salt, and stack one on top of the other, separating the fish with wax paper. Refrigerate until ready to cook them.

In a small saucepan, combine the ketchup, vinegar, lime or lemon juice, horseradish, oil, and hot sauce. Bring to a boil and simmer 5 minutes to blend the flavors. Cool to room temperature.

Preheat a water-smoker or grill with a hood to moderate, and smoke the fish as directed by the manufacturer. Brush lightly with the sauce two or three times while smoking. Smoke about 1½ hours, until the fish is cooked through, but still moist.

The woods most often used for smoking are hickory, buttonwood in southwest Florida, citrus wood, oak, or Australian pine. Place the dampened chips on a charcoal fire or in the water pan of a smoker when the fish is added, or wrap the smoking material in heavy foil, poke holes in the packet, and place them on the ceramic "coals" of a gas or electric grill.

When the flesh is firm but not dry, remove the fish, cool it to warm, and cut off the heads. Place a fish on each plate, and add a thick tomato slice, onion slice, dill pickles, and lime or lemon. Or chill the fish and reheat it on a greased baking sheet in a 350-degree oven.

Saffron, the most expensive culinary spice, is the classic coloring and flavoring for yellow rice, arroz con pollo, and paella in Florida Spanish cooking. The spice is the hair-like stamens of a crocus plant harvested in Spain. Packing and sorting the delicate strands requires painstaking work, one reason for the outrageous price of saffron. Today several substitutes are available, and some cooks have no qualms about using them.

Achiote seeds (also called annato), *bijol* (powdered annato), turmeric, or yellow food coloring are used in place of saffron. All provide color, and some cooks reinforce the golden color of saffron by using a few drops of annato oil in combination with saffron in yellow rice. Turmeric or food coloring are primarily for looks.

Sticklers for tradition would as soon give up salt as saffron, and many cooks and chefs insist upon thread saffron, suspecting that "powdered saffron" may be a less expensive substitute. Few major spice packers offer powdered saffron, since the dust that escapes into equipment or on workers' clothes can amount to a substantial loss.

Use of annato, a red-orange coloring and faint flavoring, is borrowed from the cooks of the Caribbean. The irregular shaped seeds are available in jars in the Cuban or Caribbean sections of most markets. It is available in tiny packets, each holding enough powder to color four servings of rice.

An easy way to use annato is in an oil, splashed into sauces, rice, or other foods while cooking, and this oil serves as a table sauce with lime juice on avocados. To make it, heat ½ cup olive oil or half vegetable and olive oil until warm. Add 1 tablespoon dry annato seeds and simmer 5 minutes, or until the oil turns bright red. Cool slightly and strain the oil into a small bottle. Cap and store it in a cool, dry cupboard. The oil will keep for several weeks at room temperature, and longer in the refrigerator.

ARROZ CON POLLO
YELLOW RICE WITH CHICKEN

MAKES 4 LARGE OR 8 SMALL SERVINGS.

This chicken and rice combination is the best-known food of Hispanic origin, often the first "foreign" dish for newcomers and tourists to taste. To many of them, arroz con pollo becomes daily food, and hundreds of restaurants list it on the menu daily.

Saffron colors and seasons the best chicken and yellow rice, though some Spanish cooks use less expensive substitutes. In this version, the saffron is mulled in hot broth, before adding it to the rice to release the flavor and aroma. This dish customarily is a one-dish meal, though a green vegetable may accompany it.

8 chicken thighs or 4 breasts, split

1 ounce salt pork, chopped fine

1 tablespoon olive oil

1 large onion, chopped

1 red bell pepper, seeded and diced

1 large tomato or ¾ cup drained canned Italian-style tomatoes, chopped fine

3 cloves garlic, minced

1½ cups long-grain rice

1 bay leaf, crumbled, with rib removed

2 teaspoons salt, or less if broth is salty

¼ teaspoon hot pepper sauce

2½ cups chicken broth

8 to 10 saffron threads

1 cup shelled fresh or frozen green peas

Skin the chicken, if desired. Heat the salt pork and oil in a large Dutch oven until sizzling. Add the chicken and brown it lightly on both sides. Remove the chicken and set aside. Add the onion, bell pepper, and tomato to the pan drippings, and sauté until the onion is almost tender. Add the garlic and sauté a minute or two longer, stirring well. Add the rice, bay leaf, salt, and pepper sauce. Sauté and stir until the rice is opaque and coated with the fat. Add the broth, bring to a boil, and crumble the saffron into the boiling broth. Mix well, then arrange chicken on the rice. Cover tightly and simmer 20 minutes. Fluff the rice, sprinkle the peas over all, cover, and simmer 5 to 8 minutes longer. Spoon the rice onto a platter or into a large serving bowl and arrange the chicken around it. Pull up some of the peas and pieces of red pepper and tomato to the top for color accent. Serve hot.

CACEROLA CUBANA DE ARROZ Y CALABAZA

CHICKEN AND RICE CASSEROLE WITH SQUASH AND SAUSAGE

MAKES 4 SERVINGS.

Calabaza, the Caribbean pumpkin, generally is a side dish in Spanish-Floridian meals, but it contributes a bright golden color and mellow flavor to combinations such as this. In Key West, Tampa, or Miami's Cuban section, the *calabaza* is easy to find, but when it is unavailable, *señoras* substitute butternut or deep-orange winter squash.

1 cup peeled and cubed *calabaza* or butternut squash

1 tablespoon olive or vegetable oil

½ cup (2 ounces) crumbled chorizo (page 219)

1 small yellow onion, diced

½ green bell pepper, seeded and diced

1 clove garlic, minced

1 Florida sweet onion or 2 small green onions or scallions, sliced thin

1 cup long-grain rice

1½ to 2 cups chicken broth

1 cup cubed cooked chicken

Salt and freshly ground pepper

8 to 10 saffron threads

2 firm-ripe bananas, sliced diagonally

1 to 2 teaspoons butter

Cook the squash until barely tender in a small amount of water or in a microwave. Drain, if necessary, and set aside. Heat the oil in a large deep skillet. Add the chorizo and sauté until lightly browned. Pour off most of the drippings. Add the yellow onion, green pepper, garlic, and sweet onion. Sauté until the onions are tender but not browned. Add the rice, stir to coat with the drippings, then add the 1½ cups chicken broth; bring to a boil and gently mix in the cooked *calabaza,* chicken, salt, and pepper to taste. Ladle up a large spoonful of the boiling broth and crumble the saffron into it. Hold over the steaming pot until the spoonful of broth is tinted deep gold, then stir into the pot. Cover and simmer 15 minutes. Taste and if the rice is dry but not quite done, add ¼ to ½ cup of broth, cover, and simmer 5 minutes longer.

Meanwhile, sauté the bananas in the butter in a small skillet until lightly browned, turning to brown both sides. Pile the rice mixture onto a platter and garnish with the fried bananas.

PASTITSIO

MAKES 8 TO 12 SERVINGS.

At potluck suppers in Tarpon Springs and other Greek settlements, diners flock to the dishes of *pastitsio,* a macaroni and meat sauce combination with an egg sauce and Parmesan cheese on top. Chances are that the recipes used were handed down through several generations in America, and some were not written down. But non-Greeks like *pastitsio,* too, as an alternative to lasagne. The touch of cinnamon is the clue to the Greek origin of this dish. The egg sauce and cheese topping is its crowning glory. Some cooks eliminate the topping, and the dish isn't bad, really, but not authentic.

EGG SAUCE

5 tablespoons butter	**Pinch nutmeg**
5 tablespoons flour	**3 cups milk**
1 teaspoon salt	**2 eggs, slightly beaten**
¼ teaspoon freshly ground pepper	

PASTITSIO

2 tablespoons oil, preferably olive oil	**¼ teaspoon cinnamon**
1 large onion, chopped	**½ cup fine dry bread crumbs**
1½ pounds lean ground beef	**1 pound elbow macaroni, freshly cooked, drained, and still hot**
1 can (10½ ounces) tomato purée	
1 can (6 ounces) tomato paste	**1 egg, beaten**
1 teaspoon salt	**1 cup freshly grated Parmesan cheese**
½ teaspoon freshly ground pepper	

To make the egg sauce, melt the butter in a large saucepan. Add the flour, salt, pepper, and nutmeg. Gradually stir in 2½ cups of the milk. Cook, stirring, over moderate heat until smooth, thickened, and boiling. Add the remaining ½ cup milk to the beaten eggs and stir into the hot sauce. Cook and stir over moderate heat until it is thickened, about 1 minute. Do not boil the sauce after the eggs are added, or it may curdle. Remove the sauce from the heat and set aside.

To prepare the casserole: Preheat the oven to 375 degrees. In a large skillet, heat the oil. Add the onion and sauté until translucent. Add the meat and cook and stir until lightly browned. Stir in the tomato purée and paste, salt, pepper, and cinnamon. Simmer, covered, 30 minutes. Mix in the bread crumbs.

In a large bowl or the pot in which the macaroni was cooked, beat the egg to blend the yolk and white. Add the macaroni and toss it well.

Butter a 13×9×2-inch baking dish. Spread half the macaroni in the baking dish; add the meat sauce and ¼ cup of the Parmesan, then the remaining macaroni. Spoon the egg sauce over the dish, letting as much run down into the dish as possible, pushing the macaroni back from the sides with a spatula to encourage generous moistening by the sauce. Sprinkle with the remaining Parmesan cheese.

Bake until hot and bubbly, 30 to 40 minutes. Remove from the oven and let cool about 10 minutes to absorb the juices. Cut in squares to serve.

NOTE: This is a party-size recipe, but can be easily divided in half; reserve the remaining half cans of tomato purée and paste for soups, sauces, or other dishes.

EARLY CATTLE ROUNDUPS

Recalling cow hunting in the late 1890s and early 1900s, C. T. Tooke, a longtime resident of Fort Myers and a cowman for many years, related the following account of range life:

Many of the cow hunters were youngsters who liked adventure, to see new places. They thrived on hard work and ate like horses. They kept on the go from dawn to dusk and when they lay down at night on the ground, they never moved until morning. In the summer they covered themselves with mosquito nets, in the winter they kept warm under a horse blanket.

On the big drives a long covered oxcart went along to carry the grub. Nothing fancy, just solid food, a barrel of flour, a couple of sacks of bacon and lard, a demi-john of syrup, slabs of salt pork and lots of coffee. This was something the men simply had to have—coffee. And lots of it. They never drank less than three or four quarts a day.

Usually when we started we slaughtered a young fat steer and sometimes we killed a couple more along the way. Cattle were cheap in those days, and it didn't make much difference whether we ate a few of them or not. To give us a variety of meat, we almost always managed to shoot a couple of deer and also plenty of wild turkey. Game was mighty plentiful way back then.

When we got to Punta Rassa, the young fellows usually cut up a bit. They were paid off in gold and had some mighty big poker games. And they drank much more than a little Cuban rum which they got for fifty cents a gallon.

from *Florida Cowman,*
A History of Cattle Raising by Joe A. Akerman, Jr.,
Florida Cattlemen's Association, Kissimmee, Florida, 1976

CUBAN-STYLE ROAST PORK

The essentials of a proper Cuban sandwich are first quality roast pork and fresh Cuban bread. The pork is marinated, roasted, then cooled and sliced paper thin for a Cuban sandwich, which is filled with three or four thin slices of the pork, plus baked ham, usually Genoa salami, and Swiss-style cheese. At home, the pork often is served hot, with leftovers reserved for the sandwiches. Floridians use sour oranges in place of limes; if you can get the oranges, their flavor is wonderful.

2 pounds boned and tied well-trimmed pork loin	**Freshly ground black pepper to taste**
1 large clove garlic, cut in slivers	**Juice of 3 limes or Seville (sour) oranges and the shell of 11**
teaspoon dried oregano	**Salt**

Slit the meat in several places and push a bit of garlic into each cut. Rub the roast with oregano and black pepper. To be authentic, use plenty of pepper. Place in a deep bowl. Add the lime or sour orange juice and the shell of 1 fruit after juicing it. Marinate in the refrigerator several hours or overnight.

Preheat the oven to 325 degrees. Remove the meat from the marinade and place it on a rack in a shallow roasting pan. Rub the meat generously with salt. Roast 1½ to 2 hours, until a meat thermometer inserted near the center registers 160 degrees. To serve hot, place the pork on a platter, cover with foil to keep hot, and let it rest 15 to 20 minutes before carving. For sandwiches, chill the roast and and slice thin.

CHORIZO

MAKES 2½ POUNDS.

This is the name for spiced sausage in Mexican, Caribbean, and European Spanish cooking, and the seasonings vary by region. Since Florida chorizo is difficult to find in many places, we provide this recipe. It is adapted from the recipe in Bruce Aidells and Denis Kelly's *Hot Links and Country Flavors*, which is an excellent California-style chorizo. We make it more Floridian with added paprika and garlic, typical of the chorizo in Key West and Ybor City.

We take other liberties, using salted fatback because few butchers offer fresh fatback for sale. The chorizo can be stuffed into casings, if you like, but we feel this task is unnecessary, since chorizo nearly always is broken up for use in cooking.

1½ pounds lean boneless pork
    loin or butt
½ pound skinned salt fatback
2 cloves garlic, minced
1 small red chile, dried or fresh,
    seeded and crumbled or
    minced

2 teaspoons paprika
½ teaspoon coarsely ground
    black pepper
½ teaspoon salt, or to taste
¼ cup red wine vinegar

Have the fresh pork ground. Grind the salt pork yourself, so you can desalt it before you do so. Rinse the salt fatback thoroughly in cold water, wiping off as much salt as possible. Cut in strips and process a few at a time in a food processor until chopped, adding more strips and scraping down the sides of the container until all the fatback is ground and smooth with a few flecks in it.

With your hands, using plastic gloves if you wish, mix the fresh pork, ground fatback, the garlic, chile, and the remaining seasonings. To mix evenly, squeeze the mixture through your hands, as a child squeezes a glob of modeling clay, then work in the vinegar.

When the mixture appears smooth and well blended, pinch off a tiny blob and sauté it in a skillet. Taste it and add more salt or other sea-

Chorizo (continued)

sonings, if needed. Divide the mixture into 3- and 4-ounce portions, wrapping each in a fat sausage shape in waxed paper. Freeze, then loosely pack the packets in coffee cans with tight-fitting lids (easy to locate in a freezer) or freezer bags, close tightly, and return to the freezer. Plan to use chorizo in 6 weeks.

FAST SUPPER YBOR CITY STYLE

Many an impromptu supper of chorizo and eggs has saved the day for busy women and men in Ybor City and other Hispanic areas. To prepare it, crumble 3 to 4 ounces of chorizo into a skillet. Sauté it over a moderate fire until the sausage is dry and crumbly. Pour off most of the fat, and add 6 or 8 eggs that have been mixed with a quarter cupful of water or cream. Stir the mixture over low heat for 5 minutes or so, until the eggs are soft-scrambled, for one of the tastiest suppers you've ever had. Toasted Cuban bread and butter are the appropriate accompaniments.

GREEK LEG OF LAMB

MAKES 6 TO 8 SERVINGS.

Florida's Greek communities retain many of the food traditions of their homeland isles. In this recipe, typical Greek seasonings are rubbed onto the lamb, imparting the distinctive East-meets-West flavors of Greece.

1 leg of lamb, 5 to 6 pounds
4 garlic cloves, peeled and
    cut in slivers
½ cup olive oil
½ cup fresh lemon juice
2 teaspoons dried oregano

2 teaspoons dried thyme
2 teaspoons dried mint
½ teaspoon salt
½ teaspoon freshly ground
    pepper

Preheat the oven to 450 degrees. Make slits in the lamb with a small knife and insert a sliver of garlic in each incision. Combine the oil, lemon juice, oregano, thyme, mint, salt, and pepper and rub all over the lamb. Put the lamb on a rack in a baking pan and roast for 20 minutes. Reduce the oven temperature to 350 degrees and continue to roast the lamb until a meat thermometer inserted near the center of the lamb reaches an internal temperature of 130 to 140 degrees for rare, 140 to 150 degrees for medium, or 150 to 160 degrees for well done. Remove the lamb from the oven and transfer to a hot platter. Let rest for 10 minutes before carving.

COOKING IN THE 1890S—A MEMOIR

Whole black-eyed peas, whole string beans, cabbage cut in quarters, turnip and mustard greens usually were overcooked by boiling with a big chunk of white or smoked bacon until the bacon was tender. Coleslaw was chopped in a wooden bowl with a one or two-bladed knife. Scallions were eaten alone or cut up with tomatoes and cucumbers. Green corn, boiled on the cob, was cut off the cob and fried or creamed. . . .Tomatoes were pear-shaped, about the size of a man's thumb, bright red, juicy and seedy. They made good ketchup with homemade vinegar. Bottles were sealed with a wax made from beeswax and resin from the pine trees and squares of clean cloth. Pepper sauce was a bottle filled with small hot peppers (both green and red) and vinegar—a fixture on every dining table.

from *Life in Florida Since 1886*
by Emma N. Gaylord, Hurricane House, Miami, 1969

SQUASHES OF THE ISLANDS

Calabaza (pronounced kah-la-*bah*-zah), the pumpkin of Cuba, Jamaica, and other Caribbean islands, has little resemblance to the milk pumpkin that is used for pies in this country. The *calabaza* is boiled, mashed, and served as a side dish, seasoned with salt, pepper, and butter or oil, and garlic. It has a brilliant color, and the taste resembles that of the cushaw, a winter squash favored by farmers in this country until more flavorful squashes were developed. The *calabaza* is rather large, so it is usually cut in halves or quarters for sale. It has a thick greenish-beige rind, golden flesh that deepens to a rich orange color as it cooks, and a center cavity filled with seeds. To prepare it, scoop out and discard the seeds, and cut the meat into cubes. Since the rind is tough, it is easier to peel *calabaza* after cutting it. Cook it in a small amount of water until tender for use in casseroles, as a hot vegetable, or cold salad.

Chayote, a pale green, pear-shaped squash with three or four prominent lobes, is a mild-flavored summer squash. Chayote is the Cuban-American name for it, but it is called *christophine* by those of Dominican and Haitian origin, and *chocho* in Jamaica; in Louisiana and the southern United States it is known as mirliton.

The tender young squash, when cooked lightly, is served as a vegetable or salad, and with a meaty stuffing is a satisfying entrée. Young specimens have tender skins and seeds that are cooked and eaten with the flesh. Tough skin on an older chayote is peeled and discarded along with the long slender seed, if it is too tough for eating.

Cooks of Spanish origin use zucchini, summer crookneck, and pattypan squashes as a vegetable. A favorite way to cook zucchini or crookneck squash is with fresh whole kernel corn, onions, garlic, tomato, and okra for a Spanish-Southern American take-off on ratatouille.

COLIFLOR VINAGRETA

CAULIFLOWER VINAIGRETTE WITH CAPERS

MAKES 6 SERVINGS.

The sauce makes cauliflower an exciting dish to serve on the side with meats, as a salad, or as an appetizer. Salt is not used in the dressing, as the capers provide as much salt as most diners want in this dish.

1 head cauliflower

SALSA VINAGRETA

¼ teaspoon freshly ground
   pepper
2 tablespoons minced onion
2 teaspoons minced parsley
2 tablespoons red wine vinegar
1 tablespoon water

3 tablespoons olive oil
½ 3-ounce bottle capers,
   drained
Leaf lettuce or other greens
   for garnish

Break the cauliflower apart into flowerets and steam it until tender, but not mushy. Start testing it with a fork after 7 minutes to guard against overcooking. Meanwhile, prepare the sauce. Combine the pepper, onion, and 1 teaspoon of the parsley in a small bowl. Stir in the vinegar until the pepper is distributed well, then beat in the water and oil. Add the capers. Place the cauliflower in a bowl, add the dressing, and toss well. Let stand 30 minutes before serving.

Spoon the cauliflower mixture onto a serving platter or individual plates, sprinkle with the remaining 1 teaspoon of parsley, and tuck greens around the edges. Cauliflower Vinaigrette is at its best served at room temperature or barely warm.

BLACK BEANS AND WHITE RICE

MAKES 6 SERVINGS.

A *sofrito* (aromatic vegetables cooked in oil or with salt pork) is to black beans and other Spanish-Floridian dishes what a roux is to Cajun and Creole cookery. The slow sauté of onions, bell peppers, garlic, and, sometimes, celery in fat extracts maximum flavor to give life to the bland-flavored beans. White rice is traditional with black beans, and is specified in Ybor City or Key West, where almost everything else goes with yellow rice.

2 cups (12 ounces) dried black
    beans
Water
3 cloves garlic, or to taste
2 medium onions
2 small green or red bell
    peppers, seeded and cut in
    small squares
¼ cup diced salt pork or
    country ham
1 tablespoon olive oil

2 teaspoons salt, or to
    taste
½ teaspoon freshly ground
    pepper
2 tablespoons cider or red wine
    vinegar
3 cups hot cooked white rice
Thinly sliced green or minced
    yellow onion for garnish
Sieved hard-cooked egg
    (optional)

Pick over the beans, removing any debris; rinse and drain them. Place in a large bowl with water to cover by at least 2 inches. Cover and soak overnight. Drain the beans and place in a large pot. Add water to cover by at least 1½ inches, 1 clove garlic, minced, 1 onion, chopped roughly, and 1 green pepper, chopped. Bring to a boil, cover, and simmer 1 hour, or until the beans are tender but not mushy. Add hot water if needed to keep the beans floating in liquid, but when done the mixture should be thick. Do not add salt until the beans are tender.

Meanwhile, heat the diced salt pork or ham with the oil in a large skillet. Add the remaining onion, minced, the green pepper, and 2 cloves garlic, put through a press or chopped fine. Sauté until the onion is tender and the vegetables are coated with oil. Add the mixture (*sofrito*), the salt, and pepper to the beans. Cover and simmer 30 to 40 minutes, until the beans are soft and the fragrance of onion, garlic, and bell pepper is evident. Mash a few beans against the side of the pot to thicken the stew. Stir in the vinegar, bring to a boil, and cook, stirring, for a couple of minutes. Taste and add more seasonings, if needed.

Serve the hot beans over the rice with bowls of minced onion and chopped hard-cooked egg for garnish. Black beans and rice are served as a first course or a side dish with grilled poultry and meats. On occasion, the beans are cooked with added oil and no salt pork and the dish is served as the entrée in a vegetarian meal.

ORANGE RED PEPPER BROWN RICE

MAKES 4 TO 6 SERVINGS.

This combination enlivens the taste and color of a chicken or turkey dinner, and some serve orange rice in place of stuffing with a holiday bird.

2 tablespoons olive or vegetable oil

1 large red bell pepper, seeded and cubed

2 green onions or scallions or 1 Florida sweet onion, minced

1½ cups brown rice

1½ cups hot chicken broth

1½ cups orange juice

½ teaspoon salt, or to taste

2 teaspoons shredded orange zest

2 small oranges, peeled and cut in ¼-inch slices

Heat the oil in a large heavy saucepan. Add the red pepper and sauté a minute or two. Add the onions and stir over low heat for 2 or 3 minutes, until wilted. Add the rice and cook and stir until the rice is coated with oil and opaque. Add the chicken broth, orange juice, salt, and orange zest. Cover, and simmer 40 minutes. If the rice is tender and the broth absorbed, it is done. Cook a few minutes longer, if necessary, to render the rice tender, adding more hot broth, water, or orange juice, if needed. Turn out on a platter and garnish with the orange slices.

CUBAN BREAD

The daily bread of Hispanic Florida is crisp-crusted, a loaf with a slightly flattened top to cut in slabs for the ubiquitous Cuban sandwich. Fresh bread is served at lunch and dinner, and a chunk of warmed bread, lavishly buttered, and *café con leche* is breakfast for Cuban-Floridians.

In Key West, bread used to come from the brick ovens three or four times a day, and many folk bought warm bread at each baking. In the Keys, banana leaves line the ovens and in Tampa a palm frond is laid along the top of each loaf before baking. The moistness of the greenery promotes the crustiness and the greens lining the bricks keep the bread from sticking.

In Tampa, the loaf is shaped about 36 inches long and is called Yard Bread. In south Florida, the standard loaf is 18 to 24 inches long. Another bread, a dense chalky white loaf, called Creole or Haitian, is found in the Miami area. It is excellent with foods and for breakfast, but not for Cuban sandwiches.

Hispanics rarely bake bread, but depend on commercial bakeries for it. Bakers were among the first artisans to set up shop in the great migration from Havana in 1959 and 1960. A recipe is provided for readers who wish to make authentic Cuban sandwiches and cannot buy appropriate bread. Day-old Cuban bread is the base for a famous pudding of Key West and makes a custardy French toast.

HOME-BAKED CUBAN BREAD

MAKES 2 TO 3 LOAVES.

To get the crisp crust that is typical of this bread, use a baking stone or pizza tile, a pan of hot water set below the bread, and spray water into the oven periodically while the bread is baking. Cuban bakers introduce dampness by lining the brick ovens with banana leaves or laying palm fronds on tops of the loaves. If you can get unsprayed banana leaves or palm fronds from a florist, use them, but washed corn husks, grape leaves, or other nontoxic foliage can be used in place of the tropical greenery.

2 cups very warm water (120 to 130 degrees)	5 to 6 cups flour, preferably bread flour
2 packages active dry yeast	Corn husks, nontoxic leaves, or corn meal (for the pan)
1 tablespoon sugar	
2 teaspoons salt	

Pour the water into a large bowl. Add the yeast, sugar, and salt. Stir well, and let stand until bubbly, about 5 minutes. Mix in 2 cups of the flour with a wooden spoon, then the remaining flour by the cupful, working with the spoon, then floured hands. Add more flour until the dough leaves the sides of the bowl and is no longer sticky.

Turn out onto a floured surface and knead until smooth and elastic, about 8 minutes. Add more flour as needed to prevent sticking. Place in a warm buttered bowl. Turn to butter the top, and cover with waxed paper and a kitchen towel. Let rise in a warm place until doubled, about 30 minutes.

Punch down the dough and turn out onto the floured surface. Invert the bowl over the dough and let it rest 10 minutes; then shape into 2 or 3 long thin loaves. Line the baking stone or sheet with leaves or sprinkle with corn meal to prevent sticking. Place the loaves on the leaves or meal and, with a sharp knife, slash a cross at the center of each loaf. If using palm fronds, trim off the long leaves and rinse the remaining rib and short-cut leaves in cold water. Shake off the water, and place a frond lightly on top of each loaf.

Place the bread in a cold oven set at 400 degrees. Bake 45 minutes, or until golden brown and the bread sounds hollow when the bottom is thumped. Every 6 to 8 minutes while baking, spray a fine mist of water, using a laundry mister or well-washed spray bottle, into the oven.

Cool thoroughly. Cuban bread is best the day it is baked. Or freeze extras, packing the cooled bread in two large plastic bags or wrapping it airtight in heavy-duty aluminum foil; label and freeze it. Thaw it inside the wrapping, unwrap it, place it on a baking sheet, and heat it in a preheated 350-degree oven for 10 to 15 minutes.

THE CUBAN SANDWICH

Hispanics and other Floridians are passionate about the integrity of Cuban sandwiches.

It is not just another "sub" or "hero," they are quick to tell you. The bread is not a bun, but a five- to eight-inch length of Cuban bread, cut diagonally, and split to receive the fillings. French bread tastes right, but is not flat enough.

The bread is spread with yellow mustard, and filled with thinly sliced roast pork, ham, Genoa salami, Swiss cheese, and sliced sour or dill pickle. The meats and cheese are layered generously and poke out the sides a bit, but the sandwich is not overstuffed. Waitresses are apt to ask, "Pressed or plain?" To press it, a sandwich is brushed with pork drippings and heated in a grill with a fold-down top that flattens and heats it.

The no-nos in this sandwich are important to aficionados. It is not a repository for leftover roast beef, turkey, chicken, or other leftovers. At the Valencia Garden Restaurant in Tampa, a Cuban sandwich has no mayonnaise, lettuce, or tomato. Adela Gonzmart, of the Columbia Restaurant in Ybor City, says lettuce and tomato are optional—but never mayonnaise. Butter and/or mustard are also optional, she says.

REMEMBERING CUBAN SANDWICHES

Tony Pizzo, son of Sicilian immigrants, was born in Ybor City in 1912. He has written three books on the heritage of Ybor City, and founded and served as the first president of the Tampa Historical Society. Pizzo remembers that in the old days Cuban sandwiches were shorter than they are now, "just the right size for a good lunch." Mustard was used, never mayonnaise, with a layer of ham, Swiss cheese, sliced roast pork, salami, and dill pickle, thinly sliced lengthwise. The bread was warm but not toasted. A slice of ham was studded with cloves and pressed with a hand-iron first heated on the stove. When the ham was warm, it was trimmed of fat, the cloves removed, then the ham was cut in strips, ready to go on the Cuban bread. "Sandwiches were made one at a time and it used to be that you stood on the sidewalk in front of the shop and ordered through an opening in a glass window. When it was ready, it was wrapped in white paper and handed through the window to you." Those were the days.

INDIAN FRY BREAD

MAKES 4 TO 6 PIECES.

The Seminoles and the Miccosukees make crisp, fried bread by making a dough of self-rising flour and water, kneading the dough, patting it by hand into thin pieces about four inches in diameter, then frying it in oil until puffy and brown. Variations include pumpkin or sweet potato fry bread, or for an Indian burger, cooked ground beef is combined with the dough before frying.

Seminole medicine man Bobby Henry oversees the forty-one-acre Tampa reservation referred to by many as "Bobby's Seminole Village." His daughter Barbara gave us her recipes for basic fry bread, sweet potato, and pumpkin fry bread that we have adapted to smaller portions.

3 cups self-rising flour	**Vegetable oil for frying**
1 cup water	

Put the flour in a large bowl, and add the water a little at a time. Blend together well and knead until the dough is soft and elastic, not sticky. Cut the dough into 4 to 6 pieces and flatten on your palms until ¼ to ½ inch thick and approximately 4 inches in diameter. Heat 2 inches of oil in a heavy skillet, add the dough pieces, and fry until puffed and golden brown on each side, turning once. Drain on absorbent paper and serve plain or with butter.

SWEET POTATO OR PUMPKIN FRY BREAD

MAKES 4 LARGE OR 10 TO 12 SMALL PIECES.

1 cup self-rising flour
1 cup puréed sweet potatoes or
  pumpkin, fresh or canned.
  Pumpkin pie filling may be used,
  but omit sugar.

¼ cup sugar, or to taste
Vegetable oil for frying

Mix and fry as for Indian Fry Bread. Serve hot with butter and syrup. Or, make smaller sizes, dust with confectioners' sugar, and serve for dessert or snacks.

INDIAN BURGER

MAKES 4 TO 6 BURGERS.

Dough for Indian Fry Bread
  (see page 231)
¼ pound ground beef

¼ cup chopped onion
Salt and freshly ground
  pepper

Cook the ground beef and onion together in a skillet until done. Season with salt and pepper to taste. Drain and set aside. Cut basic fry bread dough into 4 to 6 pieces, and flatten each piece ¼ inch thick. Divide the hamburger mixture and put in the middle of each piece, fold the dough to enclose the meat, and press the edges together to seal. Fry for 2 to 3 minutes on each side until golden brown, remove, and let drain on absorbent paper before serving. Cut the top open for additional seasoning or ketchup, or barbecue sauce.

GRAPEFRUIT BISCUITS

MAKES 8 TO 10 BISCUITS.

In 1823, a French count, Dr. Odette Philippe, planted the first grapefruit in Florida, in Safety Harbor on Tampa Bay. Since that first planting, Florida has become number one in production, providing more than 50 percent of the world's grapefruit.

In citrus-growing areas especially, the juice is used in a variety of recipes, for everything from salad dressings to pies. Amanda Hicks, who works as a cook for citrus growers Ginger and Atlee Davis, uses grapefruit juice from their backyard fruit in this recipe for biscuits, which turn out light and flaky.

1½ cups flour	3 tablespoons shortening
1 teaspoon baking powder	½ cup grapefruit juice
½ teaspoon salt	

Preheat the oven to 400 degrees. Sift the flour, baking powder, and salt into a bowl. Cut in the shortening until the mixture resembles coarse crumbs. Slowly add the grapefruit juice, mixing well. Turn the dough onto a floured board and knead lightly. Roll out the dough ¼ inch thick. Cut with a 2- to 2¼-inch round cutter. Place rounds on an ungreased baking sheet and bake for 15 to 18 minutes, until brown. Serve hot with butter.

HONEY BUTTER

Florida could very well be called the "land of milk and honey," given that it is a major honey-producing state. From the well-known orange blossom variety to the unique tupelo, locally produced honey is found in abundance throughout the state. Biscuits and honey are popular with almost any meal. Caroline learned as a child to poke a hole in the side of a hot biscuit with her thumb and fill it with honey or honey butter, a simple mixture of equal parts honey and softened butter, beaten together until blended and creamy. It is also good on muffins, pancakes, and waffles. The payoff in Caroline's method is that since the biscuit isn't cut, the honey doesn't drip from around the sides.

TARPON SPRINGS—STYLE RICE PUDDING

MAKES 6 TO 8 SERVINGS.

A dusting of cinnamon and flavoring of lemon zest marks the rice pudding of Greek mamas and grandmamas. This recipe is inspired by the dessert that Mama Pappas used to bake for the family restaurant in Tarpon Springs. The original Louis Pappas restaurant overlooking the Anclote River catered to the Greek sponge divers who settled the town. Tourists soon discovered it, and the restaurant has moved to larger quarters a few blocks east, nearer the northward bound freeway from Tampa.

½ cup rice, preferably short-
grain
1 cup boiling water

1 quart milk
½ cup sugar
Zest of ½ lemon, slivered

1 teaspoon cornstarch	1 tablespoon butter
1 teaspoon cold water	Ground cinnamon
1 egg yolk, lightly beaten	

Place the rice in a 2-quart saucepan, add the boiling water, cover, and cook over low heat 10 minutes, or until the liquid is absorbed. Add the milk and bring to a boil, stirring now and then; lower the heat and simmer 30 minutes, stirring often to prevent scorching. The pudding should be creamy and soft at this point. Add the sugar, lemon zest, and the cornstarch blended into the 1 teaspoon cold water. Cook and stir 10 minutes, or until smooth. Remove the pudding from the heat and stir 2 large spoonfuls of the hot mixture into the beaten egg yolk. Add the egg yolk mixture to the pudding with the butter and cook over moderate heat, stirring, 2 minutes. Spoon the pudding into individual dessert bowls and sprinkle lightly with the cinnamon. Serve warm, or cover and chill the puddings before serving. Top with whipped cream, if desired.

STRAWBERRY AMBROSIA

A turn-of-the-century variation of Florida's classic dessert with oranges is this one made with another important state crop, strawberries. In a glass bowl, alternate layers of large, capped berries and coarsely chopped pineapple. Sprinkle confectioners' sugar and grated coconut between each layer. Over the top, pour a cup of fresh orange juice. Serve cold.

RUM SPANISH FLAN WITH CARAMELIZED ORANGES

MAKES 8 TO 10 SERVINGS.

There's no contest for the top dessert of Spanish Florida: baked caramel custard unmolded to show its golden crown. The rule in a Spanish kitchen that you can't use too many eggs makes a flan that stands up handsomely, and is easier to work with than a *crème caramel*, which may be so creamy that it relaxes on the plate. Nuns in the first mission in St. Augustine probably brought this style of dessert to Florida almost 450 years ago. Latter-day Hispanics brought their versions from the Caribbean and Europe. A Florida flan has a velvety texture and can be cut in pretty slices. The caramelized oranges with it are a new wrinkle, and a good one. Flan usually is served as is with a bit of the caramel spooned over it.

CUSTARD

1⅔ cups sugar	2 12-ounce cans evaporated
3 tablespoons water	milk
8 large eggs	2 tablespoons dark rum
Pinch salt	

CARAMELIZED ORANGES

1 large orange, peeled and sliced ¼ inch thick	⅓ cup water
	1 tablespoon dark rum
1 cup sugar	

Butter a 9×5-inch loaf pan. Place the ⅔ cup sugar in a large heavy skillet and stir over moderate heat until it turns golden. Work out any lumps, taking care not to let the sugar burn. Stir in the water with a long-handled spoon (the hot syrup will spatter). Cook, stirring, a minute or two, until blended. Pour into the prepared loaf pan, tilt the pan to coat the sides and bottom, and set aside.

Preheat the oven to 325 degrees. Place a baking dish large enough to hold the loaf pan in the oven. Pour hot water to a depth of ½ inch into the baking dish. In a medium-size bowl, beat the eggs with the remaining 1 cup sugar until blended. Add the salt and stir in the undiluted evaporated milk and the rum. Mix well and pour over the caramel in the loaf pan. Place the loaf pan in the baking dish with water in the oven. Bake 1½ hours, or until a table knife inserted in the center comes out clean. Remove the pan from the water bath and cool the custard, then chill it overnight or for at least 8 hours.

Meanwhile, prepare the oranges. Cut the orange slices crosswise into half circles. Place the sugar and water in a large heavy skillet. Cook and stir over moderate heat until golden brown. Add the oranges to the hot caramel. Using tongs or a spatula, turn to coat them with the caramel. If the caramel sticks, stir in a bit more water. Sprinkle with the rum and cool the mixture.

To turn out the flan, loosen it around the edges with a thin-bladed knife, invert a platter over the pan, and invert it quickly, so as not to lose any of the caramel; lift off the loaf pan. Garnish the platter with the caramelized oranges or pass them separately. Slice the flan to serve. Refrigerate any leftovers and serve within a day or two.

BANANA BITES

MAKES 3 TO 4 SNACK SERVINGS.

Caroline remembers as a child how her family would drive to Tampa to watch banana boats from South America dock and unload their cargo down long conveyor belts. The boatmen would sell bananas to onlookers. One way her mother used them is for these crispy fritters that practically melt in your mouth. Caroline now makes them for her sons, Andy and Chris, who enjoy them as much as she always has. The coconut gives them a little crunch and a lot of flavor.

Vegetable oil for frying
1 cup all-purpose flour, plus flour
   for dusting
¾ cup beer, or more
½ teaspoon baking powder
⅛ teaspoon salt
3 to 4 bananas, cut in ½-inch
   slices

½ cup shredded coconut
   (page 159) or frozen
   unsweetened coconut
Confectioners' sugar for
   dusting

Preheat 3 to 4 inches of oil in a deep-fat fryer to 350 degrees. Combine 1 cup of the flour, the beer, baking powder, and salt. Dust the banana slices with the remaining flour, shaking off the excess. Dip the slices into the batter, then roll them in the coconut. Fry 3 or 4 banana slices at a time until golden brown, about 2 to 3 minutes. Skim out the fritters and drain on paper towels. Dust with confectioners' sugar and serve warm.

MRS. HARVEY'S FRUITCAKE

Mrs. Paul J. Harvey won second prize for this recipe in a Tampa *Tribune* recipe contest in 1951. Nobody remembers the first-prize recipe, but this one was reprinted annually for more than thirty years in response to frantic readers who had lost the recipe, and each year it gained new devotees. Most of the newspapers in central and north Florida have printed the recipe, food writers as far away as the Atlanta *Journal and Constitution* published it, and the recipe has appeared in recipe anthologies.

Traditional dark English-style fruitcakes faded in the fifties and sixties, and this is an example of the "new" fruitcake, with no bitter peel to cut the richness, and loaded with candied pineapple, cherries, and pecans. Mrs. Harvey's was one of the earliest printed recipes for this style of cake.

Until her death several years ago, Mrs. Harvey tinkered with the recipe, reporting to the *Tribune* each "improvement." Once she increased the flavoring extracts to two bottles each, but the recipe included here is the best one of all time for all-round flavor, says Ann McDuffie, retired food editor of the *Tribune*. Mrs. Harvey's cake still is a regional favorite in west and central Florida.

MRS. HARVEY'S WHITE FRUITCAKE

MAKES ABOUT 4½ POUNDS OF CAKE, 50 OR MORE ELEGANT, THIN SLICES.

This cake often is baked in miniature sizes to serve as a finger-food dessert at holiday parties, but there is nothing so majestic as fruitcake baked in a large tube pan and turned out on a footed cake stand.

4 cups (1 pound) shelled pecans	**1 cup sugar**
¾ pound candied red cherries	**5 large eggs**
1 pound candied pineapple	**1 bottle (1 ounce) vanilla**
1¾ cups all-purpose flour	**extract**
½ teaspoon baking powder	**1 bottle (1 ounce) lemon**
1 cup (2 sticks) butter,	**extract**
softened	

Prepare this cake in two stages—nuts and fruits the night before, mixing and baking the next day. Chop the pecans coarsely and place in a large bowl. Snip the cherries and pineapple into ½-inch pieces, using kitchen shears dipped in water from time to time. Add the fruits to the pecans. Cover with a clean towel and let stand overnight.

Butter a 10-inch tube pan or two 8½×4½-inch loaf pans and line the bottoms with heavy brown paper or cooking parchment; butter the paper. Toss 3 tablespoons of the flour with the fruit mixture; set aside. Sift together the remaining flour and baking powder. In a large bowl, cream the butter. Add the sugar gradually, beating thoroughly. Beat in the eggs, one at a time, mixing well after each addition. Add the flour mixture in three or four parts, stirring each time until smooth. Stir in the vanilla and lemon extracts. Add the fruit mixture and mix well with a spoon or floured hands.

Pour the batter into the prepared pan(s) and pack lightly. Place in a cold oven, set at 250 degrees, and bake 3 hours for a tube pan or 2½ hours for loaf pans. A skewer inserted in the center should come out clean but moist when the cake is done. Cool in the pan on a wire rack, turn out, and wrap in foil or plastic wrap. Chill before serving and slice very thin. This cake will keep for 2 or 3 weeks in a cool cupboard or pantry, for several weeks in the refrigerator, or for months in the freezer.

FRESH STRAWBERRY PIE

MAKES 6 TO 8 SERVINGS.

The Amish folk who settled the Pinecraft section of Sarasota a half century ago still hold to their food traditions, though the village is only a few blocks from the concert hall, museums, and beaches that make Sarasota a tourist mecca. But Sarasotans and tourists flock to Yoder's and other Amish spots for the mashed potatoes and pot pie, although the dessert pies, heaped with real whipped cream, are the big drawing cards. In strawberry season you have to go early to get a slice of this one.

1 jar (8 to 10 ounces) red currant jelly	2 to 3 tablespoons confectioners' sugar
¼ cup granulated sugar	1 baked 9-inch pie shell
2 teaspoons strawberry- or raspberry-flavored liqueur	(recipe fon next page)
1 quart strawberries	Whipped cream for topping

Place the jelly and granulated sugar in a small saucepan. Bring to a boil over moderate heat, stirring until the sugar is dissolved. If lumpy, cook and stir a minute or two longer. Stir in the liqueur and cool. Store the glaze in a covered jar in the refrigerator, and warm to room temperature before using.

Wash and cap the berries. Slice them and fill the pie with overlapping circles of the berries. Work from the center, with pointed ends of slices to the inside. Sprinkle each layer with confectioners' sugar, using less if berries are very sweet. Brush the final layer lightly with glaze. Cover the pie and keep it at room temperature until ready to serve. This pie is best served within 2 or 3 hours of filling it. Top lavishly with whipped cream.

PASTRY FOR PIE

Makes one 9-inch pie shell.

1½ cups flour
¼ teaspoon salt
⅓ cup vegetable shortening
4 tablespoons (½ stick)
    butter, cut in small pieces

3 to 4 tablespoons cold
    water

Combine the flour and salt in a mixing bowl, add the shortening and butter, and cut in with a pastry blender or two table knives, until larger pieces of shortening are the size of small peas. Sprinkle 3 tablespoons of water over the mixture and work in with a few swift strokes of a fork. Add only enough water to make the dough cling together. Round up the dough in a ball, wrap in plastic wrap or waxed paper, and chill at least 30 minutes before rolling.

Place the dough in the center of a pastry cloth or floured countertop. Smooth the edges of the ball, and roll out to a round 2 inches larger in diameter than the pie plate. Fit the dough loosely into the pie plate, and flute edges to the rim of the plate. To bake as a shell, prick bottom of the crust with a fork in several places. If you wish to prevent the crust from swelling up while baking, weight with dry beans or rice in a sheet of foil. Bake in a preheated 425-degree oven 10 to 12 minutes, until pale brown. Cool before filling. Or fill unbaked pie shell as pie recipe directs.

PASSOVER LEMON PIE

MAKES 6 SERVINGS.

Sue Sutker's Passover desserts are famous in Tampa, and one that she is sure to serve when her family is home for the holidays is this lemon pie. It is a light but sweet and tangy finale to the first seder dinner on Passover eve or any dinner during the season. The matzo-meal and ground almond pie shell is unique; an equal amount of fine graham-cracker or other cookie crumbs can be substituted for matzo meal after Passover.

5 eggs, separated	¾ cup plus 10 tablespoons
1½ teaspoons slivered lemon zest	sugar
⅓ cup lemon juice	1 baked 9-inch Almond Matzo
⅓ cup water	Pie Crust (recipe follows)

Combine the egg yolks, lemon zest and juice, the water, and the ¾ cup sugar in the top of a double boiler. Cook over boiling water, stirring often, then constantly as the filling thickens for 15 minutes. Remove from the heat.

Preheat the oven to 400 degrees. In a medium-size bowl, beat the egg whites until frothy, then gradually beat in the 10 tablespoons sugar. (To measure 10 tablespoons without losing count, measure a ½ cupful, then 2 tablespoons.) Beat until soft peaks form and the sugar is dissolved. Fold about one-third of the egg white meringue into the warm lemon filling. Spoon the filling into the pie shell. Spread the remaining meringue over the top, sealing it to the edges of the crust. Bake 15 minutes, or until the meringue is lightly browned. Cool, but the pie is best served within 4 to 5 hours of baking.

ALMOND MATZO PIE CRUST

MAKES 2 9-INCH PIE SHELLS.

Ground almonds lend richness to a crumb pie shell, made with matzo meal for Passover, when other flours and crackers are forbidden. Cookie crumbs of other kinds work in this recipe, when they are not prohibited.

1 cup blanched almonds	½ cup almond or peanut oil
¼ cup sugar	1¼ cups matzo meal
1 egg, beaten	

Preheat oven to 375 degrees. Grind the almonds in a processor, adding 1 tablespoon of the sugar with the nuts to keep them from becoming oily while being ground. In a medium-size bowl, beat the egg. Stir in the oil, matzo meal, ground almonds, and the remaining sugar until well mixed. Press the mixture into 2 9-inch pie plates, making a uniform layer on the

Almond Matzo Pie Crust (continued)

bottom and up the sides. Bake for 12 to 15 minutes, until rims of the pie shells are lightly browned. Cool and fill the pie shells, or wrap and freeze one for later use. Makes 2 9-inch pie shells.

NOTE: This recipe can be halved for one pie shell, but dividing an egg is a nuisance. The frozen pie shell can be used for ice cream or fruit, or for another pie later.

NAPLES CHOCOLATE CHEESE PIE

MAKES 8 TO 12 SERVINGS.

In the 1980s Doris and Bill Reynolds operated a restaurant, The Gazebo, in Naples. Their chocolate cheesecake was such a hit that former customers still plead, "I would pay anything if you'd bake a cheesecake for me." Doris, the cheesecake maker, now is a food and travel writer whose column is syndicated by the Scripps-Howard News Service. The recipe for her cheesecake in her book, *Let's Talk Food,* inspired this cheesecake pie, "that is worth every calorie," say those who taste it, and it is not complicated to make. It's rich so serve in thin wedges.

CHOCOLATE CRUMB CRUST

1 8½-ounce package chocolate
    wafers, crushed (see Note)

⅓ cup butter, melted
¼ cup sugar

CHOCOLATE FILLING

1⅓ cups (8 ounces) semisweet
    chocolate pieces
2 eggs
⅔ cup sugar
2 8-ounce packages cream
    cheese, softened

1 teaspoon vanilla extract
⅛ teaspoon salt
⅔ cup sour cream or sour
    half-and-half
Whipped cream, sweetened,
    if desired

For the crust, mix the crumbs, melted butter, and the sugar until blended. Press the mixture firmly into the bottom and sides of a 9½-inch pie plate. Refrigerate while preparing the filling.

Preheat the oven to 350 degrees. Melt the chocolate, and set it aside to cool slightly. Combine the eggs and sugar in a processor or mixer bowl and process or beat at high speed until the sugar is dissolved. Cut the cream cheese in chunks, and process or beat it in until well mixed. Add the chocolate and blend it in well, then the vanilla, salt, and sour cream. Pour the filling into the crumb crust. Bake 1 hour, or until a pick inserted in the center comes out clean, but moist. Set the pie on a rack to cool, then refrigerate several hours or overnight. Serve with whipped cream, or set each wedge of the pie on a pool of custard sauce flavored with vanilla, brandy or orange-flavored liqueur on the dessert plate.

NOTE: If chocolate wafers are not available, 1½ cups crumbs made of miniature chocolate graham snack crackers can be used.

ST. JOHN GREEK ORTHODOX CHURCH

While there are many Greek communities in Florida, the Tampa–Tarpon Springs area is home to one of the largest. Greek Orthodox churches are centers of activity, and in Tampa, at St. John Greek Orthodox Church, Mary Nenos, president of the Ladies Philoptochos Society, regularly leads battalions of volunteers into the church kitchen to prepare time-honored dishes for their festivals and celebrations. Special observances traditionally call for certain foods; for instance, the bread of oblation, marked with a special seal, is prepared for communion. Likewise, *kolyva* is a bread used in services honoring the memory of one who is deceased. A mound-shaped loaf made with shelled whole wheat, sugar, cinnamon, raisins, and nuts, it is topped with confectioners' sugar, with the initials of the deceased arranged in white-iced almonds on top.

The group also provides hundreds of cookies and pastries for Tampa's annual Greek Festival, a huge cultural celebration that is open to the public. Other occasions garner the same attention, with specialties like baklava, Greek nut cake, and *finikia*, orange-nut cookies dipped in syrup and cinnamon.

CENTRAL FLORIDA

APPETIZERS

Tomato Slush

Pickled Shrimp

Grapefruit with Shrimp

Sliced Tomatoes with Basil

Pineapple Coleslaw

Three Squashes Salad

Willy's Paella Salad

Saffron Rice

Pressed Chicken Salad

SOUP

Cream of Garbanzo Soup

ENTRÉES

Christmas Eve Shrimp Curry

Yellow Bonnet Barbecue Sauce

Baked Ham with Starfruit and
    Marmalade Sauce

Puerto Rican Rice

Smothered Rabbit

VEGETABLES AND STARCHES

Corn Pudding with Tomatoes

Greens with Corn Meal Dumplings

Tomato Gravy with Biscuits or Rice

Onions and Bacon

Curried Rice

Spiced Oranges

BREADS

Sweet Potato Yeast Biscuits

Blueberry Cornbread

DESSERTS

Florida Ambrosia

Fresh Strawberry Ice Cream

Masaryktown Rosky (Cream Cheese
    Pastries)

Strawberry Cobbler

Carrie's Pineapple Cake

Old South Caramel Cake

Grapefruit Chiffon Pie

Double-Crust Guava Pie

Pastry for a Double-Crust Pie

Nestled between the glittering Gold Coast and its quieter relation, the Sun Coast, lies the huge expanse of heartland that is central Florida. This is citrus country, though cattle, phosphate, and all manner of agriculture prevail here as well. It is also firmly and devotedly Southern, with Dixie roots that are far less entwined with the migrations that have affected other parts of the state.

Hunting is a tradition in the South, and the Ocala National Forest is teaming with game, including deer, that in season attract thousands of hunters. You're apt to find good, hearty venison stews around here, made with locally grown vegetables, and venison chile. There are also private hunting lodges, where for a fee sportsmen (and women) can bag wild turkey, ducks, dove, quail, and wild pigs (piney rooters). Every hunter has his or her favorite way of preparing game, and whether roasted, stuffed, or smothered with gravy, such dishes, served with cornbread and rice, are a source of pride for hunters.

Because a tremendous variety of vegetables are grown locally, bush and pole beans, limas, southern peas, eggplant and squash, among other things, are available in farm markets everywhere in the area, no home-cooked meal is complete without some combination thereof. In the Zell-wood-Sanford-Oviedo triangle, greens, peppers, spinach, cabbage, carrots, celery, and cucumbers are all grown, but the major crop is sweet corn. Zellwood is home to the annual Corn Festival, where the price of admission includes a meal of ham, potato salad, beans, rolls, and "all the sweet corn you can eat."

Not far away, but very much in contrast to the rural nature of most of central Florida, Orlando has shot up virtually overnight with the arrival in 1971 of Walt Disney World. What was once little more than a collection of farm towns amid acres and acres of citrus has grown to become Florida's number one attraction; drawing visitors from all over the world, it is now a sprawling, contemporary city. Here more than anywhere else, Southern traditions have given way to a plethora of theme restaurants and fast food. On the Disney grounds, the Epcot Center offers an array of international restaurants serving dishes from around the world, while all across town, anything from burgers and tacos to haute cuisine is standard fare. The Crackers who once lived on farm food like pork chops and corn pudding have been joined by throngs of people from all over the country, enticed by growth and opportunity, whose food patterns are as diverse as the places from which they hail.

Moving southward away from the relative hustle of Orlando, life returns to a more characteristic pace. Flashy tourist attractions give way to vast, level pastures and mile after mile of citrus groves.

This is also an area where freshwater lakes are seemingly everywhere. Fishing for bass, bluegill, speckled perch, and catfish is as popular as the hushpuppies and slaw that accompany the pan-fried fish.

Here, as throughout the state, much has changed in recent years though life is still very much connected to the land. Barely out of the shadow of Orlando, the Citrus Tower still commands a panorama of the citrus area, a reminder of central Florida's original attraction.

The "Silver Spurs Rodeo," the largest rodeo in the state, is held each year in Kissimmee, long known as "Cow Town." True to its colloquial name, cowboys and cattle figured prominently in the life of the town. Back in the 1870s, Kissimmee originated a ride-in bar, where cowpokes could drink without getting off their horses. Nowadays cowboys are more likely to dismount from pickup trucks and saddle up to a table crowded with steaks, with biscuits and gravy (before retiring for some shut-eye). Outside town, the emphasis is on accommodating tourists, with motels and fast-food joints.

In Lakeland, the Reececliff restaurant has been the place to go since 1934. It is known for simple homestyle dishes like chicken fried steak, squash soufflé, and most of all, fresh-baked pies.

Home-cooking in central Florida often is what Caroline's father called "farm food"—fried chicken or pork chops, hamburgers in gravy, turkey or steaks, and lots of fresh vegetables from the farmer's market or the backyard garden. Black-eyed peas and rice, greens with hot pepper sauce (from wild grove peppers), sweet potatoes, okra, and tomatoes. Any or all of these are common at family dinners, many of which are topped off with coconut layer cake or fresh strawberries over homemade ice cream.

Throughout citrus-growing areas in early spring, the scent of orange blossoms fills the air, and fruit stands dot the roadsides, selling oranges, tangerines, and grapefruit. Evan's Fruit Stand on Highway 60 near Plant City also sells bags of hot, freshly cooked boiled jumbo peanuts, a favorite snack in these parts.

Around Plant City, strawberries are the major crop. It is also home to one of the state's wholesale farmer's markets that sells and ships produce across America. And at the edge of the wholesale market is Jean and Harry Burtz's produce stand, known in the area for almost twenty years. They buy from local farmers and are open for retail business every day, rain or shine, selling all manner of vegetables and even fresh swamp cabbage. Fish lovers around here go to Fat Willy's Fish Camp, in Valrico, for "all the fried catfish you can eat," plus alligator "fingers" and smoked mullet and to Buddy Freddy's in Plant City for a taste of Old Florida.

The strong connection between the people and the land in central Florida is evident in the endless string of festivals devoted to various crops, and even animals. San Antonio, northeast of Plant City, hosts the annual Rattlesnake Festival and International Gopher Race Games. "Gopher" is a land turtle that Crackers have eaten for generations, but here the gophers are put to more recreational use. Not far away, in Spring Hill, the World Championship Chicken Pluckin' is held, and elsewhere there are citrus festivals, strawberry festivals, and other celebrations.

Masaryktown is the only ethnic community in central Florida with a population that is predominantly Czechoslovakian. It was once called the "egg capital of Florida," because of all the poultry farms. That label is outdated now, but the Czechs here still make traditional pastries like rosky, kolacky, and poppy seed tortes, and at the Masaryktown Hotel Restaurant (no longer a hotel) the menu still features dishes such as chicken paprikash with dumplings, duck stuffed with kraut, and stuffed cabbage rolls.

The history of central Florida is a story of gradual evolution, more than one of dramatic events. The pioneering folk who settled the area and tamed the wilderness in the nineteenth and early part of this century were mostly farmers and ranchers lured by the land, the climate, and the promise of the new frontier. These enterprising pioneers worked the land, developed the industry, and created the core of what is still Florida's wealth today: citrus, phosphate, and agriculture.

Although the attraction of the orange trees goes back to the days of missionaries and Indians, the crop that was to help shape the entire region was largely un-exploitable until the coming of efficient transportation systems. In the 1880s, Henry Plant built, expanded, and consolidated rail lines that stretched from Tampa to Jacksonville, passing through central Florida and providing the necessary means for the shipping of fruits and vegetables to Northern markets. Since then, the area's natural wealth has been developed to a degree that makes central Florida an important agricultural center.

There is a sense of permanence here in the middle of the state, a continuing reliance on the land that makes this place a bit more impervious to trends that come and go. While the people, customs, and foods here are evolving along with the rest of the world, the satisfying tastes of tradition remain deeply rooted in the sandy soil.

FLORIDA CRACKER

Folklore explains the origin of the term "Florida Cracker" as coming from early cowboys "cracking" their bullwhips as they drove cattle to Florida. But whatever the actual origin of the term might be, it has come to refer to any rural, native-born Floridian with strong ties to the land, especially those who are second or third generation.

The food traditions of "Cracker cooking" have Deep South roots, but have been adapted to make use of indigenous fruits, vegetables, and animals. Swamp cabbage (hearts of palm), citrus, and exotic fruits such as pineapple, mangoes, and guavas were integrated into the Cracker diet, as was gator, gopher (land tortoise), and cooter (soft-shell freshwater turtle), among others. More common Southern foods, such as fried chicken, all manner of pork, cornbread and biscuits, greens, rice, and grits, all figure prominently in Cracker cooking. Today, Cracker heritage is a source of pride for many Floridians.

TOMATO SLUSH

MAKES 6 SERVINGS.

This icy tomato juice mixture is a real Old Florida starter, served as a cocktail before lunch or dinner, as a first course in small bowls with spoons, or as a refreshing drink, especially in hot weather. It consists of tomato juice, simmered with cloves, and a bit of onion, bay leaves, and lemon juice, which is then frozen to a slushy consistency, thick with slivers of iced juice. At Margrette and Bill Stuart's, in Bartow, guests are served the old-fashioned specialty in crystal goblets from a silver tray with linen cocktail napkins.

P.S.: Tradition dictates that a sterling silver fork be used to beat the icy mixture after freezing.

3 cups (24 ounces) tomato juice	**2 bay leaves**
4 whole cloves	**¼ teaspoon salt**
1 tablespoon chopped onion	**2 tablespoons lemon juice**

In a saucepan, combine the tomato juice, cloves, onion, bay leaves, and salt. Simmer for 15 minutes. Strain and cool. Stir in the lemon juice. Pour into a shallow pan and freeze until ice crystals form and it is a thick slush. Remove from the freezer and beat with a silver fork until fluffy. Serve in glasses, or in small bowls.

PICKLED SHRIMP

MAKES 10 TO 12 HORS D'OEUVRE SERVINGS, OR 5 TO 6 SALAD SERVINGS.

Few large wedding receptions or cocktail receptions in Florida are complete without a huge bowlful of pickled shrimp on the refreshment table. It is easily made in advance, keeps well in the refrigerator, and virtually everyone enjoys it. When serving, leave the lemon slices, onions, and bay leaves in with the shrimp for a more appealing presentation.

5 to 6 cups water	**2 lemons, sliced thin and**
½ to 1 cup celery tops	**seeded**
2 tablespoons pickling spice,	**¾ cup tarragon vinegar**
tied in cheesecloth	**3 tablespoons capers with juice**
½ cup cider vinegar	**1¼ cups vegetable oil**
2½ pounds medium shrimp,	**2½ teaspoons celery seed**
shelled and cleaned	**Thinly sliced French or party-**
10 to 12 bay leaves	**type bread, water biscuits,**
1 medium onion, sliced thin	**or other crackers**
and separated into rings	

In a large pot bring 5 cups of water, the celery tops, pickling spice, and cider vinegar to a boil and simmer for 5 minutes. Add the shrimp and more water if necessary to barely cover the shrimp, and return to a boil. Cook until the shrimp is pink, approximately 2 minutes. Drain, rinse the shrimp briefly in cold water, and cool. In a shallow glass dish or glass bowl, make layers, alternating the shrimp, a few bay leaves, onion, and lemon slices, finishing with lemon and a few bay leaves. Mix together the tarragon vinegar, capers, oil, and celery seed. Pour the mixture over the shrimp, cover, and refrigerate overnight. If the marinade does not cover the shrimp, turn it or spoon the marinade over the top from time to time.

To serve, wipe off the top inside edge of the bowl or transfer the shrimp to another bowl. Provide guests with toothpicks, or if serving with crackers, a fork or small tongs so that guests can place a shrimp or two and onion rings on a cracker or thin slice of bread. Pickled shrimp can also be served on lettuce or other greens as a luncheon salad.

FLORIDA'S GOLD STRIKE

His voice is husky with emotion, as Dr. Edwin Moore remembers the tasting in the spring of 1946 of orange juice "made" in a pitcher. Since 1943, Dr. Moore and two other young research scientists, Louis J. MacDowell and C. Donald Atkins, had worked in the Citrus Experiment Station at Lake Alfred to perfect the frozen concentrate that was to make orange juice a breakfast habit worldwide and create a boom for Florida growers. Sweet oranges for juicing are seasonal; concentrate made the juice available fifty-two weeks a year.

Immediately industry representatives, who shared the tasting, went out on the road and sold 225,000 gallons of the concentrate in the 1945–46 season. Production and sales boomed, and in the 1949 season, almost 10 million gallons were sold; for several years orange concentrate was the top-selling frozen food.

The introduction of frozen juice concentrate was timely. Consumers became frozen-food addicts after World War II, as refrigerators and freezers became available again. Nutrition education before and during the war had made orange juice a daily habit with millions.

The nutrient value of juice concentrated by whirling it in giant drums at cool temperatures is comparable to freshly squeezed juice; though many home folk treat themselves to freshly extracted juice on occasion.

A new word, convenience, was entering the food-marketing lexicon, and a few years later shortcuts became even more important as moms and home-makers began to go to the workplace. The convenience of mixing instead of extracting fresh orange juice was appealing.

When tourists are given orange juice at the Welcome Centers to the state, they are often outraged to find the chilled drink is made of concentrate. It is the taste that most Floridians know, and that made millionaires of some successful citrus people in the 1950s and 1960s.

GRAPEFRUIT WITH SHRIMP

MAKES 2 SERVINGS.

This combination makes a handsome appetizer for luncheon or dinner. Pink shrimp is a pretty color accent to the pale grapefruit and avocado, though other seafood can be substituted.

1 grapefruit
10 to 12 tiny shrimp or 5 to 6
    split medium or large shrimp,
    cooked and cleaned
¼ avocado, cut in thin
    crosswise slices

Salsa Vinagreta (see
    page 191)
Arugula or watercress sprigs

Cut the grapefruit in halves. Flick out the seeds with a fork and cut around the sections with a grapefruit knife. Holding the fruit over a bowl to catch the juice, remove alternate sections of fruit and save for other uses. Toss the avocado with the juice in the bowl.

Insert a shrimp or shrimp piece and avocado slice in each space left after removing grapefruit sections. Drizzle with the Vinagreta and place a sprig of greenery in the center of each grapefruit half. Place each appetizer on a doily on a small plate and provide a grapefruit spoon and small fork.

SLICED TOMATOES WITH BASIL

MAKES 6 TO 8 SERVINGS.

Florida tomatoes in season can be juicy and full of flavor. We get them at farm stands that specialize in field-ripened fruit or patronize U-pick sellers. Posters and ads for U-pick sales appear in neighborhood newspapers and on community bulletin boards just after Christmas in south Dade County, then near Immokalee in southwest Florida a month later, then in Ruskin in the spring. Pluck the tomatoes well colored and smelling faintly of the vine. They usually are soft at this stage, so treat them tenderly by packing them on crushed paper in a shallow box to bring them home. Serve them within twenty-four hours, and never, never refrigerate them.

If the tomatoes are perfect, use just a splash of olive oil, salt, pepper, and a sprinkle of minced fresh basil on them. This sweet-sour dressing bumps up the flavor of less than perfect tomatoes.

6 ripe tomatoes, sliced ¼ inch thick
2 teaspoons sugar
½ teaspoon salt
¼ teaspoon freshly ground pepper

2 tablespoons balsamic or rice vinegar
¼ cup olive oil
¼ cup finely shredded basil

Arrange the tomatoes in overlapping circles on a plate or platter, sprinkling them with the sugar, salt, pepper, and vinegar. Cover loosely with waxed paper and let them stand at room temperature 1 to 1½ hours before serving. Drizzle with the olive oil, and sprinkle the basil over the salad. Serve at room temperature.

WILLIE KEEN RIDING ROMAN OVER AUTO ARCADIA RODEO

PINEAPPLE COLESLAW

MAKES 8 SERVINGS.

Rodeo riders are a breed apart, and in Florida, where there are more than fifty rodeos a year, tough, adventure-loving cowboys (and girls) get their "kicks" in events such as bull riding, steer wrestling, calf roping, and barrel racing. Many of the riders take their families along with their horses, and camp out on the rodeo grounds.

By necessity, camp food is simple and hearty, with convenience at a premium. Caroline's sister, Kathie, who has done some barrel racing herself, and whose husband and son compete in steer wrestling and team roping events, fixes this coleslaw for back-of-the-pickup and camper barbecues.

3 cups shredded cabbage
   (about ½ head)
½ cup shredded carrots
¾ cup drained crushed
   pineapple (1 8-ounce can)
   (see Note)

2 teaspoons vinegar
1 teaspoon sugar
⅔ cup mayonnaise
Pepper to taste

Combine the shredded cabbage and carrots in a bowl. Add the pineapple, vinegar, sugar, mayonnaise, and pepper. Taste and adjust the seasoning, if desired. Cover and chill for 30 minutes.

NOTE: You may substitute ½ cup finely chopped fresh pineapple for the canned.

THREE SQUASHES SALAD

MAKES 4 TO 5 SERVINGS. DRESSING RECIPE MAKES
1½ CUPS.

Chalet Suzanne, a fairyland-like inn and restaurant, has stood on a lake near Lake Wales for more than half a century, and the menu hasn't changed much. Carl and Vita Hinshaw, who inherited the inn-restaurant from his mother, defy trendiness, serving foods that customers come back for year after year. A salad is brought after the soup in the multi-course dinner. The combination of summer squashes, artichoke hearts, and hearts of palm is especially colorful, and the dressing can be used on many salads.

DRESSING

½ teaspoon salt

1 tablespoon curry powder

1 small clove garlic, peeled

1 teaspoon soy sauce

1 cup soybean oil

7 tablespoons lemon juice

1 tablespoon water

½ pound each yellow crookneck, pattypan, and zucchini squash

¼ cup sliced canned artichoke hearts, drained and rinsed

½ cup sliced fresh or canned hearts of palm, drained and rinsed

¼ cup thinly sliced uncooked Jerusalem artichokes

Garden lettuce

Combine the salt, curry powder, and garlic in a bowl or mortar and work with the back of a spoon or pestle until the garlic is mashed to a paste

Three Squashes Salad (continued)

with the salt and curry powder. Add the soy sauce, oil, lemon juice, and water. Whisk the mixture together until blended. Hold at room temperature up to 2 or 3 hours or refrigerate for longer storage.

For the salad, steam the squashes separately until barely tender, drain well, and cut in ½-inch slices. Combine with the artichoke hearts, palm hearts, and Jerusalem artichoke slices in a bowl. Add 2 or 3 tablespoons of the salad dressing, toss lightly, and add a bit more if needed to coat the vegetables well, but do not drown the salad. Spoon the salad onto lettuce-lined salad plates. Refrigerate extra dressing for use on other salads later.

A TASTE OF WALT DISNEY WORLD

The opening of Walt Disney World in 1971 brought a new flavor to central Florida, affecting all phases of culture. Tourists, including the hordes of Floridians who flocked there, began to think of Walt Disney World as the ultimate Florida dining experience. Florida fare such as fruit salads, avocados, and shrimp are available at many of the more than 1,800 eating spots, and the menu is a mind-boggling mix of the tastes of the world. One can grab an ice cream, orange juice, or hot dog at a kiosk or dine simply or elaborately in dozens of cafés, coffee shops, bistros, or restaurants. In Victoria & Albert's at the Grand Floridian Hotel, guests dressed for dinner choose from an extensive wine list and order from a menu plotted daily to take advantage of the premium ingredients in the market; in the informal Narcoossee's, overlooking the hotel's sandy beach, diners in sports shirts are encouraged to try the alligator pâté with bread to start the meal, but the soups, salads, and sandwiches there are geared to conservative palates. At lakeside, holidayers in swimsuits have lunch or snacks at umbrella-shaded tables.

In the World Showcase section of Walt Disney World, the choices include Mexican at the San Angel Inn from Mexico City, French at Chefs de France with menus designed by three-star chefs Paul Bocuse, Roger Vergé, and Gaston LeNôtre, Italian at L'Originale Alfredo di Roma, English at the Rose and Crown, Moroccan, Japanese, German, Canadian, and Norwegian. A favorite of Walt Disney World crowds is The Land Grille Room in Epcot Center, where one can order sampling portions of roast tuna loin, Oriental spiced chicken, novelty pizzas, and other New Age foods. The enormously varied menu of Walt Disney World has a bit of the flamboyance that typified Florida real estate deals of the past, as well as traditional American food to appeal to mass tastes; Floridians, as well, take pride in the food here.

An exciting exhibit for students of food production is the Land Pavilion in Epcot Center. A boat ride or walk takes visitors through experimental plots of food plants in a tropical rain forest, a desert, an American prairie environment, and a living exhibit of foods of the future. A section devoted to aquaculture shows tilapia, a fish that has been farmed for food for centuries in Africa, and paddlefish, which produces a roe that some think is comparable to Caspian Sea caviar. Horticulturists and fish scientists tend the crops and fish tanks, and are available to answer questions. Seeds of some of the experimental plants can be bought at a nearby shop, as well as literature on how to grow and cook them. A few of the vegetables and fish harvested in the Land exhibit are incorporated into special menus in the restaurants.

O-17—Orange Avenue, Orlando, Fla.
"The City Beautiful"

WILLY'S PAELLA SALAD

MAKES 4 TO 5 SERVINGS.

Willy Hopkins, majordomo for over twenty-five years to Anne Pipping and her family in Lakeland, really knows his way around a kitchen. He enjoys making this saffron rice salad, especially in summer, when cold one-dish meals are welcomed.

½ pound medium shrimp, cooked, shelled, and cleaned

1½ cups Saffron Rice (recipe follows), cooled

1 6½-ounce can minced clams, drained

¾ cup cubed poached chicken breast

½ cup diced celery

¼ cup diced green bell pepper

3 tablespoons thinly sliced green onions or scallions with tops

½ 10-ounce package (¾ cup) frozen green peas, thawed (not cooked)

1 2½-ounce jar pimiento, drained

1 medium tomato, chopped

DRESSING

½ cup mayonnaise

1½ tablespoons dry white wine

1½ tablespoons capers, with juice

½ clove garlic, pressed (¼ teaspoon)

¾ teaspoon salt

½ teaspoon freshly ground pepper

1½ teaspoons lemon juice

Garden lettuce

Slice the shrimp lengthwise in halves. Combine the shrimp, rice, clams, chicken, celery, bell pepper, green onion, and peas in a large bowl. Chop ¼ cup of the pimento. Add with the tomato to the salad and toss lightly.

For the dressing, mix together the mayonnaise, white wine, capers, garlic, salt, pepper, and lemon juice. Add to the salad, using just enough to moisten well. Serve the salad on a bed of greens and garnish with the remaining pimiento, cut in strips.

SAFFRON RICE

MAKES APPROXIMATELY 2⅓ CUPS.

1 tablespoon olive oil
1 tablespoon finely chopped
   onion
⅔ cup long-grain rice
1½ cups hot chicken broth or
   water

½ teaspoon salt
⅛ teaspoon saffron threads,
   well crushed

In a 1-quart saucepan, heat the oil over moderate heat. Add the onion and cook, stirring, for 2 to 3 minutes, or until soft. Add the rice and stir to coat, for about 1 minute. Add the broth and salt and bring to a boil. Stir in the crushed saffron, reduce the heat to a low simmer, and cover. Simmer for 20 minutes, or until the broth has been absorbed and the rice is tender.

PRESSED CHICKEN SALAD

MAKES 12 TO 15 SERVINGS.

This light party dish has never gone out of style in Florida, and some people still call it by the old-fashioned name "congealed" salad. It is often served at functions like church suppers, bridge club and bridesmaid luncheons, and club socials. You can easily make it the day before, then when ready to serve, cut into squares and placed on salad greens.

1 chicken, about 4 pounds (to make 4 cups chicken)

1 medium onion, peeled and quartered

1 rib celery, including leaves

Several sprigs of fresh parsley

1 teaspoon dried thyme leaves

½ teaspoon salt

½ teaspoon freshly ground pepper

2 envelopes unflavored gelatin

1 cup hot chicken stock (cooking liquid from chicken)

2 cups finely chopped celery

1 cup broken pecans

1 tablespoon capers

4 hard-cooked eggs, chopped

2 tablespoons sweet pickle relish or chowchow

2 tablespoons Worcestershire sauce

Juice of 1 lemon

1 cup uncooked frozen peas

1 cup mayonnaise

To a large pot of water, add the chicken, onion, celery rib, parsley, thyme, salt, and pepper. Bring to a boil, cover, then simmer until the chicken is tender, approximately 1 hour. Remove the chicken, cool, take off the skin, and cut the meat into bite-size pieces. Transfer to a large bowl. Soften the gelatin in a little cold water, then dissolve completely by combining with the 1 cup boiling stock. To the cut-up chicken, add the hot stock with gelatin, chopped celery, pecans, capers, eggs, relish, Worcestershire sauce, lemon juice, and peas. When the chicken mixture has completely cooled, mix in the mayonnaise and pour into an $11 \times 13 \times 2\frac{1}{2}$-inch glass dish or similar mold. Refrigerate overnight or until firm.

CREAM OF GARBANZO SOUP

MAKES 4 LUNCHEON OR SUPPER SERVINGS, OR 6 TO 8 FIRST-COURSE SERVINGS.

This suave soup contains most of the elements of standard Spanish bean soup, but the flavor is less assertive, and it is creamy and smooth, with a few flecks of beans in it. Small cups of it are an appealing first course for dinner and bowls of it make a pleasant lunch with a salad on the side.

2 medium potatoes, peeled and
   cubed
1 small carrot or turnip, peeled
   and cut in chunks
3½ cups chicken broth
1 large bay leaf
1 teaspoon salt
¼ teaspoon freshly ground
   pepper
2 cans (20 ounces each)
   garbanzo beans

2 tablespoons olive oil
2 ounces (¼ cup) salt
   pork or country ham, diced
   (optional)
2 large cloves garlic, minced
1 large onion, diced
½ cup light or heavy cream,
   or more if needed

Combine the potatoes, carrot or turnip, chicken broth, bay leaf, salt, and pepper in a soup pot. Bring to a boil, cover, and simmer 25 minutes, or until the potato pieces are soft. Meanwhile, rinse and drain the garbanzos. Add a little more than half of them to the potato mixture, then purée this mixture in a food processor or blender. Set aside.

In the soup kettle or another large pot, heat the oil and salt pork or ham, if used. Add the garlic and onion and sauté until the onion is tender but not browned. Add the puréed soup to the onion mixture, along with the remaining garbanzo beans. Heat thoroughly, stir in the cream to thin as desired, and serve immediately.

GRAPEFRUIT JUICE—A GREAT MARINADE

The source of this marinade is as close as the back door for Floridians with a grapefruit tree in the yard. It just means squeezing the fruit of its juice and covering fish or chicken in it for 15 minutes before cooking. The tart juice, used alone or mixed with other citrus juices, gives a distinctive flavor. Some say that grapefruit juice will even tenderize beef and lamb.

CHRISTMAS EVE SHRIMP CURRY

MAKES 6 SERVINGS.

Christmas at the Stuart ranch has always been festive and chaotic, with as many as thirty-five family members, from four generations, gathered for the holidays. In the midst of all the activity, a simple buffet-style dinner is served for family and friends. A huge pot of rich, curried shrimp, redolent with coconut, raisins, and apples is made early that morning, then finished off and served with hot rice and salad in the evening. An array of condiments makes for a colorful table. This recipe has been cut down to serve six, but is easily multiplied for larger groups.

2 cups shredded coconut	½ teaspoon turmeric
4 cups milk	3 tablespoons Mango Chutney
4 tablespoons (½ stick) butter	(see page 171) or one of
1 large onion, chopped	your choice, chopped but
1 apple, peeled and cubed	undrained
2 cloves garlic, minced	¼ cup raisins
1 tablespoon curry powder, or to	2½ pounds shrimp, shelled
taste	and cleaned
4 tablespoons flour	6 cups hot cooked rice
1 teaspoon powdered ginger	Condiments*

*Popular condiments are chutney, raisins, sliced bananas, roasted peanuts, shredded coconut, chopped orange or lime peel, or chopped hard-cooked whole eggs or yolks.

Put the coconut in a large saucepan and pour the milk over it. Mix and let soak for 15 minutes; simmer 10 minutes, then cool. Strain and squeeze the coconut, reserving the milk (about 3 cups). Melt the butter in a large skillet, add the onion, apple, and garlic, and sauté until tender. Sprinkle the curry powder and the flour over the mixture and cook another minute or two, stirring constantly, until it makes a smooth paste. Slowly add the coconut milk, ginger, turmeric, chutney, and raisins. Cover and simmer 15 to 20 minutes, stirring frequently to prevent sticking. Uncover and continue to cook until the sauce has thickened. If it is too thick, thin with a little milk or water. The curry sauce may be made ahead up to this point, cooled, and refrigerated. At serving time, bring to a boil, add the shrimp and simmer until pink, 3 to 4 minutes. Serve over hot rice with an assortment of curry condiments.

FRIED TURKEY

We are unsure of the origin of the rather unusual Floridian practice of deep frying turkey, but for years, many have served the crisp cooked bird for celebrations and large gatherings, and swear by it. The process involves submerging a whole turkey in enough hot oil to cover it completely, and frying it until the skin is golden, and the interior is moist and juicy. When using this method, the turkey is never stuffed.

Any large, deep vessel will do, such as a cast-iron kettle, large soup pot, or even a cut-down pony beer keg. For outdoor cooking, be sure your fire or grill will heat to 350 to 375 degrees. Fill the container approximately halfway with vegetable oil and heat to approximately 350 degrees (see Note). Gently lower the turkey into the hot oil, being very careful not to splash oil from the pot. A 12-pound turkey will take 20 to 30 minutes to cook. When done, remove it with long-handled forks and put on heavy absorbent paper to drain. Slice as you would a roast turkey, and serve.

NOTE: To determine the amount of oil needed, first put the turkey in the container in which it will cook and fill with water. Be sure to leave approximately 6 inches at the top to avoid splashing. Remove the turkey and note the water level. When ready to cook, fill with oil to that point.

SOUTHERN FRIED CHICKEN

Surely no single food is more steeped in Southern tradition than crisp, golden brown, fried chicken. Just the thought of a fat bird sizzling in a black cast-iron skillet is enough to make any Southerner's mouth water. There are almost as many methods and recipes for frying chicken as there are Southern cooks, and some of them get very persnickety about the do's and don'ts; here are a few essential basics:

First of all, there must be enough shortening or oil in the pan to reach halfway up the sides of the chicken pieces. And constant attention must be paid to ensure that each piece is evenly browned and cooked, but not over-cooked. Remember that the dark meat takes a little longer to cook than the white meat.

One simple method of frying chicken is to season the pieces liberally with salt and pepper, then put them a few at a time into a large paper bag with one to two cups of flour. Roll up the top of the bag to close it, and shake the bag vigorously to coat the chicken with the flour.

Use a heavy skillet (we still like the old cast-iron favorites), and melt enough vegetable shortening to fill the pan a minimum of ½ inch deep. If you prefer oil, peanut or vegetable oil are good alternatives. When the short-ening or oil is hot (a little flour sprinkled in the pan will sizzle when ready), place the chicken in the pan (don't crowd the pieces), and cook over medium-high heat until brown on one side. Turn the parts as needed, to evenly brown each side, and reduce the heat if necessary so as not to burn the flour. The total cooking time should be approximately 20 to 25 minutes; test by piercing the flesh with a knife point or fork. They are done when the juices run clear. Drain the pieces on paper towels or paper bags as you remove them from the skillet. Remember to remove the white meat first.

YELLOW BONNET BARBECUE SAUCE

MAKES ABOUT 2½ CUPS, ENOUGH FOR 8 WHOLE
CHICKEN BREASTS, OR 2 TO 3 POUNDS OF SHELLED,
SKEWERED SHRIMP.

Among the hottest of peppers are Scotch bonnets, also called bonnet peppers or yellow bonnets, which give fierce heat to food. The little bonnet-shaped firebrands are about the size of cherry tomatoes, and can be found in farmer's markets in Florida and in Hispanic markets everywhere. Allen Smith, whose family has lived in central Florida for generations, has created this highly spiced sauce for chicken breasts and shrimp, which he uses at his annual family reunion cookout in Alturas.

½ cup water

¼ cup cider vinegar

½ cup malt vinegar

3 tablespoons light corn syrup

1 can (6 ounces) tomato paste

1½ teaspoons Worcestershire
    sauce

¼ cup firmly packed dark brown
    sugar

3 cloves garlic, minced

½ cup minced onion

1 yellow bonnet pepper, or
    more to taste, seeded and
    minced (if unavailable, use
    other hot pepper)

1 bay leaf, crushed

1 teaspoon turmeric

½ teaspoon freshly ground
    pepper

1 teaspoon salt

Combine all of the ingredients in a stainless steel or enamelware saucepan. Over medium heat, stir for 5 minutes to dissolve the sugar and blend the flavors. Do not cook longer, or the zest of the pepper is lost. Use this basting sauce for barbecuing and grilling meats and seafood. It is especially good with chicken breasts or shrimp. The sauce is thick, so it can be spread on one side of the chicken or shrimp, then spread on the other side when it is turned.

RANGE STEAKS

In earlier days, on cattle drives and roundups, cowboys often slept outside and cooked their meals over open fires. They were quite resourceful in improvising techniques for cooking without pots and pans, relying on what was on hand. To cook steaks (and probably birds, rabbits, and squirrels as well), they cut a sturdy palm frond trimmed of its "fan," speared the meat with one end of the stick, and stuck the other end into the ground beside the fire. When one side was done, they would rotate the stick to cook the other side, all the while letting the grease drip to the ground, involving no utensils to be washed. Contemporary cowboys and urbanites alike can put this trick to use at cookouts today, wherever open fires are allowed.

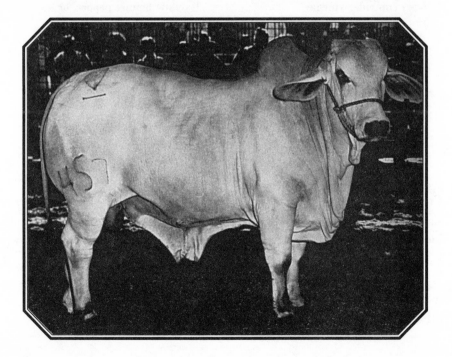

BAKED HAM WITH STARFRUIT AND MARMALADE SAUCE

THE SAUCE MAKES 4 TO 6 SERVINGS; THE HAM,
30 TO 40 SERVINGS, AND IS A TREASURE TO HAVE
ON HAND TO SLICE AS NEEDED.

Ann McDuffie, food editor of the Tampa *Tribune* until her retirement in 1990, guided home-cooks in this part of Florida as well as Tampa for almost thirty years. Her culinary roots are in Georgia, as are those of thousands of Floridians, giving her a special insight to her readers' tastes. She practices the old Southern custom of having a ham on hand for impromptu meals and snacks when the house—whether home or a beach house—is full of guests. Floridians, like people everywhere, buy ready-baked, spiral-cut hams, but Ann insists on baking it fresh. Buy carefully for top quality and keep the glaze simple for ease of carving is her advice. The sauce can be as fancy as you like. Sliced carambola in an orange-flavored sauce is one way to gussy up a ham without spoiling the convenience of it.

1 boned ham, 10 to 12 pounds, hot country ham	2 teaspoons dry mustard
¼ cup packed brown sugar	1½ to 2 teaspoons cider vinegar

SAUCE

1 cup (1 12-ounce jar) sweet orange marmalade	1 carambola (starfruit) or peeled large navel orange, sliced thin
1 tablespoon cider vinegar	
1 tablespoon dry mustard	

Preheat the oven to 300 degrees. Place the ham in a baking dish, lined with foil for easy clean-up. Blend the brown sugar, mustard, and just enough vinegar to make a spreadable paste. Spread over the ham. Bake 1½ to 1¾ hours, brushing occasionally with any glaze that drips off. Place the ham on a platter, cover with foil, and let stand 10 to 20 minutes before carving. Slice and serve with sauce on the side.

    While the ham bakes, prepare the sauce: Combine the marmalade, vinegar, and mustard in a medium-size skillet. Heat and add the sliced fruit. Serve the sauce warm with the sliced ham.

FLORIDA'S CATTLE INDUSTRY

The importance of Florida's cattle business has been largely overlooked. Somehow, the image of the wide open West and the archetypal Western cowboy has overshadowed Florida's centuries-old cattle industry and the state's unsung "cowmen." But while attention to Florida's beef and dairy herds may be lacking, the business of raising cattle, particularly in the central and southern parts of the state, is thriving.

The Spanish brought hardy Andalusian cattle to Florida in the early 1500s. They were gaunt, bony, long-horned beasts, but despite their appearance, proved to be perfectly suited to withstanding the heat, pestilence, and rugged conditions of their new home. They would eventually comprise the herds raised by missionaries, Indians, and early rancheros, and later come to be known as "Cracker cattle." Crossbreeding with other stock, particularly Brahmans brought from India, would improve Florida herds, but Cracker cattle predominated well into this century. Recently they have garnered renewed attention by cowmen interested in preserving the breed.

The state's cattle industry grew gradually from the small herds kept to feed pioneer families to ranches raising hundreds, then thousands of head, as lucrative markets developed. Cuba became a major source of trade, and long cattle drives, culminating at the west coast ports of Punta Rassa and Tampa, brought Spanish gold for the state's cattle barons and wild-looking, rough-and-tumble cowmen.

During the Civil War, Florida became a major supplier of beef, tallow, and hides for the Confederacy. As the state was spared from major fighting on home ground, the industry was able to continue and, following the war, recover from the reconstruction depression by resuming its increasingly active trade with Cuba.

Florida was a "free range" state until 1949, meaning there were no fencing laws, and cattle were allowed to roam at will. Ear marks and branding identified ownership, and roundups meant that cowmen covered a lot of ground to gather widespread herds. Progressive operators, who fattened their cattle or sent them to feedlots, often fenced them in before it became a law, but many cattlemen thought it their right to let their animals graze wherever they roamed, and free range was a hotly fought issue for many years.

Today, Florida's calves are raised for out-of-state sale rather than for breeding stock. They are sold as calves because large quantities of grain and nutrient-rich grasses are necessary to sufficiently fatten mature cattle. Florida ranchers will tell you, "It's cheaper to send the cow to the feed, than the feed to the cow." Consequently, most calves are sold at auction and shipped to other states (primarily in the Midwest and the Southwest, where grain is abundant and the grass is more nutritious) to be fattened. Like many ranchers, Caroline's father always kept back a few head for the family. They were grain-fed at home, butchered locally, and were shared with ranch hands and friends.

There is also a market for "vealers," very young calves sold for veal that are fed only milk and sometimes grass. The pale, delicate meat contains far less fat than beef and absorbs flavors well. Most Florida veal is shipped out of state for the hotel and restaurant trade.

As for dairy cattle, people tell tales of milk cows called English Lineback (so-called because of the white line of hair running from head to tail) which were brought down from Georgia and presumably flourished in Florida back in 1776. Whether it's true or not, it is safe to say that many settlers did bring a cow or two into the state, pulling them behind their wagon, to provide milk for the family. From such humble beginnings, mom and pop dairy operations grew up gradually around the state. It is only in this century, with the advent of refrigerated transportation, milking machines, and other automation, government controls, and the huge population growth since the 1920s, that dairying in Florida has become a modern-day industry, with Holsteins being the predominant breed.

PUERTO RICAN RICE

MAKES 6 SERVINGS.

Florida's Puerto Rican population brings its traditional foods, such as this, to the table. The casserole is flavored with chorizos, garlic, bell peppers, capers, and olives. It is good as a family supper entrée or robust side dish with fish or pork.

2 slices bacon, cut in small pieces	1 can (1 pound 12 ounces) crushed tomatoes in purée or juice
½ cup diced ham	
2 medium onions, chopped	
2 cloves garlic, minced	2 chorizos (2 ounces), thinly sliced
1 large green bell pepper, chopped	2¼ cups water
1 teaspoon dried oregano	2 teaspoons freshly ground pepper
2 tablespoons olive or vegetable oil	2 teaspoons salt
½ teaspoon paprika	12 pimiento-stuffed olives
1½ cups long-grain rice	1 tablespoon capers

In a medium-size skillet, fry the bacon until crisp, then remove it, crumble, and set aside. Add the ham, onions, garlic, bell pepper, and oregano to the drippings. Cook over moderate heat until the vegetables are tender but not browned, about 10 minutes. Set aside.

In a 3-quart saucepan, heat the oil. Add the paprika and rice. Stir over low heat 2 minutes, until the rice is coated with oil and colored. Add the tomatoes, chorizos, water, pepper, salt, and the ham mixture. Stir well. Cover and simmer 45 minutes, stirring only as needed to prevent sticking. Gently stir in the olives, capers, and crumbled bacon. Serve hot as a supper entrée or side dish.

HOT BIRDS

Hunting is a tradition in the South. More than a pastime, it is a legacy handed down from father to son, a heritage of kinship with the land. In rural Florida, game is still plentiful, and in season, white-tailed deer, wild hog, duck, quail, and dove attract thousands of hunters. Trey Harden, a young hunter we know, devised an unusual twist on a familiar way to grill dove or quail. He places a split jalapeño pepper on the breast, then wraps a strip of bacon around each bird, and secures it with a toothpick. They cook at the edge of the grill for about half an hour. The bacon makes them moist, and the jalapeño gives them zip.

SMOTHERED RABBIT

MAKES 4 TO 6 SERVINGS.

Rabbit and other small game were an occasional bonus of growing up on a ranch in Florida. Smothering, which means simmering meat until tender in a savory sauce, is a tried-and-true Cracker way of cooking rabbits and squirrels. This version is modernized with herbs and freshly ground pepper, but the salt pork as a starter is old-fashioned Cracker style. It enriches the taste and keeps the meat moist. If freshly killed wild rabbits are not available, this dish is excellent with rabbit from a market; or watch for signs on roads advertising fresh-killed rabbits for sale by growers raising them for meat.

1 teaspoon each dried rosemary and thyme leaves	2 small onions, chopped
½ teaspoon salt	3 carrots, peeled and cut in chunks
¼ teaspoon coarsely ground pepper	2 ribs celery, cut in chunks
2 cloves garlic, minced	½ cup chicken broth
1 young rabbit, about 2 pounds, cut in 8 pieces	½ cup dry white wine, or chicken broth plus
Flour	1 tablespoon lemon juice
¼ pound salt pork or bacon, diced	

Combine the rosemary, thyme, salt, pepper, and garlic in a mortar or saucer. Work with a pestle or back of a spoon until the seasonings are blended and herbs ground coarse. Rub the mixture on the rabbit. Place the pieces on a plate, cover with waxed paper, and refrigerate 2 hours up to overnight.

Dust the rabbit with flour. Fry the salt pork in a large deep skillet until the pieces are lightly browned. Add the rabbit and sauté until browned on all sides, cooking in two batches if necessary to prevent crowding the pan. Add the onions, carrots, celery, broth, and wine. Cover and simmer until the rabbit is very tender, 30 to 45 minutes for a young rabbit, up to 1½ hours for an older animal. Taste, stir in the lemon juice, and add more seasonings, if desired. Serve with grits or rice.

LIFE IN THE GREEN SWAMP

Hazel Brown grew up in the Green Swamp area of central Florida, where her family had lived since John Baggs Raulerson, her grandfather, settled in 1847. Hers was a large extended family, and Hazel can still recall their gatherings and the country foods they enjoyed. Among the special things she remembers were the wild turkey breasts that were cut into strips, then fried like chicken. The giblets, along with the ribs, backbone, and other bony parts, were boiled to make broth, which was then used in cornbread dressing. The cornbread was baked in a large skillet in the wood stove's oven, then crumbled up with bell pepper, sage, and green onion, and moistened with turkey broth. Then the turkey broth was used to cook dumplings made from biscuit dough—the flour thickening the broth as they cooked.

The Raulersons grew their own rice, which they dried, then hulled, leaving it with a brownish color—they called it "dirty rice." It, too, was cooked in the flavorful turkey stock.

Potato salad was made with hot mashed potatoes, mixed with scrambled eggs, seasoned with prepared mustard, and topped with slices of hard-cooked eggs. Turnips and collards were homegrown and cooked with a wild hog backbone. They also smoked their own bacon, sausage, and hams.

Hazel's mother, Elizabeth, planted cabbage and rutabagas each fall, and cooking the two together was a Christmas tradition. Coffee beans were roasted in a flat pan every morning, then ground for making strong, boiled coffee. Pecans, from the five trees in the Raulersons' yard, were used in fruitcakes, along with raisins, which were a treat because they had to be store-bought. The trees are still standing, and one is sixty feet wide. Hazel also remembers sweet potato pies, and orange pie, made from the sour oranges that grew wild on the property.

CORN PUDDING WITH TOMATOES

MAKES 4 TO 6 SERVINGS.

Corn pudding is a popular dish throughout the South, reflecting the long-standing fondness local people had for corn and corn products in the region. In Florida, where more tomatoes are grown than in any other single state, the marriage of corn and tomatoes is a natural one. This recipe, which includes green peppers and a topping of sliced tomatoes, makes an especially colorful version of this time-tested favorite.

2 tablespoons butter
¼ cup finely chopped onions
½ cup chopped green bell
   pepper
2 tablespoons flour
1 cup milk
2 eggs, lightly beaten

2 cups fresh or frozen corn
   kernels
1 teaspoon salt
¼ teaspoon freshly ground
   pepper
¼ cup chopped parsley
2 tomatoes, thinly sliced

Preheat the oven to 350 degrees. Melt the butter in a saucepan, add the onions and green pepper, and cook until tender but not browned. Stir in the flour and continue to cook and stir 1 or 2 minutes until well blended. Remove from the heat and slowly add the milk, then the eggs, corn, salt, and pepper, beating until smooth. Turn into a well-buttered 1-quart casserole and bake for 20 minutes. Remove from the oven and overlap slices of tomato on the top. Bake 10 minutes longer, or until a knife inserted in the center comes out clean. Let the pudding stand 10 minutes before serving.

"MRS. PHOEBE"—FIRST BRIDE OF LAKE WALES

The first bride of Lake Wales, Phoebe Lewis of Galesburg, was brought down by her proud husband, George Wetmore, in the spring of 1913. When "Mrs. Phoebe" was asked what amusements there were in those days in this new settlement, she laughed and answered, "Oh yes, fishing, of course, spread dinners (fish fries), hayrides, hunting deer and wild turkeys, ice cream 'sociables,' pie socials, taffy pulls, cane grinding parties where we sometimes got sick from too much syrup, jerked beef parties, group singing, old fashioned picnics, barbecues, games like Rook, and, of course, dancing." She went on, "We went to a movie, sat on boards, and the picture was flashed onto the side of a building. You couldn't tell what on earth was going on up there."

from *They Built A City* by Dorothy Kaucher,
Kirstein & Son, Printers, Orlando, Florida, 1970

GREENS WITH CORN MEAL DUMPLINGS

MAKES 4 TO 6 SERVINGS.

A quarter century ago, the seasoning for greens would have been salt pork or ham hock, but even Floridians now use oil and onion or garlic to flavor greens. The hardier greens are started first, to allow time for them to get tender, and the tenderest go in near the end of cooking. The dumplings add interest to this dish, and are a shortcut substitute for the cornbread that traditionally was served with greens. Even though there is a pod of hot pepper in the greens, many people like pepper vinegar, cider vinegar, or Old Sour (page 131) as a condiment on the table as well.

GREENS

3 pounds greens (2 to 3
   bunches), well washed*
1 tablespoon vegetable oil
1 small onion, sliced

½ to 1 cup water
1 teaspoon salt
1 dried or fresh hot chile
   pepper

CORN MEAL DUMPLINGS

⅓ cup yellow corn meal
⅓ cup all-purpose flour
1 teaspoon baking powder
½ teaspoon salt

1 egg, slightly beaten
¼ cup milk
1 tablespoon vegetable oil

*Use an assortment of greens, if possible: collards, mustard, turnip greens, dandelion greens, kale, curly chicory, escarole, romaine, or beet greens.

Cut the stems off the greens and shred the leaves coarsely, cutting several leaves at once on a chopping board. Heat the oil in a wide (to allow space for the dumplings) saucepan. Add the onion and sauté until tender but not browned. Add the toughest greens (collards or mustard greens), the ½ cup water, salt, and the chile pepper. Cover, bring to a boil, reduce the heat, and cook 10 minutes. Stir in the turnip or dandelion greens and cook 5 minutes. Next add the kale, chicory, escarole, or romaine, and water, if needed; stir and cook 5 minutes longer. Add the beet greens, stir and cook another 5 minutes. The greens should be crisp-tender.

Meanwhile, to prepare the dumplings, combine the corn meal, flour, baking powder, and salt in a small bowl. Combine the beaten egg, milk, and oil. Stir into the dry ingredients to make a thick dough. Add ¼ cup more boiling water to the greens, if needed, to provide pot liquor that bubbles to the surface of the greens. Drop the dumpling batter by teaspoonfuls onto the boiling greens. Cover and simmer 15 minutes. Serve the greens with 2 or 3 dumplings on each serving. Pass pepper vinegar, cider vinegar, and Old Sour (page 131) to sprinkle on the greens, if wanted.

TOMATO GRAVY WITH BISCUITS OR RICE

MAKES 3½ CUPS, SERVING 6 TO 7.

This steaming, scarlet-colored gravy, poured over hot biscuits or rice, has been familiar farm food for generations of Southerners, and Florida Crackers are no exception. Tradition aside, this is just as good with pork chops or chicken, or on potatoes. No salt is called for because if you're using canned chicken broth, it is salty enough. Luscious vine-ripe tomatoes beat hothouse varieties any day, making summertime just right for tomato gravy.

3 tablespoons butter
½ cup chopped onion
½ cup chopped green bell
   pepper
3 tablespoons flour
1 cup plus ½ cup chicken
   broth
1 cup (8-ounce can) tomato
   sauce
1 teaspoon sugar

½ teaspoon dry mustard
1 teaspoon finely chopped
   fresh basil or ¼ teaspoon
   dried
½ teaspoon freshly ground
   black pepper
2 cups chopped fresh tomatoes
Pinch cayenne pepper or
   hot pepper sauce (optional)

Melt the butter in a large skillet over medium heat and sauté the onion and bell pepper until tender but not brown. Blend in the flour and cook for 1 to 2 minutes. Slowly add the 1 cup chicken broth, tomato sauce, sugar, mustard, basil, and pepper. Bring to a boil, then cover and simmer for 15 to 20 minutes, stirring often to prevent sticking. Add the tomatoes and simmer another 5 minutes. Adjust the seasoning and add cayenne, if wanted. If a thinner gravy is desired, add the remaining ½ cup chicken broth. To serve, spoon gravy over hot biscuits broken in half, or hot rice.

BISCUITS AND 'TATERS

This is one writer's description of the free life of the old-time Florida cowpokes and the daily victuals that they favored:

Dozens of biscuits and sweet potatoes were cooked and packed in saddlebags along with a slab of salty bacon, coffee, and maybe some onions. The horse's provision of nubbin' corn was in a burlap bag; a bedroll, a rope for tying the horse at night, a cowwhip, and a quart pail for boiling coffee were all tied on the saddle. The cowhunter wore an old, floppy hat; a bandana tied around his neck; an old, longsleeved shirt, pistol-legged pants with lace-up boots or regular pants with brogans completed his attire. His spurs were tin so they could be molded to the boots or brogans. . . .

On the trail, camp was made wherever they were at dark. Coffee was put on to boil, a slab of bacon broiled over the fire on a palmetto stalk, 'taters eaten, moldy biscuits scraped and toasted on a stick over the fire. It was "biscuits and 'tater" time.

from *Biscuits and Taters*, by Joe G. Warner, Great Outdoors Publishing Co., St. Petersburg, Florida, 1980

ONIONS AND BACON

MAKES 4 SERVINGS.

The aroma of simmering onions and bacon is as tantalizing as any kitchen scent can be. When this simple dish is made using fresh Florida sweet onions, the results are even more inspiring. These unique onions, basically the Texas Grano or Texas Gran-X variety, are similar to Vidalia onions and are very moist and sweet. The bulbs are often as large as tennis balls, with long green tops. This recipe uses the entire onion and cooks them to a tender consistency, bringing out the mild, sweet taste. They are excellent as a side dish, served over rice, or on sandwiches.

3 strips of bacon, cut in 1-inch pieces	Salt and freshly ground pepper
3 large white or yellow onions (if sweet onions are unavailable)	Worcestershire sauce (optional)
	Hot pepper sauce (optional)

In a large skillet, cook the bacon until the fat is rendered but the bacon has not browned. Slice the onions, including the tops, then add the tops only to the pan. Cover and simmer 5 minutes. Add the remainder of the onions. Cook slowly for 15 minutes for onions that are slightly crisp, or 30 minutes for well done. Add salt, pepper, Worcestershire sauce, and hot pepper sauce to taste.

CURRIED RICE

MAKES 4 SERVINGS.

Southerners have enjoyed curries since shippers bringing luxuries from the Orient to Savannah, Charleston, Georgetown in South Carolina, Norfolk, and other ports packed the spice among their treasures. And when Southerners use curry powder, they intend you to taste it. This classic curried rice is served as a side dish to poultry, seafood, or pork. In Florida a firm, ripe mango or papaya, fresh pineapple or tomato might be used in place of the apple.

1 tablespoon olive oil	1 cup long-grain rice
½ small onion, diced	2 cups water or chicken broth
½ medium apple, unpeeled, cored and chopped	½ to 1 teaspoon salt
1 tablespoon curry powder, or to taste	¼ teaspoon freshly ground pepper, or to taste

Heat the oil in a large skillet or sauté pan. Add the onion and apple and sauté until the onion is translucent. Stir in the curry powder and sauté 15 seconds to develop the flavor. Add the rice and cook, stirring often, until it is opaque and coated with curry. Add the water or broth, the ½ teaspoon salt, and pepper. Bring to a boil, cover, and simmer 18 to 20 minutes, or until the rice is tender and the liquid absorbed. Or bring the mixture to a boil, pour it into a buttered 6-cup baking dish, and bake, uncovered, at 350 to 375 degrees until done. To hold rice in the oven for 15 to 30 minutes, stir in ½ cup hot water and continue to bake, uncovered, at 325 degrees. Taste and add more salt and pepper, if needed. Fluff up the rice and serve hot.

FLORIDA PEAS

Farmer's markets throughout Florida offer bushelsful of southern peas, of every description, and good cooks all have their individual favorites. While southern pea is the preferred name, many refer to these delectable vegetables as field pea, cowpea, and table pea. U-pick fields provide varieties that include names like black-eyes, cream or "conch" peas, field peas, lady peas, purple hulls, crowders, and zipper peas. They are sold in farmer's markets and in limited supply in supermarkets when in season.

Southern pea descriptions are difficult because there are so many varieties. They are distinguished by size, color, whether or not they have "eyes," and, of course, taste. All of these share a certain delicate, perishable quality that makes shipping difficult; hence the scarcity of most of these peas in markets nationwide.

Floridians have always had a fondness, even a passion, for peas and they relish the unmistakable aroma of a potful of them cooking on the stove. Peas are gently boiled usually with a ham hock or bacon strips to enhance their subtle flavor, and served alongside virtually any main dish, often as a complement to rice.

SPICED ORANGES

MAKES 12 SERVINGS.

These oranges, redolent with cloves and cinnamon, make a flavorful condiment to accompany any main dish, and look bright and sensational, too. We think they go especially well with a baked ham or roast pork and are often given as gifts at Christmas. Overlap the slices around the edge of the serving platter for a festive presentation.

6 oranges, preferably navels
2 cups water
3 cups sugar

¾ cup cider vinegar
12 whole cloves
2 cinnamon sticks

Place the washed, unpeeled oranges in a saucepan and fill two-thirds full with water. Cover and gently boil for 20 minutes. Drain off the water and cut the oranges into ¼- to ½-inch slices. Combine the 2 cups of water, sugar, vinegar, cloves, and cinnamon sticks, and stir over low heat until the sugar is dissolved. Bring to a boil. Add the orange slices and simmer 30 minutes. Remove the oranges and set aside. Continue to cook the syrup 10 minutes longer. Strain and pour over the fruit. When ready to serve, remove the slices from the syrup and serve warm or at room temperature. Leftovers can be kept in the refrigerator for 2 or 3 weeks.

DON'T SQUEEZE THE ORANGES

When buying citrus, select the fruit that is heavy, firm, and thin skinned. Keep in mind that citrus, unlike other fruit, will not ripen more after it has been picked. And don't be dismayed by variations in the color of the skin; cold temperatures produce a rosy tint; the skin may even retain some green color if the temperature is warm. The fruit will be mature, however, because it must meet Florida Citrus Commission standards for taste.

SWEET POTATO YEAST BISCUITS

MAKES 100 1½-INCH BISCUITS.

This recipe yields one hundred bite-size biscuits that are ideal for tiny party sandwiches, filled with country ham or smoked turkey. They are equally good served hot, cut this size or larger, to complement any meal. The sweet potato gives them a subtle orange color. This dough will not rise substantially like bread dough, but will have a slightly porous appearance.

5 cups self-rising flour
1 teaspoon baking powder
⅓ cup sugar
1 cup cooked and well-mashed
    sweet potatoes
1 cup vegetable shortening

1 egg, lightly beaten
1 package active dry yeast,
    dissolved in a little warm
    water
1 cup buttermilk
Melted butter

Sift together the flour, baking powder, and sugar, and set aside. Place the sweet potatoes and shortening in the bowl of an electric mixer and cream together until smooth. Add the egg and the yeast mixture and blend well. Add the buttermilk and mix well. Gradually add the dry ingredients,

Sweet Potato Yeast Biscuits (continued)

kneading the dough enough to hold and make a smooth ball. Put in a large buttered bowl and brush with additional butter. Cover with a kitchen towel and let rise in a warm place for several hours or overnight in the refrigerator. Remove from the bowl and knead briefly. On a floured board, roll the dough out to a thickness of approximately ½ inch. Cut with a 1½-inch biscuit cutter (or larger). Place the biscuits side by side on greased pans and set aside for 1 to 2 hours. Preheat the oven to 400 degrees. Brush the biscuits with melted butter. Bake the biscuits for 15 minutes, or until brown. If one hundred biscuits is too many to use for one time, uncooked biscuits may be frozen.

CARL ALLEN'S CRACKER CAFE

Carl Allen is a Florida legend. His Auburndale restaurant, Allen's Historical Cafe, touts Cracker specialties like 'gator, armadillo, cooter (soft-shell turtle), rattlesnake, and catfish, as well as watermelon soup and fried pickles. Allen's cooks up some of the best hush-puppies around, and though your grits may be served in the beat-up saucepan they were cooked in, it's all in the down-home spirit of this rural relic. The exotic fare is mostly fried, the atmosphere is country casual, and a meal here is something for visitors to brag about back home or for natives, perhaps, to reminisce over.

Allen himself is a dyed-in-the-wool Cracker, born a stone's throw from the café, and is a colorful spokesman for the area's rural heritage. In his seventy-odd years, he has been a cow hunter, citrus worker, and deputy sheriff, among other things, and now, in addition to running his restaurant, he writes a weekly column on Florida lore for the Lakeland *Ledger*. Carl's love for the state is apparent in his claim that "God made Florida so people could get a little hint of what heaven's gonna be."

BLUEBERRY CORNBREAD

MAKES 10 TO 12 SERVINGS.

Wild huckleberries were growing in Florida years before blueberries became an important commercial crop. Now growers in the Bartow, Auburndale, and Lakeland areas bring in ripe berries weeks before Northern farmers pick them. This bread is a wonderful way to use fresh berries. Serve it warm with butter or butter flavored with grated orange zest for brunch, with a luncheon salad, or as dinner bread.

1¾ cups yellow corn meal,
    preferably stone-ground
1¼ cups all-purpose flour
1 tablespoon baking powder
½ teaspoon salt
1¼ cups blueberries, washed,
    drained, and dried on a
    clean kitchen towel

⅓ cup sugar
2 large eggs, beaten lightly
4 tablespoons (½ stick)
    butter, melted and cooled
1½ cups milk

Butter and lightly flour a 9- to 10-inch ring mold or a 13 × 9 × 2-inch baking pan. Preheat the oven to 425 degrees. Combine the corn meal, flour, baking powder, and salt in a large shallow bowl. Sprinkle 2 to 3 tablespoons of the dry ingredients over the blueberries and toss lightly. Stir the sugar into the dry mixture, then stir in the eggs, butter, and milk. Add the blueberries and mix lightly. Turn into the prepared pan. Bake 25 to 30 minutes, until a pick inserted near the center comes out clean. Cool 10 minutes in the pan, then turn out onto a plate and slice or cut the rectangular sheet into squares. Serve hot or warm with butter.

For years, oranges have been synonymous with Florida; postcards and travel posters glorify the industry to millions who have never visited, and anyone who has traveled within the state is familiar with the numerous roadside fruit stands with big "we ship" signs out front. Souvenir shops sell orange blossom perfume, citrus honey, citrus candy, and miniature orange trees for tourists to take home. Orange wood is used for cuticle sticks, and Florida brides wear orange blossoms in their hair and carry them in their bouquets.

Oranges are second only to apples in popularity, and limes are one of the most widely used of all flavorings. Grapefruit and lemons are more secondary, but nonetheless play important roles in contemporary diets. Oddly enough, grapefruit was originally called "forbidden fruit" in Barbados, where it was "discovered" in the mid-eighteenth century. In fact it should be considered anything but "forbidden," given that half a grapefruit has only forty calories, and one cup of juice provides more than the National Research Council's recommended daily allowance of vitamin C. (The name "grapefruit" appeared somewhat later, in Jamaica, so-called because the fruit hung in clusters, like grapes, instead of one to a twig.)

As for oranges, both the fruit and the juice have superior healthful qualities as grapefruit, along with the distinctive sweet taste favored around the world. It is believed that oranges were first introduced in Florida with the settlement in St. Augustine in about 1565. They were much loved by the local Indians who were probably responsible for inadvertently scattering the seeds from the oranges as they carried them back to their villages. Conditions of the soil were perfect for the trees that sprang from this accidental "planting," and later explorers found thickets of wild orange trees flourishing in several sections of the state. They used the juice from these sour oranges to marinate and sprinkle over their meat and fish for flavor. The Indians ate them in a number of ways. They would cut a hole in the top and pour in honey before eating, and they also roasted them, unpeeled, at the edge of the fire.

From such humble beginnings grew what has become Florida's most important agricultural industry. Early groves were planted along the St. Johns River, around St. Augustine, and in the northeast section of the state, but the Great Freeze of 1894–95 devastated the citrus industry and pushed cultivation southward, where growing is centered today.

There are a number of varieties of oranges, and different types ripen at different times of the year, so the fresh-picked fruit is available almost year-round. Valencias are the most widely grown and are a favorite juice orange. Other types such as Hamlin, navels, Pineapple, and Parson Brown are also grown in Florida, each strain contributing to the continuous cycle of maturing. Grapefruit, too, comes in different varieties, the leading ones being the Marsh, Foster, Redblush, Thompson, and Duncan varieties. In addition to oranges and grapefruit, Florida grows a few lemons, Persian hybrid limes (as well as Key limes, farther south), and even some "zipper" fruit (so-called because the peel comes free from the flesh so easily), such as tangerines.

Before the days of modern machinery, citrus fruit was picked by men standing on tall ladders, and transported by wagon to Tampa for shipping to England, or to the closest railway for delivery to the North. Before it was shipped by boat, the fruit was put in the sun to dry the skin and protect it from spoiling.

Beyond the obvious uses for processed fresh juice, frozen concentrate, canned sections, and, of course, the fruit itself are an infinite variety of ways to add vigor to virtually any food by using citrus. For generations, Floridians have made the most of their prized fruit—in marinades, in quick breads, salad dressings, cakes, and more.

Florida ranks first in the United States in orange production (second in the world after Brazil), and is the number one producer of grapefruit in the world. In spite of the freeze of 1989, there are over 720,000 acres of citrus trees in the state, and 10,000 to 12,000 grove owners.

FLORIDA AMBROSIA

MAKES 4 TO 6 SERVINGS.

Ambrosia is so important to the Christmas tradition in many Southern homes that the bowl it is served in becomes a family treasure. A Floridian whose mother died with few worldly goods to bequeath once confided to his wife, "Mama could have left me the ambrosia bowl!" So it is no wonder that Southerners feel they've found a bit of paradise when the ingredients for ambrosia hang on trees in every garden. Purists proclaim that only oranges and freshly shredded coconut should be used. Cooks in Fort Pierce, where pineapple plantations flourished before citrus brought in big bucks, say it's not ambrosia without pineapple. Some cooks add sliced bananas just before serving ambrosia. And many embellish it with maraschino cherries for color or dash in orange liqueurs or brandy. In citrus-growing areas, several types of oranges are used together for varied flavor. But there is agreement on one thing, that true ambrosia contains no custard, creams, or gelatin.

1 coconut, or 2½ cups frozen shredded coconut, thawed	Confectioners' sugar (optional)
4 medium sweet Florida oranges	

Shell the coconut as directed on page 159. Pry out the flesh with the tip of a paring knife, peel off the brown skin, and shred the coconut.

Place a third of the coconut in a glass dessert bowl. Peel the oranges and cut in slices ¼ inch thick. Place half the orange slices on the coconut in the bowl. Sprinkle confectioners' sugar on each layer if oranges are not as sweet as wanted. A quicker way is to cut unpeeled oranges in half and remove the pulp with a grapefruit spoon, holding the orange half over the coconut to catch the juices, but the sliced oranges make a prettier presentation.

Add another third of the coconut to the bowl, the remaining oranges, except for a few slices for garnish, then the remaining coconut. Garnish and chill until ready to serve. Ambrosia is best made the day it is to be served.

OPTIONAL INGREDIENTS
ADD ONE OR TWO, IF DESIRED:

**1 to 2 tablespoons orange-
    flavored liqueur**
**½ fresh ripe pineapple,
    cubed or shredded**
**2 bananas, peeled and sliced
    (add just before serving)**

**Use tangelos, Temple oranges,
    Mandarins, or grapefruit
    sections in combination
    with other oranges**

FRESH STRAWBERRY
ICE CREAM

MAKES 1½ QUARTS, 6 SERVINGS.

Fresh berry ice cream brings back memories of the ache of cranking the ice cream freezer, licking the dasher, and that first spoonful melting on your tongue. The freezers are more sophisticated now, but we still use the old-fashioned recipes. Add the strawberries to the vanilla custard in two parts, the first for delicate color, and second for berries to bite.

2 cups milk	1 cup heavy cream
⅔ cup sugar	1 tablespoon vanilla extract
3 eggs, beaten	1 quart strawberries, washed,
⅛ teaspoon salt	capped, and quartered

Heat the milk and sugar in the top of a double boiler over moderate heat, stirring until the sugar is dissolved. Remove from the heat and gradually stir it into the beaten eggs. Return to the double boiler, and place over (not touching) boiling water. Add the salt, and cook and stir until the custard thickens and coats the back of a spoon. Set the pan in cold water for a few minutes to stop the cooking quickly, then cool completely in the refrigerator. Stir in the cream and vanilla. Add half of the berries to the mixture and freeze in an ice cream maker according to manufacturer directions. When the ice cream is almost firm, add the remaining berries and continue to freeze until firm. Pack in a freezer container, and freeze for later eating.

STRAWBERRIES IN FLORIDA

$\int$trawberry cultivation began in central Florida in the 1880s and has grown to become one of the state's largest crops. Hillsborough county, the self-proclaimed "Winter Strawberry Capital of the World," is the center of the berry-growing area, and in Plant City, even the water tower is in the shape of a giant strawberry. From December to the first of June, there are roadside stands selling berries and pies, as well as acres of U-pick fields.

Henry Plant's railroad first made it possible to ship strawberries around the country, and business in the Plant City–Dover area has been booming ever since. In the old days, children often were the field laborers, since they didn't have to bend over as far as adults to do the picking. "Strawberry schools" closed each year during the picking season, but this practice was abolished in the 1950s.

While competition from California and Central and South America has increased steadily (and, in fact, California produces more berries overall than Florida), the area's pride in its major crop has not faltered, and in Plant City during the annual Strawberry Festival, the first two weeks in March, growers and visitors can sample a multitude of shortcakes, pies, cakes, jams, and breads, all made with locally grown strawberries.

Florida's expert on growing the state's favorite berry is Roy Parke. He plants over two million strawberry seedlings each year from October to early December at his one-hundred-acre "strawberry patch" that is the pride of his Parkesdale Farms. In 1962 the "strawberry king" was a pioneer in the shipping of Florida berries by air to cities nationwide, and the following year, began shipping overseas. He initiated the use of a sprinkler system to protect strawberries against freezing: by spraying water on the plants when the temperature plummets. The resulting coat of ice serves as a blanket to keep the berry temperature from dropping below 32 degrees.

Parke relies on three varieties of strawberries: Selva, Pajaro, and his favorite, the Oso Grande. Though all three look alike, large and scarlet-colored, Roy says the Oso Grande is the sweetest and best, the "Cadillac" of all winter berries.

Today, Parkesdale Farms operates two retail markets, where visitors can purchase berries and produce (also grown on Parke's farm), and, of course, homemade strawberry shortcake.

MASARYKTOWN ROSKY CREAM CHEESE PASTRIES

MAKES 50 PASTRIES

Rosky are baked pastries made with cream cheese dough and filled with cooked fruit, preserves, or beaten egg whites, sugar, and nuts. They are one of the specialties that Ludmilla Ortuba makes for her family and for festivals in the tiny Czechoslovakian community of Masaryktown, northeast of Tampa.

1 cup (2 sticks) well-chilled butter,
    cut in pieces
2 cups unsifted all-purpose flour
1 package (8 ounces) cream
    cheese, softened and cut in
    pieces

1⅓ cups filling (see next page)
Confectioners' sugar or
    granulated sugar

In a large bowl, using a pastry blender, cut the butter into the flour until the mixture resembles fine crumbs. Add the cream cheese and again cut into the flour mixture until the dough begins to form. Using your hands, work the dough together just until the cream cheese is evenly distributed. Form into a ball. Wrap airtight and chill for several hours or overnight. The dough will be very firm.

Preheat the oven to 375 degrees. Divide the dough in half. On a lightly floured board, using a lightly floured rolling pin, roll half of the dough into a 15-inch square using additional flour as needed to prevent sticking. With a floured sharp knife, cut the square into 25 3-inch squares. Place about 1 teaspoon of the filling in the center of each square. Fold all four corners over the filling so the "points" meet in the center, forming a 2-inch square "envelope." Pinch to seal at the center, then pinch the edges together to seal in the filling. Place the filled squares on ungreased baking sheets (use foil-lined baking sheets for easy cleanup) and bake for 15 minutes, or until lightly browned. Remove to a wire rack to cool. Repeat with the remaining dough half. If desired, sift sugar onto the pastries just before serving.

FILLINGS

Enough for 50 pastries.

PRESERVES

1⅓ cup preserves, top with a few chopped, toasted almonds (½ cup total).

APPLE FILLING

Cook 2 to 3 large apples, peeled, cored, and finely chopped, with 3 tablespoons butter and 3 tablespoons of sugar until the consistency is of chunky applesauce. Add 1½ teaspoon vanilla extract.

EGG WHITE FILLING

Beat 4 egg whites until frothy. Gradually add 1¼ cups sugar and continue to beat until stiff but not dry. Fold in ½ pound chopped walnuts.

NOTE: The dough may be prepared in the food processor. Be sure the butter is very well chilled and cut in pieces, and the cream cheese is well chilled and cut in pieces, not softened as above. Place the butter and flour in a food processor fitted with the steel blade. Using the pulse switch, cut the butter into the flour until the mixture resembles fine crumbs, about 50 short pulses. Add the cream cheese and again, using the pulse switch, cut the cream cheese into the flour mixture until it begins to come together and will hold a shape when pressed, about 50 short pulses. Turn out onto a floured board and press the dough together to form a ball. Proceed as above.

STRAWBERRY COBBLER

MAKES 6 SERVINGS.

To make a good strawberry cobbler, the strawberries must be cooked and thickened before baking so that the filling isn't watery and the topping soggy. Use plenty of berries for peak flavor and color. With rich cream or ice cream, this dessert has pampered several generations of Florida children.

1½ cups sugar	1 teaspoon vanilla extract
2 tablespoons cornstarch	1 tablespoon lemon juice
¼ cup water	½ cup (1 stick) butter
4 cups strawberries, washed, capped, and large ones cut in half	1 cup flour
	1 tablespoon baking powder
	1 cup milk

Preheat the oven to 350 degrees. In a saucepan, combine ½ cup of the sugar, the cornstarch, and the water. Stir over moderate heat until the mixture thickens. Add the berries and cook until thick and tinted pink throughout, about 10 minutes. Remove from the heat and stir in the vanilla extract and lemon juice.

Put the butter in an 8-inch cast-iron skillet and place in the oven until the butter is melted, tilting the pan once or twice so it covers the bottom evenly. Meanwhile, in a bowl, combine the flour, the remaining 1 cup of sugar, baking powder, and the milk. Mix well and pour into the melted butter, gently spreading the batter to cover the bottom of the pan. Pour the berry mixture over the batter, but do not stir. Bake in the lower third of the oven for 1 hour, or until lightly browned on top. The crust will rise to the top as it bakes. Serve warm.

CARRIE'S PINEAPPLE CAKE

MAKES 14 TO 16 SERVINGS.

When we asked Carrie Young for the recipe for her three-layer cake with pineapple filling and white icing, she shrugged and answered, "Oh, I just throw it together." In fact, she has worked for Caroline's parents doing just that for more than thirty years, with a well-earned reputation as an exceptional cook. This is her favorite; she uses an old-fashioned 1-2-3-4 cake and covers it with mountains of white frosting.

3 cups all-purpose flour	4 eggs
2 teaspoons baking powder	1 cup milk
1 cup (2 sticks) butter, at room	1 teaspoon vanilla extract
temperature	1 teaspoon lemon extract
2 cups sugar	

PINEAPPLE FILLING

2 tablespoons flour	1 teaspoon lemon extract
½ cup sugar	
1 20-ounce can crushed	
pineapple in heavy syrup	

FLUFFY WHITE ICING

1 cup sugar	3 egg whites
⅓ cup light corn syrup	½ teaspoon vanilla extract
⅓ cup water	

Preheat the oven to 350 degrees. Grease and flour 3 8- or 9-inch cake pans. Sift together the flour and baking powder and set aside. In a mixing bowl, cream together the butter and sugar until light and fluffy. Add the eggs, one at a time, beating well after each addition. Add the dry ingredients, alternating with the milk, beginning and ending with the flour mixture. Add the vanilla and lemon extracts. Pour the batter into the prepared cake pans. Bake for about 30 minutes, or until the cake springs back when touched lightly with fingertips, or a cake tester comes out clean.

Meanwhile, make the filling: In a saucepan, combine the flour and sugar. Drain the syrup from the canned pineapple and slowly add it to the flour mixture. Mix well until smooth, making sure there are no lumps. Add the crushed pineapple and over moderate heat, stir until thickened. Add the lemon extract. Remove from the heat and set aside to cool.

When the cake is done, cool the cake in the pans on a rack for a few minutes, then turn the layers out onto cake racks to cool completely. Spread the pineapple filling between the layers.

Make the fluffy white icing: In a saucepan, heat the sugar, corn syrup, and water slowly to boiling and cook until the temperature reaches 240 to 242 degrees on a candy thermometer, or until a small amount forms a firm ball when dropped into cold water. Beat the egg whites until stiff but not dry. Slowly pour the syrup into the whites, beating constantly. Continue to beat until cool and thick enough to spread. Add the vanilla extract. Frost the top and sides of the cake with the icing.

OLD SOUTH CARAMEL CAKE

MAKES APPROXIMATELY 16 SERVINGS.

Cakes like this, light but firm enough to slice easily, even and smooth for frosting perfectly, are unobtainable by later recipes with more baking powder or, perish the thought, cake mix. For this one, we still sift the flour twice, the way our grandmothers did, before measuring it.

3½ cups all-purpose flour, sifted twice before measuring	2 cups sugar
	6 eggs
2 teaspoons baking powder	1 cup milk
1 cup (2 sticks) butter, softened	1 teaspoon vanilla extract

CARAMEL FROSTING

3 cups firmly packed brown sugar	4 tablespoons (½ stick) butter
2 cups milk	2 teaspoons vanilla extract

Preheat the oven to 325 degrees. Butter 2 9-inch layer cake pans and line the bottoms with parchment or waxed paper. Butter the waxed paper. Sift the flour with the baking powder and set aside.

In a large mixing bowl, cream the butter until fluffy, then gradually add the sugar, beating until creamy. Add the eggs, one at a time, and beat in thoroughly. Add the flour mixture alternately with the milk, beginning and ending with the dry ingredients. Stir well after each addition, but do not overmix. Stir in the vanilla extract. Turn the batter into the prepared pans. Bake until the tops of the layers spring back when lightly touched, about 35 minutes. When the cake is done, cool 10 minutes in the pans, then turn out onto cake racks to cool completely.

To make the frosting: Combine the brown sugar and milk in a large saucepan. Bring to a boil and cook, stirring constantly, to a soft-ball stage or 234 to 240 degrees on a candy thermometer. Remove from the heat, add the butter and vanilla, and beat at high speed until thick enough to hold to the cake when spread. If the frosting becomes too thick, beat in a few drops of hot water. Spread the caramel frosting over one layer of the cake, top with the other layer and cover the top and sides of the entire cake with the remaining frosting.

GRAPEFRUIT CHIFFON PIE

MAKES 6 SERVINGS.

This is a delicate, exceptionally light, slightly tart dessert that is popular in central Florida. If pink grapefruit is available, the sections make an especially attractive garnish, in contrast to the light-colored pie.

1 9-inch pie crust, baked
    (pages 304–5)
1 tablespoon (1 packet)
    unflavored gelatin
¼ cup water
2 eggs, well beaten
1 cup grapefruit juice
2 tablespoons lemon or lime
    juice

1 cup sugar
1 cup very cold evaporated
    milk
1 grapefruit, sectioned, with
    white membrane and pith
    removed from each segment

Sprinkle the gelatin over the water and set aside to soften. Beat the eggs lightly in a saucepan. Gradually add the grapefruit juice, lemon or lime juice, and the sugar. Cook over moderate heat, stirring constantly until the mixture is slightly thickened and will coat a spoon. Be careful not to let the mixture come to a boil or the eggs will curdle. Remove the saucepan from the heat and stir in the softened gelatin. Pour into a bowl, preferably a metal one (it will chill faster), and refrigerate until the filling has partially set, approximately 15 minutes, stirring occasionally. Be careful not to let mixture congeal. Remove from the refrigerator and beat with a whisk or an electric hand-mixer until fluffy.

In another bowl, whip the evaporated milk until thick. Fold it into the grapefruit mixture, then gently pour into the baked pie shell. Chill several hours until firm. Just before serving, garnish with grapefruit sections.

DOUBLE-CRUST GUAVA PIE

MAKES 6 SERVINGS.

Though not grown commercially in central Florida, guavas are popular as backyard fruit and often end up in homemade jellies and pies. Harriet Oglesby, from Bartow, uses a sturdy hybrid variety for this simple, double-crust pie. Such flavorful fruit requires very little embellishment.

3 tablespoons flour

⅔ cup sugar

⅛ teaspoon salt

Pastry dough for a 9-inch
Double-Crust Pie (recipe
follows)

4 cups seeded and sliced
guavas

4 teaspoons lemon juice

3 tablespoons butter, cut in
pieces

Preheat the oven to 450 degrees. Mix together the flour, sugar, and salt and set aside. Line a 9-inch pie plate with the pastry and add the guavas, slightly mounding them in the center. Pour the flour mixture evenly over the guavas. Sprinkle with the lemon juice and dot with butter. Cover with the top pastry. Cut several slashes in the top for steam to escape. Bake 10 minutes, then lower the heat to 350 degrees and bake 30 to 40 minutes longer.

PASTRY DOUGH FOR A DOUBLE-CRUST PIE

Lard was the standard shortening in pie crusts for most good cooks of Cracker heritage before 1950. Good-quality fresh lard still is available in Florida, but solid white shortening is more common in pastries today.

2 cups all-purpose flour
1 teaspoon salt
⅔ cup vegetable shortening

4 to 6 tablespoons very cold
water

Combine the flour and salt in a shallow bowl, add the shortening, and cut it in with a pastry blender or until the mixture resembles coarse meal. Sprinkle cold water over the top, a teaspoon or so at a time, and work it in with a fork until the pastry clings together. Round it into a ball on waxed paper, cover loosely, and chill for 30 minutes. Roll out half the pastry to a circle 4 inches larger than the pie pan. Gently fit it into the pan, trim the edges, and fill the crust. Roll out the remaining pastry, fit over the filling, turn the edges under the bottom crust, and crimp them together to form a high fluted edge. Cut slashes in the top and bake as directed.

FOR A BAKED 9-INCH PIE SHELL

Roll out half the pastry to a circle 4 inches larger than the 9-inch pie pan. Fit into the pan, trim, and flute the edges to the rim of the pan. To prevent the pastry from buckling, line the bottom and sides with a sheet of aluminum foil and fill with uncooked rice or dried beans. Bake in a preheated 425-degree oven for 10 minutes, remove the foil and rice or beans, and bake 3 to 4 minutes longer until lightly browned.

FLORIDA'S
GREAT
LAKE

APPETIZERS

Okeechobee Vegetable Fantasia

Tomato and Pasta Salad

Curried Chicken Salad

ENTRÉES

Baked Fish with Fresh Vegetable
   Stuffing

South Florida Frog's Legs

Country Chicken and Dumplings

Honey Mustard Barbecued Chicken

Orange Rosemary Chicken

Florida Goulash

Tony's Florida Spaghetti Gravy

Smoked Pork Chinese-Style

Barbecue Venison Seminole-Style

VEGETABLES

Swamp Cabbage Cracker-Style

Bell Peppers amd Corn in Cream

Barbecue Corn

Florida Celery Bake

Squash Casserole

Citrus Sweet Potatoes

Hoppin' John with Trimmings
   (Black-Eyed Peas and Hog Jowl)

BREADS

Clewiston Cornbread

Buttery Rich Cornbread

Sugar Cube Orange Biscuits

DESSERTS

Poached Guava Shells

Mango Bavarian Cream

Jam Pies

Okeechobee Shortcake

Coconut Pound Cake

Fresh Banana Layer Cake

Orange Melts

Ambrosia Cookies

Sour Orange Pie

$\int$ outh Florida's Lake Okeechobee is the second largest freshwater lake in the United States, after Lake Michigan, and the center of Florida's most incredible growing area. It is a winter vegetable paradise. The region seems calm by comparison with its neighbors, the dynamic Gold Coast, the energized Sun Coast, and the enterprising central area of citrus, cattle ranching, and phosphate mining.

But don't get the idea that the lake area is sleeping. Every holiday, cooks all over America buying crisp snap beans for a Thanksgiving or Christmas dinner in a snowy climate are indebted to the farmers around the lake. Today more than $50 million worth of green beans are shipped to markets all over the country in an average year. A half century ago the first grower to bring his beans in before Thanksgiving could charge top dollar to Northern buyers, and become wealthy over a weekend. Bean bonanzas are less common now that new varieties mature faster, and the produce from other regions fills in the lean seasons in Florida. But winter holiday vegetables are still big business.

A drive around the lake takes you through miles upon miles of vegetables and fruits. A tourist hardly sees the lake behind the dike, without driving down an access road to the shore, where water stretches farther than the eye can see, like an ocean. The sights on land are lettuces in several colors and shapes disappearing into the horizon, millions of rows of radishes, eggplants, peppers, celery, cucumbers, squashes, turnips, and other greens stretching to infinity. Sweet corn is harvested all year long, so you might see one field of corn with plump ears ready for pulling, the next with ears filling with the silk, another with tassels beginning, and other fields with new plants gaining strength to grow tall.

In the Okeechobee area lies most of the Everglades, a grassy expanse with its feet in water. The "River of Grass" is speckled with hammocks, small islands of forest where the Indians built homes after the largest battle of the Seminole wars, on Christmas Day, 1837. The muck land that now grows vegetables and sugarcane so well is created by the natural action of the great body of water on decaying vegetation.

This part of Florida was hardly known at all, except by troops warring with the Indians, until the early 1900s. A few Anglos from Georgia, Alabama, Tennessee, and the Carolinas had come to farm, hunt, and fish. Many had small herds of cattle. Indians in the Everglades have run cattle for generations, and some carry on successful ranching today. Early settlers found the lake, the rivers, and creeks full of fish—catfish, widemouth bass, and bream, the sunfish that give an angler a lot of fight for their mere half- to one-pound heft. Hunting was backwoods sport from the beginning, and hunting dog trials were once a big event near Moore Haven.

The cooking here was peas and beans, chicken and eggs, a hog or two that most families raised, wild foods like venison, boar, guavas, and berries. Even oranges, abandoned by Spanish explorers two or three centuries before, had gone wild in the Everglades, and Crackers and Indians alike used them.

At the turn of the century, serious farmers began to recognize the asset of the black muck soil and long growing season in the area, and came to buy acreage. They brought their families and attracted workers. As Florida always does, the migration attracted a few bizarre personalities. In 1916, when Mrs. Marian Newhall Horwitz O'Brien, sister of a partner of the J. P. Morgan firm and a self-proclaimed socialite, came to Moore Haven, the town was a nondescript hamlet of frame houses and stores on the west shore of the lake. She announced she would transform Moore Haven into "the Chicago of the South." During the prosperity created by easy sales of farm products in World War II, Mrs. O'Brien got along well in Moore Haven. She persuaded several retired English gentlemen to settle there. Afternoon tea was a daily ritual at the colony, and the men rode to the hounds in English-style saddles. Longtime residents sneered at such shenanigans, and Mrs. O'Brien and her husband moved south to Clewiston. Her efforts to rebuild this town failed, but the broad street that was to be the great white way of the new city has been preserved as Clewiston's main street, lined with one-story commercial buildings. The O'Briens went on to Palm Beach and lived out their lives where social life is livelier than around the lake and where afternoons in town there call for a Coke or beer break more often than tea and finger sandwiches.

The Cracker-style cooking of the early settlers is still here. Grits and fine cornbread hold a high place on tables. Home folk and most restaurant cooks prepare fish and swamp cabbage routinely. The best chicken and dumplings in Florida may be here when a civic club has a community supper. The Seminoles, who live and farm in the Everglades, carry on their food traditions on occasion. Many also eat Anglo style, with lots of fast food and too much fried food, said one Indian woman, in speaking of her children. Indian women, many of whom have moved from the traditional open-face, thatch-roofed chickees in the Everglades to houses in towns or cities, get their recipes where everybody does: from magazines, newspapers, and books. And when a Seminole man or woman barbecues venison these days, the seasonings may seem more Cajun than the smoky meat flavor of the past.

After the United States cut off imports of sugar from Cuba, tilling of cane around the lake went into high gear. On almost any winter or spring day one can see a tower of smoke across the Everglades, the pall that shows the cane-brakes are being burned for harvest.

Sugar, vegetables, and ranching have attracted thousands of migrant workers, some not so migrant who live here several months a year or more. These folk from Puerto Rico, the Dominican Republic, Mexico, Haiti, Nicaragua, and Jamaica have created a demand for rice by the twenty-five-pound bag, tortillas, beans in amazing variety, and a selection of chiles never seen in Florida until a few years ago.

Cooking is mostly homegrown, though you find excellent freshly made sandwiches at a lunch counter in Okeechobee City, and home-baked pies at Flora and Ella's Cafe in La Belle, so famous that people come in to view the fresh pies early in the morning. And everywhere there is good fried catfish with trimmings. As one would expect, vegetables of all varieties are served in cafés, restaurants, and at home. If you have a chance, buy a ticket to a community barbecue or supper. You won't believe the four-foot vegetable tray with dips.

OKEECHOBEE VEGETABLE FANTASIA

MAKES 25 SERVINGS.

The vegetables and dip at a large party near the lake is a testament to the agricultural prowess of the growers. Dinner chairmen ask everybody to contribute, and the assortment is stupendous, colorful and brimming with health, as each farmer tries to outshine the others.

The tray for a crowd may include a dozen crisp, raw vegetables plus more blanched vegetables. Among the uncooked ones are celery, carrots, radishes (round or long, red or white), green onions or scallions, thin slices or sticks of yellow squash and zucchini, cherry tomatoes and tomato wedges, cucumbers, bell peppers in three or more colors, and turnips, cut in thin slices, wedges, or sticks. Vegetables blanched or lightly cooked include short-cut ears of sweet corn, green beans, small okra pods, and on picks, tiny potatoes in their jackets, cubes of sweet potato, and peeled baby beets.

The dip plays second fiddle to the color and beauty of the vegetables; this one is spicy, different, and reasonably easy to prepare. Set out several bowls of it and use every colorful vegetable you can get, the more the better.

2 cups sour cream or sour
　half-and-half
2 tablespoons thick hot sauce
　such as Dat'l Do It, Tiger
　Sauce, or medium or hot
　salsa

2 tablespoons buttermilk
3 tablespoons minced fresh
　parsley or cilantro

Blend together the sour cream or half-and-half, the hot sauce, buttermilk, and parsley or cilantro. Cover and chill 1 hour or longer before serving. Serve in bowls as a dip with raw and blanched vegetable cut for dipping, chips, or crackers.

THE FLORIDA "CRANBERRY"

The cook who first made roselle sauce, which looks and tastes like New England cranberry sauce, is unknown, but he or she is remembered every holiday season when hobby cooks of south Florida make it. We can only speculate that the originator was homesick for cranberries and had seen the natives brew a tea with roselles. The dried calyxes, known as *flor de jamaica*, jamaica flower, or jamaica, make a bright red, acidic tea that is served iced in summer or hot and laced with rum at Christmastime in the islands or Central America. The dried flower is found in shops specializing in Mexican and Caribbean foods. For a sauce, you need the fresh roselles, and dooryard shrubs are the primary source. A member of the hibiscus family, the bloom opens one morning and fades by evening. In three to four weeks, the calyxes ripen fleshy and plump and are ready to gather. Cut off the stem ends, press out the seed pods of the calyxes, and discard. For each cup of roselles, use ⅔ cup water. Boil the mixture, uncovered, 10 minutes or until the roselle pieces are tender. Add ½ cup of sugar or more, bring to a boil, stirring, and remove from the heat. Cool the sauce before serving.

TOMATO AND PASTA SALAD

MAKES 8 TO 10 SERVINGS.

A vegetable pasta salad always makes a hit at a backyard barbecue or potluck. Fresh Florida tomatoes are a big item in this one. They are smoke- or oven-roasted, which concentrates their sweet-acid flavor. With the tomatoes go bell peppers in several colors, aromatic vegetables, and cilantro. Other vegetables can be added, but cut corn or green beans should be lightly cooked, if you choose them.

4 large (1⅓ pounds) ripe red
  tomatoes
8 to 10 yellow egg tomatoes
  (optional)
1 cup cubed avocado
  (1 small)
3 tablespoons lime juice
  (1 medium Persian)
1 tablespoon minced jalapeño
  or other chile pepper
1 large clove garlic, minced
½ cup diced, peeled, and
  seeded cucumber
½ cup diced green bell
  pepper

½ cup diced purple or
  lavender bell pepper
½ cup diced yellow or red
  bell pepper
½ cup diced red or Florida
  sweet onion
½ cup thinly sliced green
  onions or scallions
⅓ cup chopped cilantro
  (fresh coriander)
5 tablespoons olive oil
2 teaspoons salt, or to
  taste
1 pound rotelle or fusilli

Preheat a barbecue grill with a cover to moderate or an oven to 300 degrees. Wash the red tomatoes, cut in halves, and place cut sides down on an oiled rack in a shallow pan; arrange the yellow tomatoes around the red. Place over indirect heat in the grill and close cover or bake in the oven until tomatoes are soft, but not dripping, 30 to 45 minutes; cool the tomatoes. While baking the tomatoes, prepare the avocado and mix it with the lime juice; set aside.

Pull the skins off the grilled red tomatoes and purée the pulp in a food processor or with a fork or spoon. If using the yellow tomatoes, pull the peel off them and reserve the flesh for garnish. Add the chile pepper and garlic to the puréed red tomato.

Combine the purée, the cucumber, three colors of bell pepper, onion, and green onion in a large bowl. Stir in the cilantro, 2 tablespoons of the olive oil, and the salt to taste. Fold in the avocado mixture. Refrigerate the sauce or keep it at room temperature up to 2 or 3 hours.

Cook the pasta in 6 quarts of boiling salted water with 1 tablespoon of the remaining olive oil until barely tender. Drain and toss with the remaining 2 tablespoons olive oil. Chill the pasta.

In a large bowl, toss the pasta with 2 or 3 large spoonfuls of the sauce, mixing it thoroughly. Add the remaining sauce and toss lightly. Arrange the yellow tomato halves over the top. Serve cold.

CURRIED CHICKEN SALAD

MAKES 6 SERVINGS.

Curry came to America in the treasured spice boxes of English settlers, who had long fancied its exotic flavor, and with sea captains sailing the world from Southern ports, such as Charleston and Savannah. Along with southward-looking pioneers, curry eventually found its way to Florida, where the piquant flavor was embraced, as it was throughout the South. It now shows up in a multitude of dishes, such as this one, that combines ease of preparation with unique taste.

CHICKEN

3 whole boneless chicken
  breasts
4 ribs celery, quartered
1 medium onion, coarsely
  chopped

3 tablespoons curry powder
1 tablespoon salt
1½ teaspoons freshly ground
  pepper

SALAD

3 cups chopped cooked chicken	**1 teaspoon curry powder**
1 cup chopped celery	**½ teaspoon salt**
½ cup cubed unpeeled apple	**1 teaspoon cider vinegar**
¼ cup raisins	**½ teaspoon freshly ground black pepper**
¼ cup coarsely chopped roasted peanuts*	**⅛ teaspoon ground red pepper (cayenne)**
1 cup mayonnaise	

*Peanuts can be easily chopped in a nut chopper, or in a blender.

For the chicken, place it in a large pot and cover with water. Add the celery, onion, curry powder, salt, and pepper. Boil gently, covered, for approximately 20 minutes, or until cooked through. Remove the chicken, cool, and cut into bite-size pieces.

For the salad, mix together the chicken and remaining salad ingredients in a large bowl. Cover and refrigerate until serving time.

BAKED FISH WITH FRESH VEGETABLE STUFFING

MAKES 4 SERVINGS.

Baked stuffed fish always makes a splendid appearance, and never more spectacularly than with a fresh vegetable stuffing. The dressing is good with freshwater fish or a snapper, and twin fillets or fish steaks with this stuffing are excellent. Cucumbers, a huge commercial crop in the state, are not often cooked, but here they contribute a fresh aroma to the stuffing and more cukes are braised in butter to make an uncomplicated sauce for the fish.

4 freshwater bass or speckled
trout, 1 to 2 pounds each, or
1 red snapper, 3 to 3½ pounds
5 tablespoons vegetable or olive
oil
1 medium onion, diced fine
2 small carrots, peeled and
cut in ¼-inch dice
½ green bell pepper, diced
¼ cup diced celery (optional)
¼ cup minced parsley
1 teaspoon salt

½ teaspoon sugar
¼ teaspoon freshly ground
pepper
⅓ cup water, white wine, or
fish stock
1 tablespoon lime or lemon
juice
1 cup crumbled cornbread or
fresh whole-wheat bread
crumbs
½ cucumber, peeled, seeded,
and diced

CUCUMBER-BUTTER SAUCE

1 medium cucumber
1 tablespoon salt
½ cup (1 stick) butter
1 tablespoon lime or lemon
juice

Dash hot pepper sauce
Minced parsley
Lime or lemon wedges
for garnish

Clean the fish and split it almost through, removing the backbone and ribs. Wipe the cavities of the fish with a damp paper towel. Set aside.

Preheat the oven to 375 degrees. Heat 3 tablespoons of the oil in a large skillet. Add the onion, carrots, bell pepper, celery, and parsley. Sauté until the onion is tender. Add the salt, sugar, black pepper, and water, wine, or fish stock. Simmer 5 minutes, or until the carrot is tender and the liquid evaporated. Add the lime juice, bread crumbs, and diced cucumber; stir over low heat 1 minute.

Stuff the fish cavities with the mixture and close with skewers and twine. Place the fish side by side in a large oiled baking dish. Brush with the remaining oil. Bake 25 to 30 minutes for the small fish, or 35 to 40 minutes for the whole snapper. The fish is done when the flesh of the thickest parts is opaque when tested with a fork. Baste once or twice with the pan juices.

While the fish is baking, prepare the sauce: Peel the cucumber, cut it lengthwise in half, and scoop out the seeds. Slice the cucumber very thin. Layer the slices into a plastic or stainless steel sieve, sprinkling each layer with salt. Pack down with the palms of the hands and let drain over a bowl or into the sink for 1 hour. Wipe salt and liquid off the cucumbers with a paper towel. Melt the butter in a small saucepan, stir in the cucumber, and sauté a minute or two to develop the flavor. Stir in the lime juice and pepper sauce.

To serve, remove the fish heads and lift the small fish to individual plates or the large fish to a platter. Serve with the Cucumber-Butter Sauce and garnish with parsley and lime or lemon wedges. Cut the large fish crosswise for serving.

OKEECHOBEE CATFISH

There is no match for freshly fried Okeechobee catfish, and freshwater fishermen consider them the finest food in the world. Dozens of cafés and diners advertising fried catfish are along the roads around the lake. The modest little spots, with shiny-topped tables and sweetened ice tea, are filled with neighborhood folk at noontime. The fish are wild, no more than ten to twelve hours out of the lake when they are cooked. Order the fingerlings, or baby catfish, if they are available, though larger fish are excellent, too. The tiny ones are dressed out whole with heads cut off and the tails left on, the best part, say some devotees. The little fish will be no more than six or eight inches long. In the best places, the fish are salted and peppered, coated lightly with flour or corn meal, and fried in hot fat just long enough to crisp them and cook the flesh. Eight or ten of the tiny fish are piled high on a plate with fried potatoes (sometimes sweet potatoes), fried okra, and hushpuppies. Coleslaw is on the side and locals order ice tea. Ketchup is on the table, but don't use it. A bit of lemon or lime juice is good, but sweet or spicy condiments mask the delicate flavor.

SOUTH FLORIDA FROG'S LEGS

MAKES 2 TO 4 SERVINGS.

The sport of frog gigging has been popular in Florida for generations, especially among teenagers. Armed with a gig (a long pole with a hook on the end), something to put the frogs in (croker sacks, a Southern name for a burlap bag, are handy in rural areas), a strong light, and a few pals (girls are usually squeamish and just watch), it's an evening's entertainment that can yield a rewarding meal. The job of cutting off the legs (only the hind legs are edible), pulling off the skin, then cutting off the feet, is usually passed off to Dad, and Mom takes it from there. Frying or sautéing are the most popular methods of cooking frog's legs, and some soak them first in milk or beer. Here we sauté them and make a simple butter sauce with garlic and scallions or green onions to pour over just before serving. Frog meat is delicate, so it's important not to overcook it. Since it sticks easily, a Teflon pan works well.

South Florida Frog's Legs (continued)

12 pairs medium frog's legs	¾ cup vegetable oil
Salt and freshly ground pepper	6 cloves garlic, finely chopped
1 cup flour	½ cup thinly sliced scallions or green onions
6 tablespoons butter plus ½ cup (1 stick)	Lime wedges

Wash the frog's legs thoroughly. Season with salt and pepper. Place the flour in a mixing bowl and coat the legs on all sides, shaking off the excess flour. In a skillet, heat the 6 tablespoons butter and oil over moderate heat. Without crowding the pan, sauté a few frog's legs at a time, cooking 2 to 3 minutes on each side for small legs, 4 to 5 minutes on each side for large ones. When brown and tender, remove from the pan, drain on paper towels, and put them in a warm oven while making the butter sauce.

In a clean skillet, melt the remaining ½ cup butter. Add the garlic and scallions and cook, stirring for 2 to 3 minutes. Place the frog's legs on a warm serving platter and pour the butter sauce evenly over the legs. Garnish the platter with lime wedges. Serve immediately.

ALLIGATOR MEAT

Indians were smoking and eating alligator meat when the first Spanish explorers came in the sixteenth century, but the meat never became daily fare with persons of European ancestry. Instead, they hunted the enormous reptiles for the skins that were sold for handsome prices to makers of fashionable shoes and handbags. A half century ago, the gator population was so decimated that hunting them was banned, except by Indians. Once freed of their natural predators—men—the gators multiplied so that in the 1960s and 1970s tales began to circulate about small dogs being gobbled up, and once in a while, children losing their lives to the snapping reptiles. Hunting seasons for alligators were reopened, and at about the same time several farmers began to raise the creatures commercially for food. The meat is butchered and sold, and adventurers looking for a gastronomic thrill will find it in novelty restaurants in the state, as well as in New York and other large cities. Many tourists have their first tastes of gator in one of the eating places in Walt Disney World—as a cocktail spread or mixed with cream cheese and shaped into balls served on picks with drinks. The taste is not threatening at all. The flavor is mild, and the texture somewhat like fish. Often an alligator spread is highly seasoned, masking the true flavor. If you want to cook the meat yourself, you can find it in fish markets or specialty food shops.

Alligator dressed and cut by an expert provides a choice of excellent meat for grilling, frying, or broiling. Meat cut from the jaw or tail is tender enough for fast cooking with dry heat. The pale pink color turns white in cooking, and the delicate flavor is complemented by marinades and basting sauces, herbs, and other seasonings pleasing to the American tongue. Other cuts, the neck and leg, are tougher, and best simmered slowly in liquid as you would a stew. Massive development of alligator as a major source of food meat is unlikely due to a late start compared with other meat animals, but work is progressing and animal scientists and growers point out that the meat has special properties. Ounce for ounce, it contains fewer calories and less fat and cholesterol than beef or chicken.

COUNTRY CHICKEN AND DUMPLINGS

MAKES 4 TO 6 SERVINGS.

Chickens ranged in the yard of every Southerner who settled in Florida between the Revolution and Civil War, and chicken and dumplings often were the special feature of a Sunday dinner. Sometimes an extra rich broth for the dumplings was made of the giblets, the wing tips, and feet, and the meatier parts of the chicken were fried or roasted. Older farmyard chickens were scrawny and tough, so stewing was the best way to extract the essence of these birds. This culinary heirloom is perpetuated as one of the many dishes sold at the country fairs in Florida. The dumplings are rolled and cut in thin strips, almost like noodles, as farm cooks used to prepare them a hundred years ago. A fair-goer can get a bowlful of dumplings with broth and shreds of juicy chicken for just a few dollars.

1 stewing or roasting chicken, 2½ to 4 pounds (see Note)	**1 pound carrots**
1½ teaspoons salt	**3 sprigs parsley**
1 onion, halved (it is not necessary to peel it)	**1 bay leaf**
	½ teaspoon whole black peppercorns
1 whole clove	**Water**
2 ribs celery, cut in 1-inch pieces	**½ cup milk**

HERBED DUMPLINGS

1 cup all-purpose flour	**2 tablespoons melted chicken fat or butter**
½ teaspoon salt	
⅛ teaspoon baking powder	**1 egg**
½ teaspoon dried thyme or 2 teaspoons minced fresh	**⅓ cup milk**

Cut the chicken into 8 pieces and place it, along with the giblets and wing tips, in a Dutch oven with the salt, onion studded with the whole clove, and the celery. Peel 2 medium carrots and cut them in chunks. Add them along with the parsley, bay leaf, black peppercorns, and water to barely cover the chicken and vegetables.

Cover and simmer 1 hour, or until the chicken is fork tender. Cool the chicken in the broth; remove and skin the chicken; and cut it off the bones in large pieces. Strain the broth or skim out the peppercorns, bay leaf, and seasoning vegetables with a slotted spoon and discard them. Refrigerate the chicken and broth separately, or proceed with the recipe immediately.

To mix the dumplings: Stir together the flour, salt, baking powder, and thyme in a small bowl. Mix in the fat or butter, the egg, and the milk to make a stiff dough. Turn out on a floured board and knead a few strokes, then roll out ⅛ inch thick. Cut into 1- by 3-inch strips.

Peel and thinly slice the remaining carrots. Bring 4 cups of the chicken broth to a boil. Add the carrots, then drop the dumplings into the broth. Cover and simmer 15 minutes. Add the chicken and heat about 5 minutes. Add the remaining ½ cup milk and let stand, uncovered, 2 to 3 minutes. Serve hot.

NOTE: If a larger stewing chicken (called fowl in some markets) is available, buy it. Cooking time will be longer, but the deeper flavor is worth it. Birds that are older or very large roasting chickens also require longer cooking, so plan accordingly.

HONEY MUSTARD BARBECUED CHICKEN

MAKES 4 LARGE OR 8 MEDIUM SERVINGS.

Chicken leads the barbecue list in Florida, as in most of the land, for its versatility, universal appeal, and economy. An Okeechobee barbecue involves team-cooking, several dozen birds split in half, on permanent cinderblock fire pots with long grills, at a clubhouse or park. The egg in this sauce gives the chicken a shiny finish, and the seasoning is tangy but not too spicy.

2 eggs	**8 meaty chicken pieces**
¼ cup prepared yellow	**or 4 quarters**
mustard	**Salt and freshly ground**
2 tablespoons honey	**pepper (optional)**
½ cup cider vinegar	

In a small bowl, mix the eggs well, then beat in the mustard, honey, and vinegar. Place the chicken in a large shallow dish, pour the marinade over it, cover, and refrigerate 4 hours to 24 hours. Remove the chicken with tongs, shaking off excess sauce. Grill the chicken over glowing coals or low heat of a gas or electric grill until browned, turn, and brown the other side. Move chicken to upper grill or edges of grill where heat is moderate, cover the grill, and continue cooking 45 minutes to 1 hour. When almost done, give the chicken a final slathering of marinade, and, if wished, sprinkle lightly with salt and pepper. (Most diners do not want more salt with this marinade.) Test the thick portions of pieces of chicken with the tip of knife. When juices run clear or golden, the chicken is done. Pile on a platter and serve at once.

ORANGE ROSEMARY CHICKEN

MAKES 4 TO 6 SERVINGS.

The sweet-acid flavor of citrus juices brightens bland chicken breasts, and rosemary—fresh or dried—adds variety to a food that too often is boring. Another plus for this chicken recipe is that the meat can be grilled on one of the smokeless top-stove units that are finding favor with fast-track cooks, or on an outdoor grill. But the point of the preparation is the sprightly flavor that the marinade and cooking style give plain chicken breast.

Juice of 1 medium orange
(⅛ to ½ cup)
Juice of ½ lemon or Persian
lime (1½ tablespoons)
3 tablespoons olive oil
1 tablespoon fresh rosemary
leaves or 1 teaspoon dried

¼ teaspoon freshly ground
pepper
2 to 3 whole chicken breasts,
boned
Salt to taste

Combine the orange and lemon or lime juices, the olive oil, rosemary, and pepper. Beat together until blended. Cut the chicken breasts in halves and place in a deep bowl or a heavy self-sealing bag. Add the marinade, mix well, cover the bowl or seal the bag, and refrigerate at least 2 hours up to 9 or 10 hours.

To cook, drain the chicken and place on the grill. Grill until browned, turning as needed to cook evenly, for 20 minutes. When done, the chicken should be golden brown on both sides and the juices should run clear when the meat is slit with a small knife. (If thinly sliced chicken breast is used for this recipe, check doneness after 10 minutes.) Sprinkle lightly with salt and serve hot or cooled. The chicken is excellent in sandwiches or salads.

When the time came for the men to go into the woods to round up the cattle for marking, branding and sorting out the beef cattle, the lady folks were very busy a day or so before. They would cook up whole hams and sides of bacon and fry up large quantities of sausage and there was always a lot of dried or smoked beef to be carried for them to eat during the week. They baked sweet potatoes which were always good with a sausage link for those tired and hungry men. Of course, they carried plenty of syrup which was used for sweetening the strong coffee they cooked, not brewed, and also to sop with a hoecake. They carried several extra syrup buckets to make this iron wedge coffee in. Most of them liked theirs strong and black.

from *Florida Cowman: A History of Cattle Raising* by Joe A. Akerman, Jr., Florida Cattlemen's Association, Kissimmee, Florida, 1976

FLORIDA GOULASH

MAKES 4 SERVINGS.

The fresh vegetables make this stew, and they are at their peak in January and February, when there is likely to be a cold snap. That is the time when a home-cook in this subtropical region wants something savory simmering in the kitchen. The recipe is easily doubled for a crowd, and leftovers freeze beautifully. Don't think of adding a drop of water or broth to the goulash. The meat juices and vegetables make a natural full-bodied sauce.

1½ pounds boneless lean beef, veal, or pork, cut in 1½-inch cubes

1 to 2 tablespoons canola or olive oil

2 medium onions, sliced thin

2 cloves garlic, minced

4 tomatoes, peeled and chopped coarse

3 green bell peppers, cored, seeded, and cut in strips

1 teaspoon paprika, preferably sweet rose

Salt and freshly ground pepper to taste

In a large deep skillet or sauté pan, sauté the meat in the oil until it is browned on all sides. Add the onions and garlic and cook until the onion is tender but not browned. Add the tomatoes and bell peppers. Cook over low heat until the juice begins to run from the tomatoes. Add the paprika, ½ teaspoon salt, and ¼ teaspoon pepper. Cook, stirring often, 10 minutes. Taste and add more salt and pepper, if wanted. Cover and simmer 45 minutes, or until the meat is tender, stirring now and then. Do not let boil, as the stew may scorch. Serve hot with buttered noodles, rice, or boiled potatoes.

TONY'S FLORIDA SPAGHETTI GRAVY

MAKES 6 TO 8 SERVINGS.

The Italian influence on food in Florida is apparent to one scouting the restaurants. Some Italians came to fish and work in the cigar industry and other jobs before 1900, but most Florida-Italians are transplants from Brooklyn, New York City, Boston, Chicago, and other cities, and who arrived in the 1920s or later. Tony Garnet came as a press photographer and stayed more than half a century, but never forgot Sunday dinners in Bensonhurst, Brooklyn. In Florida, Tony does a thirty-minute sauce, claiming it is better than those that are simmered for hours. "Don't do it," he advises, "you burn the tomatoes!" His sauce is freshened with basil and parsley and heavy with garlic and fresh tomatoes in season. When tomatoes are weak and watery, he prefers to use canned tomatoes. The amount of olive oil can be reduced, but it assists in lubricating the pasta well.

3 to 4 large cloves garlic, minced	7 cups diced, peeled, and seeded tomatoes or 2 16-ounce cans (not in purée)
2 large onions, diced	
⅓ cup olive oil	
1 to 1½ pounds lean ground beef	1 6-ounce can tomato paste
8 to 10 ounces small mushrooms, sliced	1 cup dry red wine
	½ cup finely shredded fresh basil or 2 teaspoons dried
½ cup minced parsley, preferably flat leaf	Hot cooked and drained thin spaghetti for 6 to 8 servings (see Note)
2 teaspoons salt, or to taste	
½ teaspoon freshly ground pepper, or to taste	Freshly grated Parmesan cheese

In a Dutch oven or large sauté pan, sauté the garlic and onions in the olive oil until tender but not browned. Add the meat and cook, breaking it up with a fork, until it loses its red color and is crumbly. Add the mushrooms, parsley, salt, and pepper; sauté 2 or 3 minutes, then add the tomatoes, tomato paste, and wine. Stir in half the fresh basil or all the dried basil. Simmer, uncovered, 20 minutes, until thickened, stirring occasionally to prevent burning. Add the remaining fresh basil and stir it into the hot sauce to develop the aroma. Toss 2 or 3 large spoonfuls of the sauce with the pasta. Serve the remaining sauce over it, and pass the cheese to sprinkle on at the table.

NOTE: This is enough sauce for 8 servings, Italian style, and 2 pounds spaghetti. Americans like more sauce, so plan on this for 5 or 6 servings and 1 to 1¼ pounds spaghetti.

SMOKED PORK CHINESE-STYLE

MAKES 4 TO 6 SERVINGS.

This is a multicultural dish that calls for pork—the meat preferred by Southern Americans, Hispanics, and immigrants from Southeast Asia—and uses a cooking method, smoking, that Indians had perfected before the first explorers arrived. In addition, the seasoning is Oriental, a taste for which Floridians, along with most of the land, have developed a liking. Small pork tenderloins are ideal for this preparation and easy to carve for serving. A boned pork loin works, too, but needs longer smoking, four to five hours, and care must be taken to roast it to 160 to 165 degrees internal temperature. Thin slices of the meat are served with hot mustard and plum sauces, chutney, or other relishes.

¼ cup sugar

2 cloves garlic, minced

¼ teaspoon freshly ground
    pepper

¼ cup ketchup

MUSTARD SAUCE

¼ cup dry mustard

2 to 3 tablespoons water,
    beer, or sherry

¼ cup soy sauce

1 tablespoon rum, bourbon,
    or brandy

2 pork tenderloins, about
    ½ pound each

Stir together the sugar, garlic, pepper, ketchup, soy sauce, and rum. Pour the marinade into a plastic bag set in a shallow dish. Place the pork in the sauce, close the bag, and marinate the meat in the refrigerator at least 3 hours, turning the bag 2 or 3 times. Remove the meat and reserve the marinade to use later; blot the meat lightly with paper towels to remove excess marinade. Place pork on the greased racks of a smoker and smoke it for 2 to 3 hours, until glazed and firm when pressed with a spatula or back of a fork. Brush it 2 or 3 times with the reserved marinade while smoking. Place the tenderloins side by side, but not touching, in a shallow baking dish lined with foil, brush again with the marinade, and roast in a preheated 400-degree oven for 30 minutes, or until a thermometer inserted in the center registers 160 to 165 degrees.

Meanwhile, blend the mustard to a thin paste with the water, beer, or sherry and serve with the thinly sliced meat. The pork is good warm, at room temperature, or chilled. Plum sauce, chutney, or other relishes also may be served. Place the meat and sauce on thin slices of bread or offer it on small plates with a fork.

OVEN-ROASTED PORK CHINESE-STYLE

Preheat the oven to 400 degrees. Place the marinated tenderloins side by side, but not touching, in a foil-lined 13×9-inch baking dish. Brush lightly with the marinade and roast for 45 minutes, or to internal temperature of 160 to 165 degrees.

BARBECUED VENISON SEMINOLE-STYLE

MAKES 6 TO 8 SERVINGS, WITH LEFTOVERS.

This peppered barbecued venison is in the spirit of Native American cooking. The Indians were roasting deer and other game over open fires long before white settlers arrived. The natives then used little seasoning, though bay leaves and other herbs were theirs for the plucking in the Everglades. Today local Native Americans appreciate the zest of peppers and other lively seasonings of mainstream American cooking and are experts at outdoor cooking.

1 tablespoon salt	1 teaspoon paprika
1 teaspoon coarsely ground pepper	3 small or 1 large clove garlic, minced

1 hind or shoulder quarter
or saddle of a small deer
Corn or vegetable oil

Combine the salt, black pepper, and paprika. Mix well, then blend in the garlic. Trim any surface fat off the venison. Rub the surface with the seasoning mixture, spreading it to coat the meat well. Wrap the seasoned deer in heavy paper or foil and place it in the refrigerator to marinate overnight. The salt may draw out moisture, so drain it from time to time.

Preheat a grill with a cover to medium, then spread the coals or turn the heat low. Spray the rack with nonstick cooking spray or oil it well. Place the deer on the rack, cover the grill, and cook until the meat is lightly browned on one side. Brush it lightly with oil, turn it, cover the grill, and cook the meat until lightly browned on the other side. Brush with oil and turn. Continue cooking, brushing with oil when the meat appears dry, or every 15 minutes, and turning until the meat feels firm but not hard and a thermometer inserted in a thick portion of a joint registers 120 to 125 degrees. Brush again with oil and remove from the fire.

Place on a warm platter, cover with foil, and let stand 15 minutes before carving. Serve with applesauce or a fruit relish. Any leftovers make excellent sandwiches or salad (julienne-cut venison, greens, orange or grapefruit sections, and a chutney or citrus-juice dressing).

TO BOOT A PALM

*S*wamp cabbage is the Floridian name for the prized delicacy best known as hearts of palm. Whatever you call it, the white core, or heart, of the sabal, or cabbage palm, is a section of the tree trunk, "booted" or stripped of the stringy fibrous layers that surround the tender center. This section is approximately two feet long, and does take a bit of work to get to.

To obtain the palm heart, a chain saw or axe is used to chop down the tree and to cut this section off the top portion of the trunk. Booting the stump requires a strong arm and a sharp knife to get through the tough outer layers of palm that hug the crisp, white heart. Each layer must be cut to loosen it (split lengthwise), then pulled off with a good tug. Anyone attempting the chore must be prepared to battle the bugs, bees, and scorpions that often live in the tree.

Because the entire tree must be sacrificed to remove the small shaft of heart, state law limits commercial harvesting and relatively few permits for cutting the trees are issued. However, Native Americans, who have relied on swamp cabbage for centuries, and first introduced it to early settlers, are exempt from these restrictions.

Fresh hearts of palm can sometimes be found in local farmer's markets in Florida, and canned hearts, from South America, are available in food stores nationwide. Today the most popular uses are raw in salads, or as a side dish boiled with a bit of smoked pork and a little sugar. More adventurous ideas include fritters, pickles, and swamp cabbage with dumplings, oysters, or rabbit.

SWAMP CABBAGE CRACKER-STYLE

MAKES 4 TO 6 SERVINGS.

Hearts of palm were free for the chopping when settlers began to migrate from Georgia and the Carolinas after the Revolution. They called the crispy inner part of the sabal palm swamp cabbage and cooked it like garden cabbage. To this day, swamp cabbage steamed the old-fashioned way, with salt pork or side meat on a campfire, is a standard side dish at fish fries. Fresh hearts of palm harvested by licensed cutters are available in farm markets in the winter and spring. When you find them, make this superb dish to commemorate use of wild food. Floridians sometimes combine canned hearts of palm from Brazil or other places with the stems of bok choy or another green to provide crispness. It's not the same as the authentic Cracker dish, but is a good vegetable side dish.

2 ounces salt pork or bacon,
   chopped coarsely
8 to 10 cups sliced fresh
   hearts of palm
½ cup water

Salt and freshly ground
   pepper to taste
Pepper vinegar or Old
   Sour (page 131)

Cook the salt pork in a large pot until lightly browned. Add the hearts of palm and water. Bring to a boil, lower the heat, cover, and simmer 20 minutes, or until crisp-tender. Season with salt and pepper. Serve hot with cornbread as a side dish to meats or fish. Pass the pepper vinegar or Old Sour to sprinkle on the greens, as wanted.

APALACHICOLA SWAMP CABBAGE

Add a dozen freshly shucked oysters to Swamp Cabbage Cracker Style just before it is done. Steam 5 minutes.

STEAMED CANNED HEARTS OF PALM

Makes 4 servings.

Use 1 12-ounce can hearts of palm and a half bunch of bok choy in place of the fresh hearts of palm. Drain and rinse the hearts of palm and set them aside. Cut the bok choy stems in 2-inch lengths and shred the leaves. Add them to the lightly browned salt pork, as in the recipe for Swamp Cabbage Cracker Style. Cook until crisp-tender. Dice the canned hearts of palm and add to the greens and salt pork. Stir and heat thoroughly.

TRAIL COOK

Melvin Story was a Florida cowman who worked for Caroline's father for fifty years. His wife, Thelma, often went along on roundups, to cook for his group of cowboys, usually eight men, but sometimes fifteen or sixteen for a meal.

Cooking equipment underwent a series of changes over the years, gradually improving from an army stove set over an open fire, to a kerosene stove and portable oven, to a wood stove and finally an electric one in a cabin.

Camp cooking varied every day. If the cowboys killed a wild hog, Thelma cooked pork ribs or backbone with rice, and stewed the pork liver. If there was freshly killed beef, it was cut up, salted, and hung on a line for three or four days to drain the blood, then country-fried with onions. The remainder was salted down and stored.

Thelma's method for fixing collard greens was to fry some white bacon, then put the bacon and drippings into a pot of water with the collards and cook them together until the greens were tender. To rid them of their strong taste, she drained them, added fresh water, chopped onions, a little sugar, then cooked them again until the onions were done.

Other home-on-the-range favorites Thelma remembers were steaks skewered on a trimmed palm frond; beef stew with gravy, potatoes, and carrots; fried chicken or turkey pieces, mashed potatoes or rice, gravy, and potato salad. There were always biscuits or cornbread, and Thelma says she used a ten-pound bag of self-rising flour every two or three days. Since the men liked something sweet, she always had jelly, cane syrup, and honey to eat with the biscuits or cornbread. Sometimes she would take two or three cans of peaches, add water and sugar, bring it to a boil, then drop in biscuit dumplings, and serve for dessert.

Today's Florida ranchers still have roundups. Fencing laws help contain the cows, and modern convenience foods and cooking equipment have taken some of the work out of cattle catering. The one thing that surely hasn't changed is the appetites of cowboys after a day out on the range working cattle.

BELL PEPPERS AND CORN IN CREAM

MAKES 4 SERVINGS.

Florida's reputation as the winter produce capital of the nation is upheld by sweet corn and peppers. The state outranks all others for production of these traditional summer vegetables, shipping tons of them each winter. Both corn and peppers are native to the Western Hemisphere, and were being farmed by natives when Ponce de León claimed Florida for Spain in 1513. This decidedly modern method of preparing the two together for a flavorsome accompaniment to fish or seafood, pork, or poultry is seasoned with cumin and hot sauce and mellowed with a bit of cream.

1 tablespoon butter
½ cup sliced green onions or
    scallions, including tops
1 small green bell pepper,
    cut in strips
1 small red bell pepper,
    cut in strips
1½ cups corn cut off the
    cobs, preferably fresh

½ teaspoon salt
½ teaspoon sugar
¼ teaspoon freshly ground
    pepper
1 teaspoon ground cumin
⅛ teaspoon hot pepper sauce,
    or to taste
⅓ cup light cream or milk

In a large skillet, heat the butter until melted. Add the green onions and sauté until tender but not browned. Add the pepper strips and sauté until soft. Add the corn, salt, sugar, pepper, ½ teaspoon of the cumin, and the hot pepper sauce. Sauté 2 or 3 minutes. Pour the cream over the vegetables, cover, and simmer 4 or 5 minutes. Taste and add salt or pepper, if needed. Place in a serving bowl and sprinkle with the remaining ½ teaspoon cumin. Serve hot.

BARBECUED CORN

Corn on the grill is a year-round feature of community and home barbecues in Florida. For a crowd, great pots of water are heated on a grill, then freshly shucked corn is dropped into it and left to sit in the very hot water for 7 minutes. Because the water is below boiling, the corn will be extra tender and can be held for 15 minutes or so, as diners file past for their portions.

Butter and other fixings are set out on a nearby table (melted butter with a pastry brush is neater for a large group), along with shakers of salt, pepper, chili powder, hickory smoke salt, and curry powder. Minced cilantro and parsley, snipped green onion tops or chives, bacon bits, salsa, and even peanut butter may be offered.

In Florida, hosts and big-party chairmen make a point of having corn gathered the morning of the dinner. It is misted at the packing plant to chill it quickly and preserve the fresh sweetness. George Cooper in Princeton used to send a helper with a truck to Lake Okeechobee to bring back two or three cases of just-picked corn for his annual springtime barbecue for hordes of friends and business associates.

Allow at least two ears of corn per person. This is the basic way of preparing corn for a home barbecue supper:

GRILLED CORN ON THE COB

        2 ears corn for each eater
        Butter, salt, pepper, and other condiments to taste

One to two hours before cooking, pull back the corn husks, and brush and pull out the silks. Push the husks back and tie them in place with kitchen twine. Soak the corn in ice water to cover until ready to cook. Place the corn near the edge of the grill and cook it over moderate heat. Turn it as the husks char. Allow 25 to 30 minutes cooking time. Test a kernel with the tip of knife. If the juice is clear, and not milky, the corn is done. Serve the corn immediately with seasonings.

OVEN-ROASTED CORN ON THE COB

Jean Wardlow, a native Key Wester who took great pleasure in cooking when she and her husband, Jack, lived in Miami, did corn this way. The shucks enhance the natural sweetness of the corn and keep it moist.

        2 ears corn, unshucked, for each eater
        Seasonings and condiments to taste

Pull back the corn husks and brush and pull out the silks. Push the shucks back and tie them in place with kitchen twine. Place the corn in a sink or large pot and soak in ice water to cover for 30 minutes to 1 hour. Preheat the oven to 375 degrees. Stack the corn in its husks in a Dutch oven or baking pan, such as a lasagne pan. The ears can be close together, but do not pack them tightly or the inside ears will not cook evenly. Cover the pan, using foil if it has no cover. Roast 25 to 30 minutes. Test a kernel with the tip of a knife. If the juice is clear, and not milky, the corn is done. Each diner shucks his corn and adds butter, salt, pepper, and other condiments to taste.

FLORIDA CELERY BAKE

MAKES 4 SERVINGS.

Some of the best food in Florida from World War II to the mid-1980s was to be found in clubs, such as The Everglades in Palm Beach, Field in Sarasota, Indian Creek, Bath, and the Surf in Miami Beach, the Tampa Yacht Club, and others. A celery casserole was a much-loved item at clubhouse buffets, a suave accompaniment to roast beef, duckling, and turkey. The old-fashioned casserole had almonds in it for crunch and understated white-on-white color. Today home-cooks serve this dish with roasts, and also with barbecued chicken.

1 medium bunch celery (1¼ pounds)	½ cup plus 2 tablespoons celery broth
Salt to taste	1 tablespoon cornstarch
1 tablespoon butter	2 to 3 tablespoons grated Parmesan cheese
1 tablespoon almond oil (or more butter)	¾ cup sliced unblanched almonds
2 tablespoons flour	White pepper to taste
½ cup light cream or milk	

Cut the celery in ½-inch slices to make 5 to 6 cups, reserving the leaves for garnish. Put the celery in a saucepan with water half as deep as the celery. Salt lightly, cover, and bring to a boil. Cook approximately 1 minute, then test with a fork. The celery should be tender, but not mushy; if necessary, cook 30 to 60 seconds longer. Drain the celery, reserving the broth.

Preheat the oven to 350 degrees. Heat the butter and almond oil in a large saucepan. Stir in the flour, add the cream or milk, and whisk over low heat until the sauce is smooth. Add the ½ cup celery broth and cook and whisk until smooth. Blend the cornstarch with the 2 tablespoons celery broth and stir into the hot sauce. Cook and stir until smooth and thickened. The sauce is thick to compensate for the wateriness of celery. Taste and add salt and white pepper to taste. Add 1 tablespoon of the cheese to the sauce and stir until blended.

Place half the celery in a buttered shallow 5-cup baking dish. Sprinkle with half the almonds. Add half of the sauce and mix. Combine the remaining celery and sauce; spoon over the layer in the baking dish. Sprinkle with the remaining almonds and cheese. Bake 35 minutes, or until bubbly and the top is lightly browned. Garnish with a bouquet of celery leaves in the center of the top or with leaves arranged at the edge of the baking dish. Serve hot.

A SUMMER STANDBY

Kitchen drawers, file boxes, and every possible niche for a cook's collections bulges with recipes for squash casseroles. A family reunion or potluck is hardly legal without one or more of these summer casseroles.

Anybody from Florida, and most any part of the South, knows that the distinctly sweet flavor of crookneck squash is far superior to the blandness of its bulb-shaped cousins that dominate markets elsewhere. We saw loads of crooknecks in a State Farmer's Market late one recent spring, so not all good squash has bowed to the demands for easy shipping and durability. To cook them, we pan-steam the tiny ones, two or three to the handful, and serve them whole with butter, herbed oil, or garlic oil.

SQUASH CASSEROLE

MAKES 4 SERVINGS.

This squash casserole uses a small amount of milk with egg in place of the ubiquitous canned soup or white sauce. Pecans on top make it special. If the crookneck variety is not available, globe-shaped yellow squash can be used. This recipe is adaptable to zucchini and pattypan, as well as to the traditional yellow squash.

2 pounds yellow summer squash, preferably crookneck, coarsely cubed	Water
	4 tablespoons (½ stick) butter
1 large onion, coarsely chopped	1 cup crumbled crackers*
	½ cup milk
1 teaspoon salt	1 cup (4 ounces) shredded Cheddar cheese
¼ teaspoon freshly ground pepper, or more	½ cup finely chopped pecans

*Saltines, whole-grain snack crackers, or crisp buttery wafers may be used in this casserole.

Place the squash, onion, salt, and pepper in a large saucepan. Add as little water as you dare, none if you can keep the heat low and stir the squash every minute or two, and ½ inch of water if you have other things on your mind. Cover and cook the squash until soft, stirring now and then to prevent scorching. Drain the squash, then return it to the pan or a bowl and stir in the butter. Taste and add more pepper if wanted. (Squash can use plenty of it.) Check for salt, too.

Preheat the oven to 350 degrees. Butter a 1½-quart baking dish well. Stir the crumbled crackers into the squash, and turn into the casserole. Pour the milk over the squash and sprinkle with the cheese and pecans. Bake, uncovered, 20 minutes, until the milk is absorbed, the squash is bubbly, and the cheese is melted. Remove from the oven, let stand 5 minutes, then serve hot.

This recipe is easily doubled. Bake it in a large shallow baking dish to permit evaporation of moisture in the squash.

CITRUS SWEET POTATOES

MAKES 4 TO 6 SERVINGS.

Floridians combine citrus fruit with almost any other flavor. This is an excellent pairing of oranges and sweet potatoes, long a staple in the South, with a sauce made from brown sugar, orange juice, and raisins. A splash of rum enriches the flavor.

4 medium sweet potatoes	½ cup orange juice
3 oranges	3 tablespoons raisins
3 tablespoons butter	1 tablespoon rum, or to taste
1 tablespoon flour	1 teaspoon grated orange zest
½ cup brown sugar	

Wash the potatoes but do not peel. Boil them roughly 20 minutes, until tender when pierced with a fork. Drain. Meanwhile, grate the zest from the oranges, then remove the pith and slice the orange into ¼- to ½-inch rounds. Set aside. When the potatoes are cool enough to handle, peel and cut them into ¼- to ½-inch slices.

Preheat the oven to 325 degrees. In a 1-quart casserole, alternate layers of potatoes and orange slices. For the glaze, melt the butter in a saucepan over medium-low heat. Add the flour and cook for a minute to blend. Make sure there are no lumps, then add the brown sugar, orange juice, and raisins. Mix well and simmer 4 to 5 minutes, stirring frequently. Stir in the rum and the grated zest. Pour over the sweet potatoes and oranges. Bake for 20 minutes, basting from time to time with the sauce.

HOPPIN' JOHN WITH TRIMMINGS
BLACK-EYED PEAS AND HOG JOWL

MAKES 4 TO 6 SERVINGS.

This humble dish is a good luck symbol on New Year's Day, and many Floridians insist that it be the first bite of the year, eating at least a spoonful before the raucous din at midnight has died. The peas signify jingling money for the year and the greens served with the peas and rice bring folding cash, according to superstition. Smoked, cured, or fresh hog jowl, the fatty lower jaw, is the traditional seasoning for Hoppin' John, but this cut is difficult to find in the North, so a ham hock is substituted by most people who've moved away.

Black-eyed peas were introduced to this country by Africans, and have become exceedingly popular with the entire population. They are eaten green in the summertime and dried in this and other dishes. The combination of peas and rice is served throughout the year as a robust economical main dish. The condiments, chopped onion, pepper vinegar or Old Sour, and pepper relish are part of the ritual. The sweet pepper and pear relish here is a modern interpretation.

PEPPER PEAR RELISH

1 firm-ripe pear, peeled and chopped	3 tablespoons sugar
3 tablespoons cider vinegar	1 tablespoon water
½ red bell pepper, diced	⅛ teaspoon celery seed
¼ cup chopped onion	⅛ teaspoon dry mustard
	¼ teaspoon salt

PEAS WITH HOG JOWL OR HAM HOCK

1¼ cups (½ pound) dried black-eyed peas	Salt to taste
½ pound smoked hog jowl or 1 ham hock, cracked	3 cups hot cooked rice (1 cup before cooking)
1 onion, studded with 3 whole cloves	Chopped onion, crushed pepper vinegar, or Old Sour (page 131)
1 small chile pepper (dried or fresh)	

The relish can be prepared several days in advance. In a small enamelware or stainless steel saucepan, combine the freshly chopped pear with the vinegar. Add the red bell pepper, onion, sugar, water, celery seed, mustard, and ¼ teaspoon salt. Simmer until thickened, about 5 minutes, stirring often. Cool and refrigerate, but remove from the refrigerator an hour or two before serving.

To cook the peas, soak them overnight in a large bowl with water to cover them generously. The next day, cut the hog jowl in thick slices, and place it or the ham hock in a large saucepan with the onion studded with cloves, the chile pepper, and water 2 inches deep. Simmer, covered, 30 minutes. Drain the peas and add them to the ham mixture with enough hot water to cover by 1 inch. Cover and boil slowly 45 minutes, stirring now and then and adding hot water as needed to keep the peas juicy. Taste a pea, and if it is tender to the core, it is done. Add salt as wished. (If the meat is very salty, little or no salt is needed.) Remove the onion.

Mix the peas with the rice and pile into a large bowl or spoon the rice in a ring onto a platter and spoon the peas in the center. Serve with the Pepper-Pear Relish and other condiments as wanted. Hot cornbread and cooked mixed fresh greens (turnip, collard, and mustard greens, or beet greens or kale) are customary side dishes with Hoppin' John.

A NATIVE'S FOOD MEMORIES

The best-known Indians in Florida, the Seminoles and Miccosukees, live in the Everglades, south of the Lake Okeechobee farming district. They are descended from survivors of Indian wars who fled to the Glades and made a life for themselves, hunting, fishing, and farming.

Gloria Osceola, a Miccosukee, who demonstrates household arts at a tourist village on the Tamiami Trail five miles west of Miami, remembers her childhood tastes:

"My father was before his time! He insisted we have vegetables and raised beans, squash, tomatoes, and pumpkin. We steamed the vegetables over an open fire. He planted purple sweet potatoes and when they bloomed we dug them. They were baked or boiled. We had a grapefruit, an orange, and a tangerine tree and banana plants, wild blueberries and strawberries. We ate swamp cabbage (hearts of palm).

"When we had deer, we would cut the meat in big chunks and smoke it. Or we roasted cubes of the meat on sticks over the fire. We call meat on a stick 'Huskabaja.'"

Natives once lived in chickees, open platforms with thatch roofs, and cooked on outdoor fires. Garfish packed in clay and leaves and roasted in the fire was a delicacy. A traditional dish still seen is sofkee, a thin gruel made of grits, roasted corn, or coontie starch (arrowroot). Children eat it as a snack. Coontie flour also is used in biscuits and with corn meal in bread.

Natives are eating more like Americans—pizza and fries, soda pop and doughnuts—admitted Mrs. Osceola. Bass, mudfish, bream (sunfish), and gar once were daily fare; now the Indians eschew fresh-caught fish for fear of mercury poisoning and opt for fried fish sandwiches at fast-food places.

"Today moms are too busy to cook, and the kids get their fried food at the fast-food places," observed Gloria Osceola wryly.

She still cooks for her family and her son supplies the fresh vegetables. "My son has a green thumb!" she said proudly. "If he plants it, it is going to grow!" Like mothers everywhere, she reads the advice to lower fat in the diets of her family. She misses fresh fish.

The memory of her grandmother and mother tending open fires is vivid, but Gloria Osceloa is proud of two ranges, electric for everyday cooking and bottled gas in case of a hurricane, when power goes off, and she even cooks over an outdoor fire sometimes to conserve the gas supply.

CLEWISTON CORNBREAD

MAKES 6 TO 8 SERVINGS.

"Sweet milk" is an old-timey term for fresh milk, to distinguish it from buttermilk, which was used in baking. This bread uses fresh sweet milk, as well as buttermilk.

1 cup white stone-ground corn-
    meal
½ cup all-purpose flour
1½ teaspoons baking powder
½ teaspoon salt
1 cup fresh "sweet" milk
½ cup buttermilk
1 egg, lightly beaten
¼ cup corn or peanut oil

Preheat the oven to 450 degrees. Butter or oil a 10×6-inch glass baking dish (bakes crispier cornbread). In a large bowl, combine the corn meal, flour, baking powder, and salt. Mix well. Add the milk, buttermilk, and egg. Beat until smooth, then beat in the oil. Turn into the baking dish. Bake 20 minutes, or until browned and the top springs back when lightly touched. If not browned to your taste, put the pan on the highest rack of the oven for 5 minutes. Cool 5 minutes in the baking dish, cut in squares, and serve hot with plenty of butter. Floridians sometimes drizzle molasses over hot cornbread, and eat it in place of dessert for family meals.

CORNBREAD—A PROUD TRADITION

Floridians of Southern ancestry care about cornbread and are quick to protest when foreigners take liberties with it. There is no sugar in the cornbread of the South. And cooks are fussy about corn meal. Some like yellow and others demand white corn meal, and the two camps heatedly debate the merits of each.

Our Southern families were serious about cornbread, too, and the tradition is passed from generation to generation. But in the 1950s at the Clewiston Inn operated by Sugarland Corporation in this lake town, Jeanne was served crispy-brown cornbread squares, so hot that butter melted in a half minute. The bread was the best she had ever had. She asked the baker for the recipe almost before she had consumed the last crumb. We're lucky to have it because the Clewiston Inn's menu has changed and this cornbread is no longer served, but we can bake it at home, and often do.

Then in 1990 we were introduced to a cornbread variously called gourmet, deluxe, supreme, and other names, that was sweeping the South. It is another champion, delicately flavored and a lovely golden brown color. It is so rich that we don't butter it, but others do.

Both recipes are here. Bake and compare them. And you'll find other cornbreads, such as hushpuppies, one of Florida's best-known contributions to the national cuisine, and a blueberry cornbread.

Hot cornbread and vegetables, with perhaps a bit of meat, served at a kitchen table at noon is the ultimate dinner for thousands who've learned the simple pleasures of Florida farm living.

BUTTERY RICH CORNBREAD

MAKES 8 4x2-INCH RECTANGLES.

We've seen children, husbands, and guests eat two, even three, servings each of this bread.

¾ cup yellow corn meal
¾ cup all-purpose flour
½ teaspoon salt
1 tablespoon baking powder
2 eggs
1 cup sour cream

1 cup whole kernel corn,
    fresh, frozen, or canned and
    drained
½ cup corn or peanut oil
½ cup (1 stick) butter,
    melted

Preheat the oven to 400 degrees. Butter or oil an 8-inch square baking pan. In a large bowl, combine the corn meal, flour, salt, and baking powder and mix well. In a small bowl, beat the eggs until blended, then stir in the sour cream, corn, and oil. Pour the liquid mixture over the dry ingredients and mix until moistened. Spread in the prepared pan and bake 30 minutes, or until the bread shrinks slightly from the edges of the pan. It will be golden, not brown. Pour the melted butter over the cornbread and let it stand in the pan 5 minutes to absorb the butter. Cut in rectangles and serve hot.

SUGAR CUBE ORANGE BISCUITS

MAKES 18 TO 20 BISCUITS.

These simple biscuits can be made in a hurry and the sweet orange taste makes them unusually good for luncheons, or with tea or coffee in the afternoon.

2 cups sifted self-rising flour

Grated rind of 1 orange

¼ cup shortening

½ cup milk, or more

18 to 20 sugar cubes (½ teaspoon each)

¼ cup orange juice

Measure the flour into a mixing bowl. Add the orange rind. With a pastry blender or fork and knife, cut the shortening into the flour until the texture resembles coarse meal. Add enough milk to form a soft dough. Turn out onto a floured surface and lightly knead until smooth. Pat or roll the dough to a thickness of ½ inch. Cut with a lightly floured 2-inch biscuit cutter and place rounds on an ungreased baking sheet. Dip the sugar cubes thoroughly in the orange juice and press a cube into the top of each biscuit. Bake in a preheated 425-degree oven for 10 to 12 minutes, until brown. Serve hot.

POACHED GUAVA SHELLS

ENOUGH FOR 6 TO 8 SERVINGS.

Guavas grew wild around Lake Okeechobee as late as the 1950s, and early settlers eked out slim incomes by eating the guavas that they gathered, along with the fish from the lake, rabbits, and other game that they hunted. Moms and grandmas "stewed" guavas in the way they had cooked apples or peaches "back home" in the Southern states or the North. The sweet-pungent fruit is served for breakfast, with meats, on shortcakes, or as sauce for puddings. Today guavas have taken on new luster in the Hispanic dessert guava shells and cream cheese. The tangy guava shells are a perfect foil for the bland, creamy cheese, though we like a variation with a more assertive cheese. Guava shells in heavy syrup are available in cans, but guavas poached in a lighter syrup with lime juice let the natural flavor of the fruit dominate.

When cut, the guava shows a center of pulp filled with seeds, which are scooped out to form the shells. The fleshy shell is pale to deep pink or yellowish, and turns a deeper pink or peach color while cooking. The pale green or yellow skin is peeled off only in places where it is blemished.

2 cups water	**Juice of 2 limes**
1½ cups sugar	**Roquefort Dessert Cheese**
12 firm-ripe guavas, 2 inches	**(recipe follows)**
in diameter (see Note 1)	

Combine the water and sugar in a large nonreactive saucepan and stir over moderate heat until the sugar is dissolved; cover and bring to a boil. (The syrup should fill the pan to 2½ inches. If insufficient, add more water and sugar in the proportions of ¾ cup sugar for each 1 cup water, to provide syrup to measure 2½ inches.)

Meanwhile, using a knife that is stain resistant, slice the blossom ends off the guavas and peel any blemished patches off the skin. Cut the guavas in half, and scoop out the seedy pulp with a serrated edge orange spoon (see Note 2). Cook the shells of 4 or 6 guavas at once, allowing space for the shells to bob about in the syrup. Simmer, uncovered, 5 minutes, or until the guavas are tender. Start testing at 4 minutes, as some shells will cook quickly. Skim out cooked shells and place them in a large dessert bowl. When all are done, sprinkle with the lime juice and pour the hot syrup over them. If the syrup does not cover the shells, cook another batch of it. Cool the guava shells and syrup and serve on shortcake, as a sauce with meat or desserts, or as breakfast fruit. For Guava Shells and Cream Cheese, place 3 or 4 shells, a spoonful of the cheese or a slice of cream cheese or feta, and Cuban crackers on each dessert plate.

NOTE 1: Guavas are ripe when they have a rich bittersweet aroma and yield slightly to gentle pressure. The skin may be beige or yellow, though some ripe fruit is green.

NOTE 2: Some cooks prefer to scoop out the seeds after cooking. Handling the cooked shells is a bit messy, but scooping out cooked pulp is easier. Poach the halved fruit in the syrup until the seedy portion swells. Allow 10 minutes cooking, as the centers slow heat penetration. Skim out the cooked guavas and cool them on a tray lined with waxed paper; scoop out the seeds and pulp with a spoon. Squeeze the lime juice over the shells. Skim any seeds from the syrup and pour the syrup over the guavas.

ROQUEFORT DESSERT CHEESE

Enough for 6 to 8 servings.

Mash or beat 1 cup ricotta cheese with 2 tablespoons plain yogurt until creamy. Stir in 2 ounces crumbled Roquefort cheese.

MANGO BAVARIAN CREAM

MAKES 8 TO 10 SERVINGS.

Mangoes most often are peeled, sliced, and eaten as dessert, a breakfast fruit, or in salads, but occasionally a fancier preparation is called for. This dessert has a creamy-smooth feel on the tongue and is sweetened just enough to bring out the best of the mango, without overpowering it. The pinkish gold color has a summery look, with sliced mangoes and whipped cream as garnishes.

1 tablespoon (1 envelope)
    unflavored gelatin
2 tablespoons cold water
2 cups milk
4 egg yolks
½ cup sugar
1 tablespoon orange-flavored
    liqueur

2 large mangoes
2½ tablespoons lime juice
    (1 small Persian lime)
1 cup heavy cream
Whipped cream for garnish,
    if desired

Sprinkle the gelatin on cold water and let it soften while cooking the custard. In a heavy stainless steel or enamelware saucepan, heat the milk until bubbles appear at the edges. In a bowl, beat together the egg yolks and sugar until blended. Whisk half the hot milk into the egg yolks, then whisk the mixture into the remaining milk. Stir over moderate heat until the custard is thickened. Test it by pulling a fingertip through the custard coating the back of a spoon. Your fingertip will leave a clear path if the custard is thick enough. Remove from the heat and stir in the gelatin mixture until dissolved, then add the liqueur. Place the pan in cold water to stop the cooking. Refrigerate the custard while preparing the mangoes, stirring it every 10 to 15 minutes.

Peel and slice the mangoes. Dice enough of the softer pieces of mango and scrape bits of flesh off the seeds to make 1¾ cups. Reserve the remaining mango for garnish. Add the lime juice to the diced mango; fold the mixture into the custard. Return to the refrigerator.

When the custard is stiff enough to mound on a spoon, whip the cream and fold it in thoroughly. Spoon into an 8-cup dessert bowl or into 8 to 10 individual dessert dishes. Garnish with reserved mango slices and, if desired, whipped cream.

JAM PIES

MAKES 10 TO 12 PIES.

These savory, individual pies were made by early settlers who filled them year-round with jam, and seasonally with fresh or dried fruit. They were served for breakfast as well as dessert, and remain popular throughout the South. This recipe calls for jam, but try different fillings like preserved guava shells (available in Hispanic markets) or fresh fruit sprinkled with a little sugar, and cinnamon or nutmeg.

2 cups all-purpose flour	¼ cup jam (approximately)
½ teaspoon baking powder	Vegetable or peanut oil for
½ teaspoon salt	deep frying
1 teaspoon sugar	Confectioners' sugar for
⅓ cup shortening	dusting
¾ cup milk	

Sift together the flour, baking powder, salt, and sugar. Turn into a mixing bowl and cut in the shortening with a fork or a pastry blender until the mixture resembles coarse meal. Add the milk and mix to form a soft dough. On a floured surface, roll to a thickness of ⅛ to ¼ inch. Cut in 3-inch rounds. Place a teaspoon of jam on one half of each round. Fold the other half over, and seal by pressing the edges together with a fork. Using a deep-fat fryer, heat 3 to 4 inches of oil to 360 degrees, or in a skillet filled to a depth of 2 inches hot oil, fry a few pies at a time until golden brown on both sides. Remove with a slotted spoon and drain on paper towels. Dust with confectioners' sugar and serve warm.

HOW SWEET IT IS

Sugarcane was brought to the West Indies in 1493, on Columbus's second voyage, and within a few years spread to most of the islands. Cane proved to be a bonanza to the young colonies, the plants growing prolifically with larger juicier stalks than in Europe. Plumper stalks yield more molasses and sugar. Soon islanders were crystallizing cane syrup to make sugar, a method brought to Spain by Moors, and sugar became the profit base of the region. Europeans loved the sugar from the Indies, where what was once a luxury was now produced at reasonable cost for anybody who wanted sweetening in their tea.

The first recorded commercial sugar production in Florida was at New Smyrna from 1767 to 1776, but the operation failed. Meanwhile, most Southern farmers in Florida, Alabama, Georgia, and South Carolina habitually raised sugarcane, and ground and boiled it down for syrup for personal use. Today many older people recall the wonderful fall ritual of boiling molasses and of their mothers making fresh molasses cakes or taffy. Ruins of cane mills that presumably were operated between the Revolutionary and Civil wars can be found in many spots in the state, including Port Orange, DeLeon Springs, and New Smyrna. The Gamble mansion, a state park facility near Bradenton that is open to the public, was the family home of Major Robert Gamble. The site of the sugar mill he operated from 1850 to 1860 is still there, and traces of the sugar works can be seen.

The modern sugar industry in Florida began in 1928 when the United

States Sugar Corporation in Clewiston on the western shore of the lake produced a thousand tons of sugar; in the next twenty years, two other mills went into production. But the industry really sprang to life with the United States embargo on sugar from Cuba. Two new mills went into production in 1961, and by 1965 ten mills were in business. The mills are clustered in western Palm Beach County, south of the lake. The rich, black muck soils and virtually frost-free climate there grow top-quality cane with a high yield, which can be cut three times in many seasons, as compared to once or twice in other states or regions of the world.

Mills near the cane fields help ensure high yields, preventing the loss of sucrose as the stalks dry out before grinding. The canes are crushed with huge rollers to produce a dark green juice that is purified by boiling and use of lime, and allowing sediment to settle out. The juice is condensed by a series of evaporating steps, then crystallized to a brownish substance called raw sugar. This then is refined to pure white sugar or a liquid, which is used as molasses. This refined sugar is the base of the common forms of sugar used in cookery.

OKEECHOBEE SHORTCAKE

MAKES 4 TO 6 SERVINGS.

A lightly sweetened rich dough lavishly filled with fruit, be it strawberries from Plant City, peaches or blueberries from north Florida, mangoes from south Florida, or guavas near the lake, is the *only* shortcake to Floridians of Southern-English heritage.

The kinship of this shortcake to biscuits and scones is apparent. This shortcake base is a cream biscuit recipe enriched with a bit of sugar and eggs. Stan Wayman, a noted photographer of animals for *Life* magazine in the 1960s, grew up near Lake Okeechobee in a big family, sometimes strapped for funds. Later he remembered his mother's Sunday suppers. "She'd bake two or three panfuls of biscuits and put a big bowl of stewed guavas and pitchers of milk on the table with the hot biscuits," he would recall. "Man, did we eat!" Until recently, guavas grew wild around the lake, so the fruit for Sunday supper was free for the picking. See page 349 for Poached Guava Shells, the modern name for stewed guavas.

2½ cups all-purpose flour
1 tablespoon baking powder
¼ teaspoon salt
¼ cup sugar
2 eggs
½ cup heavy cream
½ cup milk

6 tablespoons butter, melted
2 cups guava shells with
   syrup (page 349) or
   1 16-ounce can
1 cup heavy cream, whipped,
   sweetened, if desired

Preheat the oven to 400 degrees. In a medium-size bowl, mix the flour, baking powder, salt, and sugar. Beat the eggs until blended, and stir in the cream and milk. Make a well in the center of the dry ingredients, and stir in the egg mixture with a fork until the dough clings together. Turn out onto a floured surface and knead lightly until well mixed. Pat out half the dough to an 8-inch circle 1 inch thick. Place in an 8-inch lightly buttered layer cake pan. Brush the top with 2 tablespoons of the melted butter. Roll out the remaining dough into an 8-inch circle and place over the buttered layer. Or cut all the dough in 8 to 12 3-inch individual shortcakes. Brush the tops of half the biscuits with butter and stack the remaining biscuits on top of them. Place on buttered baking sheets. Bake 30 to 35 minutes for the large shortcake; 25 to 30 minutes for the individual cakes. The tops will be lightly browned and the cake will spring back when done when touched with a finger.

Remove the shortcake(s) from the pan, split with a long-bladed knife at the buttered seam, and brush the remaining melted butter on the cut sides. Fill the warm shortcake with fruit and its syrup, reserving one or two of the best-looking guava shells for topping. Spoon some of the whipped cream onto the fruit filling, and top with the second layer and the remaining cream. Cut the large cake into wedges to serve. Garnish with reserved guava shells.

COCONUT POUND CAKE

SERVES 15 OR MORE.

The coconut is actually the seed from the coconut palm tree, which has been called the tree of life, and flourishes in south Florida's mild climate. Fresh coconuts, as well as the packaged variety that has been grated and dried, are available in supermarkets throughout the country. The use of coconut in this very flavorful pound cake gives it a distinctive taste.

3 cups all-purpose flour

1 teaspoon baking powder

¼ teaspoon salt

½ cup vegetable shortening

1 cup (2 sticks) butter, at room
    temperature

2½ cups sugar

5 eggs

1 cup milk

1 teaspoon vanilla extract

1½ teaspoons coconut extract

1 teaspoon lemon extract

2 cups grated coconut (see
    page 159) or frozen
    unsweetened coconut

Grease and flour a 9- or 10-inch tube pan. Sift together the flour, baking powder, and salt; set aside. In a mixing bowl, cream together the shortening and butter until very fluffy. Beat in the sugar until thoroughly mixed. Add the eggs, one at a time, mixing well after each addition. Add the dry ingredients, alternating with the milk, beginning and ending with the flour mixture. Mix in the vanilla, and coconut and lemon extracts. Stir in the coconut and blend well. Pour into the prepared tube pan, smoothing the surface. Place in a cold oven and turn to 350 degrees. Bake 1¼ hours, or until the cake springs back when lightly touched and the sides begin to pull away from the pan. Cool for 15 to 20 minutes before removing from the pan to a cake rack to cool completely.

FRESH BANANA LAYER CAKE

MAKES 16 OR MORE THIN SLICES.

Lots and lots of fresh bananas in this recipe make it unique, so don't skimp if you want to get the full flavor of this old Southern cake. There are bananas in the cake, in the frosting, and even slices between the layers.

3 cups all-purpose flour

1½ teaspoons baking soda

¾ cups (1½ sticks) butter, at
    room temperature

2¼ cups sugar

FROSTING AND FILLING

½ cup mashed bananas
    (2 bananas)

2 teaspoons fresh lemon
    juice

½ cup (1 stick) butter, at
    room temperature

3 eggs, well beaten

5 ripe bananas, mashed

¼ cup buttermilk

1½ teaspoons vanilla extract

1 cup finely chopped pecans

1 box (1 pound) confectioners'
    sugar

1 teaspoon vanilla extract

3 ripe bananas, sliced thin

Preheat the oven to 325 degrees. Grease and flour 3 9-inch cake pans. Sift together the flour and baking soda, and set aside. Put the butter and sugar in a large mixing bowl and cream together until smooth. Slowly pour in the eggs, mixing well between each addition. Stir in the bananas. Add the dry ingredients and buttermilk alternately, beginning and ending with the flour mixture. Stir in the vanilla extract and the pecans. Divide the batter among the prepared pans and bake for 25 minutes, or until the tops all brown and the edges pull away from the pans, or a cake tester inserted in the middle of a cake comes out clean. Remove from the oven and allow to cool for 5 to 10 minutes, then turn out onto racks to cool completely.

Make the frosting. In a small bowl, mix the mashed bananas and the lemon juice together and set aside. In another bowl, with an electric mixer cream together the butter and the sugar. Add the mashed bananas, blending well. Stir in the vanilla extract.

Fresh Banana Layer Cake (continued)

To assemble, spread a layer of icing on one of the cake rounds, then top with a layer of sliced bananas. Place the second cake layer on top of the bananas and repeat with more icing, then bananas. After placing the third layer on top, smooth the icing over the sides and top of the cake with the remaining frosting.

ORANGE MELTS

MAKES 2 TO 2½ DOZEN.

These luscious little cookies go fast at a party, so make two batches. South Floridians especially like a cookie that requires no baking in summer.

1⅓ cups (about half a 10-ounce box) fine vanilla wafer crumbs

½ cup finely chopped pecans

1 cup confectioners' sugar

4 tablespoons undiluted orange juice concentrate

2 tablespoons Grand Marnier or Triple Sec

¼ cup more finely chopped pecans (optional)

Place a few wafers at a time in a blender or processor, and pulse the motor on and off to make crumbs. Repeat until you measure 1⅓ cups crumbs. Place the crumbs in a bowl. Add the ½ cup pecans and sugar. Mix well, mashing out lumps of sugar with the back of the spoon. Work in the orange concentrate, then the liqueur. Blend thoroughly. Oil your hands lightly, then shape balls of the dough, rolling a mounded soup spoon or tablespoon measure between hands. Roll the cookie balls in the remaining ¼ cup pecans, if desired. (Half the cookies may be rolled in nuts and the other half left plain.) Place the cookies on trays lined with waxed paper. Cover loosely with waxed paper and let ripen at room temperature overnight.

AMBROSIA COOKIES

MAKES 6 TO 6½ DOZEN.

This cookie, with minor variations, is baked almost everywhere in Florida. One baker calls it "the world's best cookie," and a Cuban grandmother's handwritten recipe is labeled simply, "Good Nut Cookies." Hers has cornflakes in it, as well as oats and coconut. Some contain no fruits, only cereal, coconut, and nuts. All are good eating anytime, with ice cream or fruit or just as a mid-afternoon treat.

1 cup butter (2 sticks) or
    margarine, softened
1 cup granulated sugar
1 cup packed light brown
    sugar
1 egg
1 cup vegetable oil
1 teaspoon vanilla extract
3½ cups all-purpose flour
1 teaspoon baking soda

¼ teaspoon salt
1 cup rolled oats, quick or
    old-fashioned (not instant)
1 cup chopped pecans
1 cup shredded coconut
1 cup raisins, rinsed in
    warm water and drained
1 cup chopped dried apricots
    or pineapple*

*Candied orange or grapefruit peel, currants, or snipped fresh dates, rinsed in warm water and drained, are other possibilities for the fruit in these cookies.

Preheat the oven to 350 degrees. Cream the butter until fluffy, gradually adding the sugars; continue to beat until fluffy and well blended. Beat in the egg thoroughly, then the oil and vanilla. The batter may look curdled at this point. Combine the flour, baking soda, and salt. Stir into the creamed mixture in 5 or 6 additions. Stir in the oats, nuts, coconut, raisins, and other fruit.

Shape the dough into 1-inch balls and place 1½ inches apart on ungreased baking sheets. Flatten slightly with fork tines dipped in flour. Bake 14 to 15 minutes, until dry on top and cookies hold a slight impression when touched on top. Cool on racks and store in tightly covered containers.

The Box of Oranges I promised to send you from Florida.

SOUR ORANGE PIE

MAKES 6 SERVINGS.

Caroline's dad always said that God had planted the sour orange tree outside the back door of the house. More likely, Native Americans were responsible, inadvertently planting sour oranges all over the state by dropping the seeds as they traveled. The oranges themselves were a highly prized gift from Spanish explorers, who brought them to the New World from Spain. But whatever their origin, sour oranges thrive in woods and backyards all over the state, and though not grown commercially, they can sometimes be found in farmers' markets or gourmet food stores. Floridians have long used them in cold drinks, marmalades, marinades, pies, and puddings. Carrie Young, who cooked for Caroline's family for many years, remembers her mother making sour orange pudding, and many old-timers have sour orange recipes that have been passed down for generations.

¾ cup plus 3 tablespoons sugar

3 level tablespoons cornstarch

1 cup hot water

1 tablespoon butter

3 eggs, separated

⅓ cup sour orange juice
  (see Note)

1 baked 9-inch pie shell
  (see pages 304–5)

In a saucepan, mix together the ³/₄ cup sugar and cornstarch, and slowly pour in the hot water and butter, stirring to dissolve any lumps. Beat the egg yolks lightly, and add, along with the sour orange juice. Stir constantly over medium-low heat until the mixture has thickened and coats the spoon. Do not boil. Carefully pour the filling into the baked pie shell.

For the meringue, beat the egg whites until frothy. Continue to beat, gradually adding 3 tablespoons of sugar, until the beater holds stiff peaks when lifted. Gently swirl the meringue over the filling, making sure it touches the edges of the crust all the way around. Bake in a preheated 375-degree oven until the meringue is brown. Remove from the oven and cool on a rack.

NOTE: If you can't get sour oranges, ¼ cup lemon juice may be substituted.

SOUR ORANGE PUDDING

Make the sour orange pie filling and pour into a greased 9-inch pie plate or shallow oven-proof dish. Spread with the meringue, all the way to the edges, and bake in a preheated 375-degree oven until the meringue is brown. Spoon into dessert dishes while warm or serve cooled. Fresh berries on the side make a nice contrast.

A GLOSSARY OF SELECTED FRUITS AND VEGETABLES

The rarest fruits and vegetables are most likely to be found in specialty shops, Hispanic markets, and street-side stands of successful gardeners.

Acerola—Also called Barbados cherry, this deep-red berry is used in commercial baby foods as a vitamin C supplement. The sour berries make good jellies and jams.

Annona—This large family of fruits includes the lush soursop, sweetsop, cherimoya, custard apple (Bullock's heart), and atemoya. The meltingly sweet cherimoya and other annonas are best raw or in ice creams or sherbets.

Banana—The choice is awesome. In addition to the familiar ones, try the tiny, sweet, finger bananas; the Cavendishes (the Canary Island variety found in Europe); and boxy ones, easy to cut in uniform slices. Plantains and red bananas are cooked, others eaten raw when ripe.

Boniata—Other names for this are white sweet potato and camote. Aficionados deem it the best of all baked potatoes, and it can be prepared in any way suitable to conventional sweet potatoes.

Breadfruit—The fruit, resembling a small basketball with a pebbly green skin, is peeled, cooked, and mashed to serve as a starchy vegetable or in desserts.

Cactus pear—Also called prickly pear or tuna, it is the most common edible cactus in Florida. The fruit is deep red when ripe, and the spines are clipped before peeling it. It is eaten as is or in fruit salads.

Calabaza—The Caribbean pumpkin is esteemed for its bright golden color of the flesh and for its mellow flavor. The *calabaza* is smaller than a North American pumpkin and the skin is a muted orange color. Cubans boil or steam it and serve it hot or cold with a tart sauce.

Calamondin—This hybrid kumquat-tangerine is cultivated elsewhere as a houseplant, but it grows outdoors in subtropical Florida. The tart juice takes the place of lemon or lime juice in beverages or desserts, and calamondin marmalade is excellent. The fruit is a miniature replica of an orange, flattened slightly at the ends.

Carambola—Nicknamed starfruit, the thin-skinned golden-ribbed cylinder is cut crosswise to form five-point-star slices. The "stars" are used as garnishes for meats or salads or are floated on punches. The juicy fruit is refreshing in a salad or relish with fish or meat. Some carambolas are sour, so are best with sweet fruits or sweetened with honey or sugar.

Chayote—This pale green, pear-shaped squash is called *mirliton* in New Orleans, *Christophine* in Jamaica, *Xuxu* or *chocho* in Haiti. The skin is tough, so it is peeled off before or after cooking. A well-seasoned vinaigrette-style dressing complements the mild squash.

Chile—Datil peppers and Scotch bonnets are the favorite chiles of Florida. The Minorcans of St. Augustine dote on the datils that they cultivate in home gardens. Scotch bonnets, beloved by Jamaicans and other West Indians, have been adopted enthusiastically by Floridians. The datil is a small, long, yellowish green chile; the Scotch bonnet is a yellowish or pale green tam-shaped pepper, less than an inch in diameter. Both are very hot. The tiny, bright-red bird pepper is used everywhere, and small hot chiles called grove peppers grow wild in the citrus areas.

Cilantro—This pungent herb is new to markets in Florida and now is grown commercially. West Indians call it *culantro*. The leaves are used fresh in salsas, and lend a sparkle to pineapple and other fruit relishes.

Feijoa—Also called pineapple guava, though it is not a true guava, this fruit is eaten raw or in jams, jellies, and sauces.

Ginger—Fresh ginger is the knobby root of an attractive plant. A slice of ginger is peeled and minced or put through a garlic press to flavor dressings, sauces, meat dishes, or fruit compotes. To keep a cut root for later use, wrap and freeze it (usable in the frozen state) or immerse the peeled root in sherry, vodka, or brandy in a jar, cover, and refrigerate it. The ginger-flavored spirits are good in drinks or as flavoring after the ginger is gone.

Guava—Wilson Popenoe, a renowned writer about tropical fruits, rated guava jelly the finest in the world. Guavas grow prolifically in gardens, and once grew wild. The skin is green to pale yellow or beige, and the flesh may be as pale as cream or as deep rose as mashed strawberries. Guavas are gathered firm-ripe, develop full flavor after they are softened, and are intensely aromatic. The seedy center is scooped out and, if the skin is smooth and unblemished, the fruit is not peeled.

Kumquat—This doll-size citrus fruit looks like a tiny Christmas-tree bauble, and is widely used as an adornment in holiday wreaths and garlands. But it is a serious fruit; it can be popped into the mouth and eaten whole (the rind carries much of the flavor), sliced in fruit compotes, and, as kumquat preserves, makes an elegant garnish.

Loquat—Children in subtropical Florida eat this golden plum-like fruit as a snack. The sweet, lightly perfumed flavor is enhanced by poaching loquats in sugar syrup; and the uncooked fruit, peeled if the skin is tough, is a juicy addition to fruit salads. Loquats are about the size of a small plum are egg-shaped, and have a golden beige color. They are ripe when they are soft and fragrant.

Litchi—This is really a nut surrounded by juicy flesh (the fruit) in a brittle deep red shell. It generally is eaten raw or dried, with the pulp becoming raisin-like in texture and flavor. Fresh litchis are on sale in farm markets, and dooryard trees flourish as far north as Central Florida. Dried litchi nuts in oriental markets are naturally dehydrated fresh litchis.

Malanga—This staple of the Caribbean table, a starchy tuber, is boiled or sliced thin and fried as chips. The malanga looks like a shaggy brown sweet potato. It often is confused with the taro or dasheen, the starchy root that is the base for Hawaiian poi, and malanga and taro are interchangeable in most recipes.

Mango—This is the ultimate fruit to thousands of Floridians and visitors. The commercial varieties are sweet, fragrant with an exotic flavor, and smooth textured. Dooryard fruit may be fibrous and taste of turpentine. Mangoes are ovoid to round, with a green-to-gold skin tinged with red. To prepare mangoes, cut the pulp off the flat sides of the seed in two thick slices, then trim off the bits of pulp clinging to the seed. Peel the fruit before or after cutting it from the seed. Sliced mangoes make a delicious summer dessert, and the fruit is good in shortcakes, ice creams, Bavarian creams, and other classic desserts. Pies and chutneys are made of firm ripe or green mangoes.

Monstera deliciosa—This fruit of a house plant called split-leaf philodendron is a rare treat. When a plant in the garden bears fruit, spikes shoot up and, as they ripen, develop a rich perfume. Tiny segments of pulp pop out of the green shell. *Monstera deliciosa,* also called ceriman, is good in ice cream or salad but is usually enjoyed with a few folk who appreciate eating adventures, since the fruit is so rare. A single *Monstera* provides a few mouthfuls of edible pulp.

Orange—Familiar commercial oranges are abundant, but try the rare ones: blood oranges (well-known in Europe, and gaining in Florida) and sour oranges (cast aside for sweet varieties until hobbyists discovered their virtues). Blood oranges may have red streaks on the skin or look like any orange. The color is in the flesh, which is pretty in salads and desserts, the juice being a deep red. The sour orange is the tangy fruit that sparks roast pork and chicken in Key West and makes the fine bitter orange marmalade of Scotland.

Papaya—Tree melon is a common name for this, and larger papayas look like small watermelons. Others look like green or golden toy footballs. The fruit is ripe when soft to gentle pressure is applied. A sprinkle of lime or lemon juice perks up the flavor. The black seeds are peppery, and it is good to leave a few of them in a wedge of papaya as a built-in condiment. Partly green papayas and the leaves are natural meat tenderizers, used by pioneers when meat quality was unreliable.

Passion fruit—This fruit was named for symbols of the crucifixion assigned to the blossom by Jesuit missionaries, and not for any aphrodisiac qualities. The tough, dark purple skin is wrinkled when the fruit is ripe. In Kenya, the skin is pierced at the pointed end and the ripe pulp sucked out, as children used to suck oranges. The pulp can be pressed out through the cut skin for use in desserts and salads, and seeds that escape are skimmed out. Or the fruit is cut in half and the flesh pulled loose from the seeds. The sweet aromatic flavor is pleasing with other fruits or creams in desserts or salads.

Pomelo or *pummelo*—This giant citrus with a thick skin is the ancestor of the grapefruit, though still grown in Florida, and is a ceremonial fruit in Asian New Year celebrations. The flavor is less distinctive than grapefruit, but the fruit is useful in salad or eaten out of hand. Shaddock is another name for pomelo; the Ugli fruit, a name created by growers, is a cross of the pomelo and tangelo, a citrus the size of an orange.

Sapodilla—This is the fruit of the evergreen tree that produces chicle, the base for chewing gum. The skin of the fruit is grayish brown and the ripe flesh is sweet, usually eaten raw on the half-shell. Bahamians still talk of "dilly boats," the craft that sailed to Florida in the brisk sapodilla trade a half century and more ago.

Sapote—This is the name applied to many fruits: the white sapote with creamy sweet flesh and a green-to-gold skin; the black sapote, with tender brownish pulp and a dark green skin; and the golden one, called canistel or egg fruit. The fruits are eaten raw or made into jams or preserves.

Star apple—Natives cultivated this fruit before Europeans arrived, but it is found only rarely in produce markets. It looks like a large plum with a purple or creamy-colored skin. Cut crosswise, the translucent flesh shows a central star. The fruit is eaten raw.

Yuca, cassava, or *manioc*—Early settlers grew cassava as a cash crop a century ago. It was the source of tapioca, cassava flour, and the grainy meal of South America called manioc. In Florida yuca is cooked and mashed for use in fritters or as a starchy vegetable; this root is also cut in strips and fried as a side dish or snack. Yuca is not related to yucca, another plant that is harvested for its root.

BIBLIOGRAPHY

Akerman, Joe A., Jr. *Florida Cowman: A History of Florida Cattle Raising.* Kissimmee: Florida Cattlemen's Association, 1976.

Allman, T. C. *Miami: City of the Future.* New York: Atlantic Monthly Press, 1987.

Allyn, Rube. *Florida Fishes.* St. Petersburg: Great Outdoors Publishing Company, 1976.

Altschul, bj. *Cracker Cooking and Other Favorites.* Winner Enterprises: 1984 and 1986 editions.

Arsenault, Raymond. "St. Petersburg and the Florida Dream, 1889–1950." *St. Petersburg Times,* June 8, 1988.

Artman, L. P., Jr. *Conch Cooking.* Key West: Florida Keys Printing and Publishing Company, 1975.

Bamford, Hal. *Florida History.* St. Petersburg: Great Outdoors Publishing Company, 1976.

Bartram, William. *Travels.* Edited by Francis Harper. New Haven: Yale University Press, 1958.

Bowe, Richard J. *Pictorial History of Florida.* Minneapolis: Historical Publications, 1965.

Carlton, Lowis. *Famous Florida Recipes.* St. Petersburg: Great Outdoors Publishing Company, 1972.

Chapman, Dorothy. *A Taste of Florida.* Orlando: Sentinel Books, 1990.

Dacy, George H. *Four Centuries of Florida Ranching.* St. Louis: Britt Printing Company, 1940.

Davidson, Alan. *Fruit: A Connoisseur's Guide and Cookbook.* New York: Simon & Schuster, 1991.

Episcopal Church Women, St. John's Cathedral. *Heavenly Recipes.* Jacksonville, 1987.

Florida Agricultural Statistics, Florida State Department of Agriculture. *Touring Florida, A Florida Agricultural Statistical Review.* Tallahassee, 1989.

Florida Strawberry Growers Association. *It's Strawberry Time.* Plant City, 1986.

Flynn, Stephen J. *Florida: Land of Fortune.* Washington, D.C.: Luce, 1962.

Frisbie, Louise. *Florida's Fabled Inns.* Bartow, Florida: Imperial Publishing, Inc., 1980.

———. *Peace River Pioneers.* Miami: E. A. Seemann Publishing, Inc., 1974.

———. *Yesterday's Polk County.* Miami: E. A. Seemann Publishing, Inc., 1976.

Garcia, Clarita. *Clarita's Cocina.* New York: Doubleday, 1970.

Gassenheimer, Linda. *Keys Cuisine.* Boston: Atlantic Monthly Press, 1991.

Gaylord, Emma N. *Life in Florida Since 1886.* Miami: Hurricane House, 1969.

Grismer, Karl H. *Tampa: A History of the City of Tampa and the Tampa Bay Region of Florida.* St. Petersburg: St. Petersburg Printing Company, 1950.

Harris, Dunstan A. *Island Cooking*. Freedom, California: The Crossing Press, 1988.

Hawkes, Alex D. *The Flavors of the Caribbean and Latin America*. New York: Viking Press, 1978.

Junior League of Tallahassee. *Thymes Remembered*. Memphis: Wimmer Brothers, 1977.

Junior League of the Palm Beaches. *Palm Beach Entertains—Then and Now*. Palm Beach, 1976.

Kaucher, Dorothy. *They Built a City*. Orlando: Kirstein & Son Printers, 1970.

Ladies Philoptochos Society of St. John Greek Orthodox Church. *Greek Festival Cookbook*. Tampa, 1989.

Lamme, Louise. *Florida Cookbook*. Boynton Beach: STAR Publishing Co., 1968.

Lane, Charlotte Balcomb. *The Florida Cookbook, A Lighter Look at Southern Cooking*. Edited by Heather McPherson. Orlando: Sentinel Books, 1990.

Lieberman, Leslie Sue, and Linda Benjamin Bobroff, eds. *Cultural Food Patterns of Florida, A Handbook*. Gainesville: Institute of Food and Agricultural Sciences, University of Florida, 1990.

Madigan, Meg. *Political Potluck*. Tallahassee: Peninsular Publishing Company, 1959.

Magnolia Garden Club. *Centre St. Cookery*. Fernandina Beach, 1978.

Marathon Garden Club. *Tropical Native Cooking*. Marathon, Florida, 1971.

Marth, Del, and Martha J. Marth, eds. *Florida Almanac*. Gretna, Louisiana: Pelican Publishing Company, 1988–89.

Michener, James A. *Caribbean*. New York: Ballantine Books, 1989.

Mickler, Delia Appleyard, and Carolyde Phillips O'Bryan. *Tallahassee Historical Cookbook*. Tallahassee: Rose Printing Company, 1984.

Mickler, Ernest M., and The Jargon Society. *White Trash Cooking*. East Haven, Connecticut: Inland Book Company, 1986.

Molaka Club. *Molaka's Arabic-American Cookbook*. Jacksonville, 1990.

Morris, Allen. *The Florida Handbook*, 21st and 22nd editions. Tallahassee: Peninsula Publishing Company, 1987 and 1989.

Muir, Helen. *Miami U.S.A.*, 2nd edition. Miami: Pickering Press, 1990.

Munroe, Ralph, and Vincent Gilpin. *The Commodore's Story*. Historical Association of Southern Florida, 1990.

Nickerson, Jane. *Florida Cookbook*. Gainesville: University of Florida Press, 1973.

Ortiz, Elisabeth Lambert. *The Complete Book of Caribbean Cooking*. New York: N. Evans and Company, 1967.

Palmer, Perrine, Jr. *Gootsie's Favorite Recipes*. Miami: Perrine Palmer, Jr., 1971.

Rawlings, Marjorie Kinnan. *Cross Creek Cookery*. New York: Scribner's, 1942.

Salley, George H. *A History of the Florida Sugar Industry*. Belle Glade, Florida: Sugar Cane Growers Cooperative, 1985.

Tebeau, Charlton W. *A History of Florida*. Coral Gables: University of Miami Press, 1971.

———. *The Story of the Chokoloskee Bay Country*. Miami: Banyan Books, 1977.

Townshend, F. Trench. *Wild Life in Florida*. London: Hurst and Blackett, Publishers, 1875.

Villagers, Inc. *Biscayne Bights and Breezes*. Miami, 1987.

Wickham, Joan Adams. *Food Favorites of St. Augustine*. St. Augustine: C. F. Hamblen, Inc., 1973.

Woman's Club of Key West. *Key West Woman's Club Cookbook*. Key West, 1949; second edition, 1988.

Ziegler, Louis W., and Herbert S. Wolfe. *Citrus Growing in Florida*. Gainesville: University of Florida Press, 1979.

Bijol and other seasonings
Bijol and Spices, Inc.
2154 N.W. 22nd Court
Miami, Florida 33142
(305) 634-9030

Bollito mix
La Gitana
1104 N. Howard Avenue
Tampa, Florida 33607
(813) 251-8129

Bollito mixes, Florida honeys,
Key lime juice, saffron
and other seasonings,
Cuban coffee
Cooks Bazaar
516 Fleming Street
Key West, Florida 33040
(305) 296-6656

Dat'l Do It sauce
Dat'l Do It, Inc.
P.O. Box 4019
St. Augustine, Florida 32085
(904) 824-2609, (800) 468-3285

Hardtack
Premier Baking Co.
1124 W. Garden Street
Pensacola, Florida 32501
(904) 438-1263

Key lime juice
Florida Key West, Inc.
3521 Central Avenue
Ft. Myers, Florida 33901
(813) 936-6548

Tropical fruits
Norman Brothers Produce
7621 S.W. 87th Avenue
Miami, Florida 33173
(305) 274-9363

Tupelo honey
Donald E. Lanier
P.O. Box 382
Wewahitchka, Florida 34625
(904) 639-5484

ACKNOWLEDGMENTS

We wish to thank our editor, Judith Jones, for her wisdom, advice, and counsel; our agent, Mildred Marmur, for her enthusiasm and encouragement; Mary Sullivan, for her many hours of research; Caroline's artist-husband, John Brainard, for the beautiful jacket painting; and our respective families and friends for tasting and support. We are also grateful to the following:

Sharon Adams, Bartow

Selma Alexander, Miami

Jane Allen, IFAS Florida Cooperative Extension Service, Home Economics Dept., Seffner

Lee Ann Applewhite, Bureau of Seafood Marketing, University of Florida, Gainesville

Jimmy Aprile, Temple Terrace

Tom Baker, curator, Florida Agriculture Museum, Tallahassee

Andy and Chris Bonnemort, Greenwich, Connecticut

Vina Jean Banks, president, Florida Cattlewomen's Association, Tampa

Bob Brandel, New York

Hazel Brown, Bartow

Helen Brown, Jacksonville

Karl Butts, IFAS, Florida Cooperative Extension Service, Seffner

Henry Cabbage, Florida Game and Fresh Water Fish Commission, Tallahassee

Paul Camp, librarian, Special Collections, University of South Florida, Tampa

Rev. Bud and Millie Carroll, New York City

Jo Coleman, director, food services, Flagler Hospital, St. Augustine

Doyle Conner, former Florida Commissioner of Agriculture, Tallahassee

Virginia Dunn Cooper, Tallahassee

Lawrence Cutts, chief, Bureau of Apiary Inspection, Florida Department of Agriculture and Consumer Services, Gainesville

Richard Dale, Lake Wales Citrus Growers' Association, Lake Wales

Atlee and Ginger Davis, Babson Park

Dee Davis, Tuscaloosa, Alabama

Art Darling, Dairy and Food Nutrition Council of Florida, Orlando

Patty Denton, Florida *Times Union*, Jacksonville

Esperanza De Varona, University of Miami Library, Coral Gables

James D. Dilbeck, IFAS, Florida Cooperative Extension Service, St. Augustine

Jack Donnelly, CEC, St. Petersburg Yacht Club

Bill and Virginia Dudenhausen, Pittsboro, North Carolina

Richard Dunaway, Florida state bee inspector, Winter Haven

Agnes Edwards, Winn-Dixie, Jacksonville

Koma Entin, Coral Gables

Estate of J. K. Stuart, Bartow
Kathie Faircloth, Lake Wales
Cathy Fernandez, Sarasota
Florida Beef Council, Kissimmee
Florida Cattleman's Association, Kissimmee
Dr. Everett Fouts, former head of Dairy Science, University of Florida, Gainesville
Brent Frei, American Culinary Federation, St. Augustine
Lloyal Frisbie, Polk County *Democrat*, Bartow
Linda Gassenheimer, Gardner's Markets, South Miami
Herbert and Stanley Gaylord, Tampa
Father George, St. John Greek Orthodox Church, Tampa
Carolynn Girtman, Bartow
Adela Gonzmart, Columbia Restaurants, Ybor City, Tampa
Ruth L. Gray, St. Petersburg *Times* (retired)
Jennie Guttermuth, Grant
Suzanne Hardee, Fernandina Beach
Alice Harden, Bartow
Jennie Hess, Walt Disney World, Lake Buena Vista
Anne C. Heyman, St. Augustine *Record*
Jimmy Hinton, IFAS, Florida Cooperative Extension Service, Home Economics Dept., Seffner
Stephanie Johnson, J.R. Brooks & Son, Homestead
Eugene M. Joyner, IFAS, Florida Cooperative Extension Service, West Palm Beach
Rev. Elizabeth Kelly, Pittsboro, North Carolina
Keith Keogh, CED, AAM, executive chef, Epcot Center, Walt Disney World
Sophia Kourmoulis, Tampa
Dr. C. Bronson Lane, Dairy and Food Nutrition Council of Florida, Orlando
Norma Lemberg, Coral Gables
Helen Litrico, *Amelia Now* magazine, Fernandina Beach
Karen Long, Tampa Tribune
Frank MacKnight, Pittsboro, North Carolina
Meg Madigan, Tallahassee
Bess Mahaffey, Florida Tomato Committee, Orlando

Ann McDuffie, food editor (retired), Tampa *Tribune*
Heather J. McPherson, Orlando *Sentinel*
Mr. and Mrs. Angel Menendez, La Tropicana Cafe, Ybor City, Tampa
Mildred Merrick, University of Miami Library (retired), Coral Gables
Barbara J. Miedema, Sugar Cane Growers Cooperative of Florida, Belle Glade
Sandra Mitchell, Winter Haven
Bill and Helen Moeller, Florida State University and City of Tallahassee Library, Tallahassee
Stephen Monroe, Florida Department of Agriculture, Tallahassee
Cal and Betsy Moore, Pensacola
Charles Moore, Florida state bee inspector, Winter Haven
Edwin L. Moore, Citrus Experiment Station, Lake Alfred
Joan Morris, archivist, Florida Photographic Collection, Tallahassee
Judge Celeste Muir, Miami
Helen Muir, author, Miami
Dr. Paul Nicoletti, University of Florida, Gainesville
John Nichols, Montgomery, Alabama
Carolyde O'Bryan, author, Tallahassee
Dr. Steve Otwell, Bureau of Seafood Marketing, Gainesville
Robert E. Patterson, coordinator, Elementary Health Education, Hillsborough County School Board, Tampa
Anne Pipping, Lakeland
Diane Piros, produce buyer, Fowler's Gourmet, Durham, North Carolina
Lorraine Praay, Bartow
Randall G. Prophet, Florida Bureau of Seafood Marketing, Tallahassee
Julia Rady, Jacksonville
Dr. Clarence Reeves, Gainesville
Henry Robitaille, Ph.D, manager, Science Technology, Epcot Center, The Land, Walt Disney World Co., Lake Buena Vista
Marilyn B. Rose, Florida Bureau of Seafood Marketing, Jacksonville

Louise Schilling, Miami Shores
Allen Smith, Alturas
Mary Spottswood, Key West
Professor James M. Stephens,
    IFAS, University of Florida,
    Gainesville
W. H. Stuart and W. H. Stuart,
    Jr., Bartow
Harold Sullivan, Tampa
Charles Thomas, Florida Bureau of
    Seafood Marketing,
    Tallahassee
Lisa Thornton, Fairfield, Connecti-
    cut
Stephen and Debbie Tiger, Micco-
    sukee Tribe of Indians of
    Florida, Miami

Geoffrey Tomb, Miami *Herald*
Jean Trapido-Rosenthal, librarian,
    St. Augustine Historical Society
Bill and Linda Virgin, Pensacola
Jeanne Marie Voltz, caterer, food
    stylist, New York
Helen Webb, IFAS, Florida Coop-
    erative Extension Service, Home
    Economics Dept., Seffner
Lovett Williams, Fish-eating Creek
    Hunting Camp, Palmdale
Dorothy Wilson, Miami
Carrie Young, Bartow

bacon and onions, 283–4
Bahamians, 149, 157, 160
baked beans, 39
Baker, Charles H., Jr., 137
banana(s)
    bread, 153–4
    cake, 357–8
    fried, 146–7
    fritters, 238
    varieties, 364
barbecue
    beef chuck, 31–2
    chicken, honey–mustard, 323–4
    corn, 337–8
    pork chops, 89
    sauce, yellow-bonnet, 269
    shrimp, 81
    venison, Seminole-style, 330–1
Barron, C. W., 123
Barron's Weekly, 123
Bartow, 253, 289, 304
Basford, Pat, 63
Basford, Steve, 63
basil, sliced tomatoes with, 257
bass, 209
Bavarian cream, mango, 351–2
Bayley's Steak House, 68
bean(s)
    baked, 39
    butter, 91–2
    black, and rice, 225–6
    green
        marinated, with dill, 8–9
        with potatoes, 90
        and walnut pâté, 186
    smoked, 37–9
    soup, with collard greens, 196–7
beef
    barbecue, 31–2
    boliche, 143–4
    cattle industry, 217, 272–3
    flank steak and tomato hash, 141–2
    goulash, 326–7
    ground
        Indian burger, 232
        pastitsio, 215–16
    range steaks, 270
    ropa vieja, 141–2
beer, shrimp steamed in, 132–3
beet salad, warm, 148
Belleview Hotel, 204
bijol, 212

Biscayne Bay Yacht Club, 108, 125
Biscayne Bights and Breezes (Parks),
        26, 142
biscuits
    grapefruit, 233
    orange, 348–9
    sweet potato, 287–8
    with tomato gravy, 281–2
    yeast, 48–9
Biscuits and Taters (Warner), 282
black beans and rice, 225–6
blackberry dumplings, 98–9
black-eyed peas
    fritters, 111–12
    and hog jowl, 343–4
Black Heritage Cookbook, The, 144
Blountstown, 8
blowfish, see sea squab
blueberry
    cornbread, 289
    pie, 53–4
boaters' lime pie, 166
Boca Raton, 107
Bocuse, Paul, 261
boliche, 143–4
bollitos de frijoles, 111–12
Bradenton, 177, 353
Bradley, Colonel, 123
bread(s)
    banana, 153–4
    biscuits
        grapefruit, 233
        orange, 348–9
        sweet potato, 287–8
        with tomato gravy, 281–2
        yeast, 48–9
    corn
        baked corn cakes, 96–7
        blueberry cornbread, 289
        buttery rich, 348
        Clewiston, 346
    Cuban, 227
        home-baked, 228–9
    fried, 231
        burger, 232
        sweet potato or pumpkin, 232
    hushpuppies, 44–7
        sweet, 154–5
    pudding, with guava paste, 156–7
    spoon, 97–8
breadfruit, description, 363
Breakers Hotel, 122, 123

Harvey, Mrs. Paul J., 239
Hastings, 4
hearts of palm, 332
    canned, steamed, 334
    Cracker-style, 333
    ice cream dressing for, 188
    salad, 187
Heimer, Phil, xii
Henry, Bobby, 231
Heron, 198
herring, orange, 184–5
Heymen, Ann, 21
Hicks, Amanda, 233
Hinshaw, Carl, 259
Hinshaw, Vita, 259
Hispanics, 22, 107, 108, 141, 146, 176,
        178, 191, 213, 220, 227, 229,
        236, 269, 329, 352
Hodges, "Shorty," 45, 207
hog jowl and black-eyed peas,
        343–4
Hollandaise, 77–8
Homestead, xi
honey
    butter, 234
    tupelo, 71
Hopkins, Willy, 262
Hoppin' John, 343
Hot Links and Country Flavors
        (Aidells and Kelly), 219
Huguenots, ix
hunting, 275
    see also game
hushpuppies, 44–7
    sweet, 154–5

ice cream
    peach, 99
    salad dressing, 188
    strawberry, 294
ice making, 101
icing, fluffy white, 300–1
Immokalee, tomatoes at, 257
Indian corn, 40
Indians, *see* Native Americans;
        specific tribes
Indian Wars, 175
Indonesians, xii, 109
International Association of Cooking
        Professionals (IACP), 169

International Gopher Race Games,
        251
Isabella, Queen of Spain, 30
Italians, 3–4, 30, 327
Italian-style sauce, eggplant in, 36

Jackson, Andrew, 7
Jacksonville, 4, 11, 14, 15–16, 33
Jacksonville Naval Air Station, 51
Jamaicans, 118, 311
jam pies, 352–3
Japanese, 67
Jefferson, Thomas, 83
Jews, x–xi
Joe's Stone Crab, 108, 113
Johnson, Vera, 128

Kancher, Dorothy, 279
Kellogg, John Harvey, 35
Kelly, Denis, 219
Kelly, Elizabeth, 103
Key lime pie, 164–6
    boaters', 166
Key West, x, xi, xii, 107, 111, 114,
        124, 128, 131, 143, 156, 157,
        160, 214, 225
Kissimmee, "Cow Town," 250
Krismer, Karl, 217

La Belle, 311
Ladies Philoptochos Society, 245
Lake Alfred, 255
Lakeland, 250, 262, 289
Lakeland Ledger, 288
Lake Wales, 259, 279
lamb
    curried, Islands-style, 145–6
    leg of, Greek, 221
    Syrian meat pies, 33–4
Land Grille Room, The, 261
Land's End stew, 202
Lanir, Donald, 71
LeCoze, Gilbert, xii
lemon
    butter cookies, 103
    pie, Passover, 242-3
LeNôtre, Gaston, 261
Let's Talk Food (Reynolds), 244

soup*(cont.)*
    turnip green, 72–3
*South American Gentleman's
        Companion, The* (Baker),
        137
South Dade Regional Library, 144
Southeast Asians, 329
Southern Ice Exchange, 101
South Florida, University of, 7
Spanish, ix, x, 3, 30, 59, 66, 75, 144,
        196, 210, 213, 219, 223, 236,
        272, 321, 360
Spanish-American War, 184
spinach and strawberry salad, 189
spoon bread, 97–8
Spring Hill, chicken-plucking contest,
        251
squash, 223
    casserole, 340, 341
    chicken and rice casserole with
        sausage and, 214–15
    salad, 190, 259–60
star apple, description, 367
starches
    grits
        cheese, 95
        fried, 43
        Nassau, 94
        spoon bread, 97–8
        à la Summerfield, 44
    herbed dumplings, 322–3
    plantains, fried, 146–7
    potato(es)
        green beans with, 90
        rosin, 152–3
        salad, 192–3
    see also rice
starfruit and marmalade sauce, 271
State Farmers' Market, 340
steam, fish, 128–9
Steinhatchee, 175
Stewart, Catherine, 73
stew
    corn, 124
    fish, 78–9, 128–9
    Frogmore, 202–3
    goulash, 326–7
    Land's End, 202
stifado, 78–9
Stokes, Jeff, 202
stone crabs, 113

Story, Melvin, 335
Story, Thelma, 335
strawberry(ies), 295–6
    ambrosia, 235
    cobbler, 299
    glaze, 163
    ice cream, 294
    pie, 241
    and spinach salad, 189
Strawberry Festival, 296
striped bass, 209
Stuart, Bill, 253
Stuart, Margrette, 253
stuffing, vegetable, for baked fish,
        316–18
sugar, 353–4
Sugarland Corporation, 347
Susser, Allen, xii, 169
Sutker, Sue, 184, 242
swamp cabbage, *see* hearts of palm
sweet potato(es)
    biscuits, 287–8
    chips, 64
    citrus, 342
    fry bread, 232
    tzimmes, 151–2
sweet puppies, 154–5
Syrians, 15, 33

tabbouleh, 17
Tallahassee, 4, 12, 37, 44, 50, 59
Tampa, University of, 205
Tampa Bay Hotel, 184, 205
Tampa Historical Society, 229
Tampa Tribune, 239, 271
Tampa Yacht Club, 339
Tarpon Springs, xi, 176, 192, 215, 234
tarte tatin, mango, 167–8
Ted Peters Famous Smoked Fish, 177,
        210
Temple Shalom, 186
Tequestas, 7
Terrell, Mrs. Glen, 50
Thai, 109
Thanksgiving dinner, 85
They Built a City (Kancher), 279
Those Toasts, 11
Tilapia, 209
Timucuas, 7
toasts, 11

PHOTOGRAPHIC CREDITS

The photographs and illustrations reproduced in this book were provided with the permission and courtesy of the following:

Ray Fisher: 222

Florida State Archives, Photographic Collection: 6, 14, 27, 32, 37, 40, 42, 61, 70, 76, 79, 80, 85, 87, 92, 102, 112, 121, 125, 129, 132, 155, 158, 170, 183, 188, 193, 211, 221, 230, 233, 252, 258, 279, 283, 290, 293, 295, 301, 313, 319, 320, 325, 331, 334, 337, 344

St. Augustine Historical Library: 43

Tampa–Hillsborough County Public Library System: 13, 180 (bottom), 205, 237

University of South Florida Library Special Collections: 9, 52, 147, 180 (top), 195, 196, 204, 270, 275, 360

Lovett Williams: 267

A NOTE ABOUT THE AUTHORS

Jeanne Voltz was born in Collinsville, Alabama.
She was for many years the food editor at *Woman's Day* magazine,
and she edited the food pages at the Los Angeles *Times* and
the Miami *Herald*. She is the author of several cookbooks, including
The Flavor of the South and *Barbecued Ribs, Smoked Butts,
and Other Great Feeds*—which is also part of the Knopf Cooks American
series—is a six-time winner of the Vesta Award for newspaper
food editing and writing, and has also won numerous other
feature and food writing awards. Mrs. Voltz lives with her
husband in Pittsboro, North Carolina, where she is a
food consultant, writer, and free-lance editor.

Caroline Stuart is a third-generation Floridian whose family
settled in the central part of the state in the 1870s. She grew up
on a ranch where her father grew citrus and raised cattle.
She graduated from the University of Alabama and
began her career as a caterer. She then worked for several years
with James Beard as his assistant and is vice-president of
The James Beard Foundation. Mrs. Stuart is a contributing
editor and restaurant critic for *Hudson Valley* magazine,
as well as a free-lance writer and cooking teacher.
She lives with her husband, John Brainard, in
Greenwich, Connecticut, and has two sons.

A NOTE ON THE TYPE

This book was set in Bodoni Book, named after
Giambattista Bodoni (1740–1813), son of a printer of Piedmont.
After gaining experience and fame as superintendent of the Press of
the Propaganda in Rome, in 1768 Bodoni became the head of the
ducal printing house at Parma, which he soon made the foremost of its
kind in Europe. His *Manuale Tipografico*, completed by his widow in 1818,
contains 279 pages of type specimens, including alphabets of about
thirty languages. His editions of Greek, Latin, Italian, and French
classics are celebrated for their typography. In type designing
he was an innovator, making his new faces rounder, wider,
and lighter, with greater openness and delicacy, and with sharper
contrast between the thick and thin lines.

Designed by Cassandra J. Pappas

Ornamental illustrations used for binding, endpapers, and the interior
are by Linda Bourke.

Printed and bound by Courier Book Companies,
Westford, Massachusetts

KNOPF COOKS AMERICAN

The series of cookbooks that celebrates the culinary heritage of
America, telling different aspects of our story through recipes
interspersed with historical lore, personal reflections, and
the recollections of old-timers.

Already published:

Biscuits, Spoonbread, and Sweet Potato Pie by Bill Neal

Hot Links & Country Flavors by Bruce Aidells and Denis Kelly

Barbecued Ribs, Smoked Butts, and Other Great Feeds
by Jeanne Voltz

We Called It Macaroni by Nancy Verde Barr

The West Coast Cook Book by Helen Evans Brown

Pleasures of the Good Earth by Edward Giobbi

The Brooklyn Cookbook by Lyn Stallworth and Rod Kennedy, Jr.

Dungeness Crabs and Blackberry Cobblers by Janie Hibler

Preserving Today by Jeanne Lesem

Blue Corn and Chocolate by Elisabeth Rozin

Real Beer & Good Eats by Bruce Aidells and Denis Kelly

The Florida Cookbook by Jeanne Voltz and Caroline Stuart

Jewish Cooking in America by Joan Nathan

Savoring the Seasons of the Northern Heartland
by Beth Dooley and Lucia Watson

"Our food tells us where we came from and who we are . . ."